THE NATURE AND PACE OF CHANGE IN AMERICAN INDIAN CULTURES

RECENT RESEARCH IN **PENNSYLVANIA ARCHAEOLOGY**

Paul A. Raber, *Series Editor*

The Archaic Period in Pennsylvania: Hunter-Gatherers of the Early and Middle Holocene Period, VOL. 1
Edited by Paul A. Raber, Patricia E. Miller, and Sarah M. Neusius
Published by the Pennsylvania Historical and Museum Commission in cooperation with the Pennsylvania Archaeological Council

Ice Age Peoples of Pennsylvania, VOL. 2
Edited by Kurt W. Carr and James M. Adovasio
Published by the Pennsylvania Historical and Museum Commission in cooperation with the Pennsylvania Archaeological Council

Foragers and Farmers of the Early and Middle Woodland Periods in Pennsylvania, VOL. 3
Edited by Paul A. Raber and Verna L. Cowin
Published by the Pennsylvania Historical and Museum Commission in cooperation with the Pennsylvania Archaeological Council

The NATURE AND PACE OF CHANGE *in* AMERICAN INDIAN CULTURES

PENNSYLVANIA, 4000 TO 3000 BP

Edited by
R. MICHAEL STEWART, KURT W. CARR,
and PAUL A. RABER

THE PENNSYLVANIA STATE UNIVERSITY PRESS | UNIVERSITY PARK, PENNSYLVANIA

Publication of this book has been supported in part by the Eastern States Archaeological Federation, the Society for Pennsylvania Archaeology, and the Pennsylvania Archaeological Council.

Library of Congress Cataloging-in-Publication Data

The nature and pace of change in American Indian cultures : Pennsylvania, 4000 to 3000 BP / edited by R. Michael Stewart, Kurt W. Carr, and Paul A. Raber.
pages cm — (Recent research in Pennsylvania archaeology)
Summary: "A collection of essays addressing aspects of Native American life in the Susquehanna and Delaware River basin from 4000 to 3000 BP, the pre-existing traditions from which they emerged, and explanations for how and why social and cultural change took place"—Provided by publisher.
Includes bibliographical references and index.
ISBN 978-0-271-07095-7 (pbk. : alk. paper)
1. Pennsylvania—Antiquities. 2. Indians of North America—Pennsylvania—Antiquities.
I. Stewart, R. Michael (Richard Michael), editor. II. Carr, Kurt W. (Kurt William), 1949– , editor. III. Raber, Paul A., editor. IV. Series: Recent research in Pennsylvania archaeology.

E78.P4N38 2015
974.8'01—dc23
2015026644

Printed in the United States of America
Published by The Pennsylvania State University Press, University Park, PA 16802–1003

The Pennsylvania State University Press is a member of the Association of American University Presses.

It is the policy of The Pennsylvania State University Press to use acid-free paper. Publications on uncoated stock satisfy the minimum requirements of American National Standard for Information Sciences—Permanence of Paper for Printed Library Material, ANSI Z39.48–1992.

This book is printed on paper that contains 30% post-consumer waste.

CONTENTS

LIST OF FIGURES

LIST OF TABLES

Introduction

WORKING WITH THE
ARCHAEOLOGICAL RECORD OF
4500–2700 BP

R. Michael Stewart

ABSTRACT

The background for the development and significance of the contributions to this volume is provided and individual contributions are summarized. Theoretical perspectives on the pace, chronology, and historical context of change are discussed with respect to issues raised in the contributions. A Middle Atlantic regional perspective is provided on selected topics.

It is a basic assumption of anthropologists and archaeologists that all societies and cultures are in a constant state of transition. Variation is inherent in any sociocultural system: potential sources of change are always there. This volume focuses on a period of time in regional prehistory that represents the interface between what have typically been considered as two distinctive trends in ancient Native American lifeways, those defined as "Archaic" and those defined as "Woodland." Variously referred to as the "Transitional Archaic period," the "Transitional period," or the "Terminal Archaic period," it is held to be a time of change, recognized throughout the Middle Atlantic region, seemingly more dramatic than what precedes it or what follows after. *The Nature and Pace of Change in American Indian Cultures: Pennsylvania, 4000 to 3000 BP* is an exploration of what we now know and understand about the Transitional Archaic period based on archaeological data drawn primarily from sites in the Susquehanna and Delaware River basins of Pennsylvania and New Jersey.

John Witthoft's 1953 publication on broadspear-using Transitional cultures in Pennsylvania focused attention on the state and the general period of time that is examined in the chapters that follow. When first defined by Witthoft, the Transitional period was characterized by broad-bladed bifaces, cache blades, steatite bowls, consistent evidence of trade, distinctive lithic preferences, the initial appearance of ceramics, and adaptations with a riverine focus. Large fire-cracked rock features, a curated lithic technology, an emphasis on staged, bifacial lithic reduction strategies, and, in some areas, burial ceremonialism have been added to this list over the years (e.g., Custer 1996; Dent 1995; Kinsey 1972; Kraft 2001).

Some researchers have linked the appearance and development of these characteristics to environmental change, specifically, the warm and dry conditions of the Sub-Boreal climatic episode. The adaptive significance of the material culture and the cultural and social behaviors of the time remains unclear, and differing interpretive perspectives remain to be explored more thoroughly. The Transitional period certainly represents a time of changes, but are these any more rapid or dramatic than previous or subsequent changes in the social and cultural life of the American Indians of the Middle Atlantic region? What are the cultural historical contexts from which the things that we consider to be Transitional emerge? In other words, what are the preexisting cultural traditions that are the platform for human agency, decision making, and innovation during the period variously referred to as the "Transitional Archaic," "Transitional," or "Terminal Archaic"? And what are the processes of change that we believe we are detecting in the archaeological record?

The contributors to this volume examine some of the foundational evidence relevant to the time, the degree to which trends can be defined for the Susquehanna and Delaware River basins and the broader Middle Atlantic region, the implications of these trends, and the frameworks that could profitably be used in crafting interpretations of social and cultural change. Their contributions are the result of a symposium, "The Nature and Pace of Change in American Indian Cultures, 3000 to 4000 BP," organized by Kurt Carr and me and sponsored by the Pennsylvania Archaeological Council at the 2009 meeting of the Society for Pennsylvania Archaeology in Harrisburg, later reprised at the 2009 meeting of the Eastern States Archaeological Federation in Johnstown, Pennsylvania.

The period referred to in the symposium's original title was chosen to roughly encompass the time during which different forms of broad-bladed stemmed bifaces occur on sites in Pennsylvania and the broader Middle Atlantic region. The time from 4500 to 2700 BP (2550 to 750 BC) is nearer the mark, as reflected by radiocarbon-dated contexts from the Middle Atlantic region (e.g., Custer 1996:171–80, 2001; Dent 1995:Table 5.4), and given the habit of many researchers of including components with Fishtail-type stemmed bifaces. The contributors to this volume employ variable scales of time depending on their analytic focus and the data upon which they draw. That they do not employ the same chronological framework should not be too surprising. The periods that archaeologists use to organize "big picture" discussions of the past falsely imply that social and cultural changes occurred in lockstep over broad geographic areas. In fact, environmental variability and the nature and individual (pre)histories of the native groups impact how, when, and to what degree changes in behavior and material culture will be manifested. This is reflected in the variable chronological benchmarks and points of view promoted by the authors in this volume.

The abbreviation "BP" (before present) is used in two different ways throughout the chapters that follow. For readers not familiar with radiometric dating, "BP" is the way in which all conventional radiocarbon ages are reported by the laboratories that assay samples submitted for analysis. Defining the "present" as the calendar year 1950 provides a comparative standard for radiometric and other types of chronometric dating techniques. The abbreviation "BP" also is used as a general way to refer to specific points in time or ranges of time, retaining the year 1950 as an anchor point.

Over the years, correction or calibration curves have been developed to account for the inaccuracy of the radiocarbon dating technique owing to the variation in the amount of carbon 14 in the earth's atmosphere through time. Since calibration curves are periodically improved, it is important to note which calibration is employed whenever calibrated radiocarbon dates are reported. Calibrated or corrected dates are included by the chapter authors whenever a specific radiocarbon assay (e.g., 3520 + 100 BP) is referenced. Calibrated dates are reported using two sigmas or standard deviations and the Calib 7.0 program (Reimer et al. 2013). For example, the calibration of the conventional radiocarbon age of 3520 + 100 BP indicates that the most likely age of the analyzed sample is between 4084 and 3567 BP or a calendar age of between 2135 and 1618 BC.

There are cases, however, where it is not possible to determine whether radiocarbon assays or calendar dates cited from published sources were corrected or calibrated. Qualifications regarding individual dates are provided in the text where possible.

The types of tool stone employed in chipped-stone technologies figure prominently in the interpretation of aspects of the behavior of the native peoples of the Transitional Archaic period. Although some authors in this volume refer to one such tool stone type as "rhyolite," and others refer to it as "metarhyolite," they are all referring to the same material, a metamorphosed rhyolitic lava, that is, metarhyolite. (For summaries of the geological literature on this material with reference to archaeology, tool stone procurement, settlement patterns, and trade, see Stewart 1980, 1983, 1984a, 1984b, 1987a.)

Frank Vento (Chapter 1) summarizes what is known about climate and the paleoenvironment during the Sub-Boreal, 4200–3000 BP (2250–1050 BC), the climatic episode that corresponds most closely with the period of Middle Atlantic regional prehistory under consideration here. Although a relatively warm and dry trend in climate is noted by Vento, it appears to have had little impact on altering regional vegetation. Arguably, the climate did, however, alter the nature of low-order and upland streams and, by implication, native settlement patterns. This is essential background for understanding the ways environmental change may be implicated in the cultural changes visible in the archaeological record. The references that Vento cites provide a more extensive chronological and geographic context in which to consider trends in environmental change.

In his overview of Late Archaic developments in the Susquehanna Valley prior to the appearance of Broadspear-related components (Chapter 2), Robert Wall provides baseline data critical to evaluating the real differences between broadspear-using peoples and the ancestral traditions from which they drew. Among other things, Wall notes the presence of large platform hearths, fishing equipment, and the use of rhyolite associated with Lamoka sites in the Susquehanna Valley as a possible forerunner of Transitional adaptations. (For similarly useful background on Pennsylvania and the broader Middle Atlantic region, see Custer 1989, 1996; Dent 1995; Funk 1976, 1993; Kinsey 1972; Kraft 2001; Moeller 1990; Mouer 1990, 1991a, 1991b; Mounier 2003; Raber, Miller, and Neusius 1998; Ritchie and Funk 1973; Snethkamp 1981; Steponaitis 1986; Stewart 1980; Turnbaugh 1977; Versaggi 1996; and Wholey 2003.)

Kurt Carr (Chapter 3) compares and contrasts the evolution of Transitional Archaic adaptations in the Susquehanna and Delaware River valleys, arguing that not only was the adaptive strategy of the time different from what came before and what followed, but the rate of change was also more rapid relative to other periods in regional prehistory. Carr's chapter also includes a brief, but useful historical summary regarding the definition of, and debate over, the characterization of the Transitional Archaic period. Various ideas are raised in his synthesis worthy of future or continued testing, including the chronology of broadspears, their geographic distribution, and their potential reflection of different types of social structure.

In her perspective on the Transitional Archaic period (Chapter 4), Patricia Miller synthesizes the results of several archaeological projects that, as part of cultural resource management (CRM) studies in the Susquehanna Valley, document significant Broadspear-related components. She suggests that a developing trade network, in conjunction with evolving hunter-gatherer adaptations driven primarily by population increases rather than climate change, is responsible for the settlement shifts in the valley during the period.

Joseph Blondino (Chapter 5) uses components from the Upper Delaware Valley associated with Fishtail-type stemmed bifaces to provide a perspective on traditional views of the Transitional Archaic period. The use history of fishtails falls on both sides of the chronological boundary typically used to distinguish the Transitional Archaic/Terminal Archaic from the Early Woodland period; Fishtail-related components are considered by many to reflect a Transitional/Terminal Archaic adaptation. Focusing on the use of floodplain/terrace landscapes and fire-cracked rock (FCR) features, Blondino reflects on cultural historical and adaptive connections and speculates about the nature of floodplain-oriented economic activities.

Population densities for microgeographic areas in eastern and central Pennsylvania are estimated in Chapter 6 by Heather Wholey. Even with the inherent problems in using diagnostic biface forms as proxies for population density, this type of estimation is necessary if we are to understand the ways that population growth and pressure contribute to the nature and pace of culture change. Site settings and occupation units viewed at a smaller geographic scale reveal variability that is often masked when we generalize about regional trends.

The existence of standardized or unvarying Transitional cultures and associated archaeological sites throughout the Northeast and Middle Atlantic regions is challenged by Roger Moeller in the final chapter of this volume. Snapshot views of relevant sites and complexes from across the two regions are provided to illustrate the problem with using a single, overarching characterization of material culture, economic, and social behaviors for the Transitional period. Moeller notes, as do other authors in this volume, that other point types in addition to broadspears are part of contemporaneous assemblages. Because these types, by themselves, are not distinctive of a precise period of time, all relevant sites may not be included in our analyses of settlement and subsistence systems or population estimates.

As with any thought-provoking archaeological research, the interpretations of the archaeological record found in these chapters do not agree on every particular point|, but most, if not all, of these interpretive differences have testable implications that can serve as the basis for future research. This is how archaeological science is meant to function in moving us closer to the reality of the past. The common themes that link the contributions echo and magnify many of the characteristics of the Transitional period initially outlined by John Witthoft and provide a more reliable context within which explanations of cultural change can be viewed. All of the contributors, of course, recognize the importance of the period in terms of its historical significance in the development of Middle Atlantic archaeology, and it remains a viable construct for organizing and addressing the nature and development of ancient Native American cultures.

Consistent with earlier views, the warm and dry trend in the climate of the region during the Transitional Archaic period is viewed as important in understanding changes in settlement patterns and ultimately increases in social interaction. What distinguishes the updated view shared by a number of the authors in this volume is that, despite the change in climate, there was no dramatic change in the forests or vegetation of the region. The most significant effect of the decrease in effective moisture was a decline in upland and low-order streams. Environmental change is viewed by these authors not as the primary factor but rather as a factor that works in conjunction with population increases to influence cultural change. Wholey takes this further in Chapter 6, arguing that population density and the nature of the environments in which the greatest densities occur may be more critical than the overall growth of the region's populations.

There are greater numbers of sites in a given area during the Transitional Archaic period than noted for earlier times. Settlement territories appear to be smaller than in earlier times and are made visible in part by distinctive trends in the types of tool stone employed in the fashioning of bifaces, if not other components of chipped-stone assemblages. These observations have been made before but are reemphasized with more recently accumulated data. The appearance of large floodplain- and terrace-oriented sites revealing what could be considered semisedentary settlements also represents the reaffirmation of a traditional observation. But intensive investigations of stratified deposits show that this pattern may not be unique to the Transitional Archaic period, as Wall points out in his discussion of the Upper Susquehanna Valley in Chapter 2. Indeed, the initiation of the pattern is evidenced by larger sites of longer habitation associated with the Narrow-Stemmed Point tradition of the Late Archaic period, although Transitional Archaic sites reveal this pattern in a more widely seen and consistent fashion. There seems to be a consensus that the linked interaction of environmental change with population growth is key to understanding the change in the nature of riverine settlements, but Miller contends in Chapter 4 that it was the operation of a trade network, together with population growth, that led to a focus of settlement along the Susquehanna. This is not to deny, however, the importance of upland sites and the degree to which they materially and stylistically can vary, as Moeller argues so forcefully in Chapter 7.

Probably the most enduring aspect of Witthoft's original characterization of the Transitional is the list of distinctive types of artifacts and features associated with the period, expanded over the years and thoroughly detailed by Carr in Chapter 3, most notably, the first appearance of container technologies utilizing steatite and clay pottery rather than organic materials, the proliferation of fire-cracked rock on sites and in features, and the appearance of distinctive broad-bladed bifaces, projectile points, caches, and pit features. What is more important, as made clear by the authors here, is that the spatial distributions and incidences of these artifacts and features are not homogeneous but reflect interesting, sometimes subtle differences in the Transitional cultures of the Middle Atlantic region. Assemblages vary depending on the geographic area and environmental setting of particular sites, the range of functional activities performed there, and the sites' position in the overall settlement and subsistence system.

Broadspears are produced using the staged reduction of bifaces or bifacial cores, a technology different from that used to produce earlier Late Archaic stemmed bifaces or projectile points. But it is clear that broadspears and narrow-bladed stemmed biface/projectile types, produced using a core-and-flake approach, are contemporaneous. A single technology for the production of bifaces/projectile points does not characterize the cultures of the Transitional Archaic period. When the totality of behaviors and adaptations is taken into account, it is clear that components associated with Fishtail-type stemmed bifaces/projectile points should be included as part of the Transitional Archaic. Assemblages associated with Fishtail-type points transcend the chronological boundaries typically associated with the Transitional Archaic and Early Woodland periods.

Fire-cracked rock can result from a variety of heat-related activities, ranging from the simple radiation of heat in a hearth, to hot-rock cooking in containers or in earth ovens, to the drying of food resources. Attention to the lithic materials employed, fracture patterns, and the context of the altered rock on-site contributes to an understanding of the activities performed, as illustrated by the discussions in the current volume and the growing literature on the subject (e.g., Stewart 2005). The highly variable distribution of steatite bowls and early pottery testifies to the use of these containers in specialized activities, the meaning or significance ascribed to them, and differences in networks of exchange and social interaction. Considered singly or together, fire-cracked rock and the new container technologies argue for the increased importance of plant foods during the Transitional Archaic period, an argument supported by the somewhat meager paleobotanical remains that have been recovered. The use of nonlocal lithics for a portion of tool kits is a hallmark of the Transitional Archaic throughout the Middle Atlantic region, with materials like metarhyolite and jasper highlighted. This trend also provides a basis for recognizing and defining exchange or trade networks. The consistent and widespread existence of exchange networks remains typical of the Transitional Archaic period. What is qualified by recent research is that evidence of these networks simply intensifies during the period, which is to say, the period is *not* the chronological point of origin of recognizable and widespread networks.

In the remainder of this introduction, I will comment on some of the problems that we must cope with in addressing the issues relevant to the archaeology of the time from 4500 to 2700 BP (2550 to 750 BC) and revisit some of the common themes and interpretive diversity found in the contributions to this volume. I hope this commentary will both provide readers with a frame of reference in considering the efforts of the contributors and serve as a broad outline for future research. Before us are the tasks not only of recognizing and thoroughly documenting change and the factors that seem to be associated with it, but also of attempting to explain what is driving the changes that we see. As Carr so aptly notes in Chapter 3, it is now clear that our characterization of the Transitional period must be more complicated than it has been.

Perspectives on Change: Pace, Chronology, and Historical Context

"Transitional Archaic"? Our use of cultural historical labels like "Paleoindian," "Archaic," and "Woodland" presumes transitions and changes of significant degree, although such labels are apt to be more constraining than productive as our knowledge of cultural diversity increases and our chronological resolution of the past becomes finer grained (cf. Custer 1996; Dincauze 1970). "Terminal Archaic"? This is another loaded term since aspects of material culture, subsistence, and settlement patterns carry on beyond the chronological boundary used to distinguish the Archaic from the Woodland period. William Turnbaugh (1977:138–39) notes that Witthoft's view of the distinctive changes that mark the Transitional period has only been partly supported by ongoing research. Turnbaugh prefers the "Terminal Archaic" label because general Late Archaic behavioral patterns continue with elaboration (cf. Snethkamp 1981:i). In Herbert Kraft's (2001:137) vision of the Terminal Archaic, "people continued to live much as they did before," meaning prior to 3950 BP (2000 BC). Dean Snow (1980:236) abandons "the options of both cultural transition and evolutionary stage" in his use of the "Terminal Archaic" label as part of his organization of New England prehistory. Many choose simply to deal with the assemblages associated with broadspears as phases of the Late Archaic period (e.g., Dent 1995). The history and aspects of this ongoing debate regarding terminology and its implications are embedded in a number of the chapters in this volume (e.g., Chapter 3 by Carr and Chapter 7 by Moeller).

Whether we are talking about environment, society, or culture, most theorists are in agreement that "change," or variability, is an ever-present given. What is of greater interest is the nature and pace of change and what is generating it. Change can be slow or it can be fast, but it is an ever-present aspect of sociocultural life regardless of the resolution provided by the archaeological record.

Evolutionary theorists (e.g., Boyd and Richerson 2005; Richerson and Boyd 2001; Richerson, Boyd, and Bettinger 2001) see the pace of change as influenced by the systemic relationship between a number of factors: evolutionary processes, human and biological ecology, human agency, social structures, and historical contingency. Climate and environment are obvious factors since they relate to biological and human ecology, the technological and economic systems of people living in specific environments, and the historical contexts in which these systems have developed. Geography is another factor with an emphasis on the degree to which it facilitates interaction between people, as well as the size and distribution of populations within a geographic area. The pace of cultural change can potentially be great among large populations in regions where geography facilitates interaction—innovations, when they occur, have the potential to spread rapidly. And innovation is often spurred by stress resulting from population growth or environmental downturns. These observations relate to scale; that is, once populations with a given economic and social system reach a certain size within a defined geographic area, things have to change. Until a tipping point is reached, change may be slow or even imperceptible, but once that point is reached, more dramatic change is initiated. In what Lewis Binford (2001:357) calls "density-dependent processes," things like population and settlement densities render traditional adaptive strategies ineffective or obsolete. In contrast, change will be slow in geographic regions occupied by small groups who interact infrequently.

Peter Richerson, Robert Boyd, and Robert Bettinger (2001; reprinted in Boyd and Richerson 2005:337–74) modeled population growth and population pressure in considering explanations for the origins of agriculture. Their observations are relevant here, especially given estimates of population size that figure in the discussions of Carr, Wholey, and Moeller (Chapters 3, 6, and 7) in this volume. Carr (Chapter 3) views many of the changes associated with the Transitional Archaic as being driven primarily by population pressure. Assuming that rates of hunter-gatherer population growth are modest and that the carrying capacity of the environment remains constant, near-capacity populations are reached on a scale of 500 to 1,000 years according to Richerson, Boyd, and Bettinger (2001). Population pressure can be alleviated by a variety of innovative behaviors that either lower population density (e.g., dispersal of people into new areas) or increase subsistence efficiency. Specifically mentioned by Carr are technological innovations and expanding the subsistence inventory to include new foodstuffs. Other behaviors such as the reorganization of subsistence-related labor could be added to this general list. "Innovation allows greater population increases over the long run, but it does *not* change the timescales on which population pressure occurs" (Richerson, Boyd, and Bettinger 2001:398; emphasis added). Put another way, the more rapidly innovations occur, the larger populations can become, but the rate at which population pressure arises does not change substantially.

The existence or perception of population pressure can occur at low population densities depending on the nature of subsistence strategies (Richerson, Boyd, and Bettinger 2001:404–5): "Hunters pursuing herd animals may generate much population pressure at low human population densities because killing only a small fraction of the herd makes the survivors difficult to hunt. On the other hand, subsistence farmers spreading into a uniform fertile plain may feel little population pressure until all farmland is occupied" (404). The initial cost of the hunters' subsistence strategy in the above example changes through time. In a similar vein,

> when a community first enters virgin territory, the strategies available for obtaining food differ in their initial costs; it may be cheaper to get a good diet by hunting deer than by collecting seeds. Over time, as deer become less abundant, and hence more expensive to obtain, new strategies are added as their costs become comparable to the cost of deer. Thus, the number of strategies foragers use in obtaining food tends to increase the longer they inhabit a given area. (Johnson and Earle 1987:12)

If we want to realize the full interpretive value of the population curves developed for the Middle Atlantic region, we need a more detailed understanding of the subsistence strategies used by Indian peoples before, during, and after the time period of interest. More comprehensive intraregional site surveys also are required so that estimates of population size and population densities can be reliably employed in explanations of sociocultural change.

Niche construction theory (Laland and O'Brien 2010; Odling-Smee, Laland, and Feldman 2003) also could prove useful in our research endeavors, especially since we are dealing with a time of environmental change and the possibility that Indian peoples are intensifying their economic pursuits. Niche theory refers to the process whereby the biological and other behaviors and choices of organisms alter (intentionally or unintentionally) their own niches and those of other organisms. The theory "stresses that, in modifying their own world, organisms frequently modify the environments of other organisms that share those environments" (Laland and O'Brien 2010:305). In what ways might climate change during the Sub-Boreal in the Middle Atlantic region have affected things that native peoples were already doing to the environment? If forests or other landscapes were being managed with fire prior to the Sub-Boreal, the continued use of such practices in conjunction with climate change could result in the creation of environments with unanticipated prospects or problems for exploitation. If Late Archaic hunters were harvesting all age and sex grades of deer and other game, how might this have affected the size and distribution of game populations and reoriented the degree to which other foodstuffs were emphasized?

If population pressure, environmental downturns, or both led to stress on Late Archaic/Transitional cultures, what is the potential range of cultural responses that we might be able to detect? Following Richard Redding (1988:71–72), strategies for reducing resource stress can include mobility, diversity, and storage. The existence of storage pits on sites, often thought to be linked with increasingly sedentary trends in settlement, could be part of a systemic response to resource stress generated by some combination of environmental changes, population growth, contraction and realignment of settlement territories, and changes in population densities. Storage is also viewed as a risk-minimizing strategy (Winterhalder and Kennett 2009). Economic intensification is another potential response that can involve new technologies, the reorganization of labor applied to traditionally exploited resources, or the addition of new resources to those traditionally exploited. The management of wild resources traditionally exploited can be thought of as a new subsistence technology. Management could be in the form of any number of behaviors that ethnohistoric and ethnographic hunter-gatherers have employed (e.g., Keeley 1995; Smith 2001). Periodically burning over certain habitats promotes the growth of favored plants, reduces competition from undesirable species, aids some hunting practices, and clears landscapes for the sowing of wild plant seeds. Other management strategies include weeding and transplanting economically useful plants and pruning and coppicing shrubs and trees. Resource management would not alter the basic list of subsistence items relative to what was being exploited during an earlier time, but the quantity or relative importance of a subsistence resource to the native diet would increase. The number and nature of processing tools and related facilities or features also need not change dramatically. All of the above have potential relevance to the Transitional Archaic period of Pennsylvania and the Middle Atlantic region.

It has been argued that, because components of cultural systems like technology, subsistence, and social institutions are critically linked and functionally well integrated, they are resistant to change, but that when change occurs, it can be rapid (e.g., Bettinger 1999, 2001; Bettinger, Richerson, and Boyd 2009). Dramatic climate change would certainly figure into this argument, as would Binford's density-dependent processes and the cultural evolutionary perspectives of Richerson and Boyd.

Some theorists (e.g., Gardner 2009; Hayden 2001) note the primary role of individual choice, human agency, or charismatic and self-aggrandizing individuals in accelerating culture change under the right conditions. Agency theory acknowledges that an individual's understanding of preexisting or traditional culture is one starting point for crafting choices about how to act or react in specific situations. Although the theoretical perspectives of Bettinger, Boyd, and Richerson do not consider human agency to be the primary force driving cultural change, they fully embrace its potential role in both initiating and constraining change and in affecting its pace. Economic and social frameworks or institutions that serve to structure people's productive lives and how they relate to one another and their environment are important components in understanding cultural evolution and the rate of change. As Bettinger (2001:145) notes: "Entrenched social arrangements may determine what is doable in a given techno-environmental context." The behavioral approach to understanding material culture also assumes that "choices build upon choices—all are made in the context of people's traditional knowledge and social systems" (Skibo and Schiffer 2008:21). The patterned behaviors that we see archaeologically could thus be viewed as the reiterative and cumulative effects of human agency operating within social and techno-environmental contexts. And, of course, there is always the role that migration of new people into an area plays in altering the "social environment" and initiating change.

Consider fishing as an example of the processes noted above. Fishing can be undertaken by individuals, by families, or by larger cooperating groups. In an evolutionary perspective, the social group can exert "selective pressure" on variations in behavior. Under stable environmental and population conditions, there may be no selective pressure favoring any specific type of labor force. But a charismatic individual might convince followers that, if fish were exploited by a large cooperating group, a surplus could be realized that might be used to underwrite feasting or trade or craft specialization.

Our assessment of the pace or rate of change is relative—is it occurring faster or slower than in earlier or later times? Are the data for the time preceding 4500 BP (2550 BC) sufficient for making comparisons? What increments of time are we able to use for comparative purposes? Centuries, millennia? And addressing the pace of change *does* matter to the degree that rapid change implicates certain processes, like dramatic climate change, interactions of large populations, or migration, that slow change need not involve (cf. Richerson, Boyd, and Bettinger 2001:Table 2).

Our ability to tightly date large numbers of sites, to develop fine-grained cultural histories, and to chart environmental change in the smallest increments of time possible is crucial to our research. Is the Pennsylvania or Middle Atlantic regional database sufficient in this respect? Consider the degree to which chronologically diagnostic artifacts allow us to date surface and plow zone deposits. A number of so-called diagnostic artifacts transcend the chronological brackets used to define the Transitional Archaic (Custer 1996:167–80). Broadspear, Fishtail, Lackawaxen, and Hellgrammite forms ca. 3250–2850 BP (1300–900 BC) co-occur at the Williamson Site in the Delaware Valley (Hummer 1991, 1994). Lamoka-like, Susquehanna, and Snook Kill broadspears and Fishtail-type points co-occur in Level 3 at the Canfield Island Site in the Susquehanna Valley, a context that suggests their contemporaneity (Bressler, Maietta, and Rockey 1983:Figure 7). Stemmed bifaces that easily could be typed as Lackawaxen points of the Late Archaic period are found in association with early pottery in the Delaware Valley (Hummer 1991:Plate 12; Payne 1990; Stewart 1986, 1987b). A Stemmed Point tradition persists throughout the Late Archaic to Early Woodland periods in the Piedmont of Pennsylvania (Snethkamp 1981:213, 217). There are triangular biface forms that can be associated with Middle Archaic to Early Woodland contexts that mimic Late Woodland projectile points (Custer 2001:84–88; Katz 2000; Luckenbach, Grow, and Sharpe 2010; Stewart 1998a; Stewart and Cavallo 1991).

In the end, we are forced to conflate time in generalizing about trends and behaviors seen in the archaeological record when dating sites solely on the basis of diagnostic artifacts. Can we confidently say that important phenomena are relatively contemporaneous? When we rely on the well-dated buried deposits that do exist, are we using them to generalize about trends across too broad an area? We are confounded by the co-occurrence of narrow-bladed stemmed points that occur in contemporaneous assemblages with broadspears. Thus sites with stemmed points but lacking broadspears are "floating" from a chronological perspective—some might relate to the Transitional Archaic period and some not, but either alternative has significant implications for our understanding of Transitional Archaic settlement patterns.

Some Aspects of Change, 4500–2700 BP

A common theme of the chapters in this volume is that variability characterizes the archaeological record across the geographic areas studied, the explanations for the changes that are evident, and the degree to which definitions of the Transitional Archaic period are upheld (cf. Carr and Moeller, Chapters 3 and 7). I next explore some of the defining trends of the period and possible explanations for their occurrence, and I suggest avenues for future research.

Environment

The nature of the environment and the nature and rate of environmental change are important both in contextual examinations of the changes that characterize the Transitional Archaic period and in attempts at explaining them. As with any archaeological issue, reconstructing and examining environmental evidence in contexts of differing scales, whether chronological or spatial, can provide interpretive insights not evident otherwise (e.g., Anderson 2001). Showing the coincidence of environmental change with cultural change does not automatically prove that the two are associated, however. There has to be some discussion of the specifics of how the two are related. Are environmental and cultural changes working on the same relative cycles throughout the region? Are environmental and archaeological data organized at the same chronological scale or in the same units of analysis? If they are not, we will never craft a convincing argument about how the two are related and implicated in culture change. Given our presumption of the importance of environmental change, what do we know from ethnography and the study of living cultures about how people perceive and react to environmental change?

Characterizations of paleoenvironmental change used by archaeologists are typically generalized at the scale of overarching trends for substantial periods of time, for example, the Sub-Boreal (4500–3000 BP/2550–1050 BC) and Sub-Atlantic (3000–1750 BP/1050 BC–AD 200) climatic episodes (Coppock, Stiteler, and Vento 2011:Table 1). Yet paleoenvironmental specialists and archaeologists recognize that overarching trends, like the warm and dry conditions associated with the Sub-Boreal and the warm and moist conditions of the Sub-Atlantic, are broken up by climatic perturbations operating on timescales more relevant to human perception and generational cultural memories (e.g., Carbone 1976, 1982; Fiedel 2001; Kellogg and Custer 1994; Stinchcomb et al. 2013; Vento, Chapter 1, this volume). Further, even dramatic and relatively short lived climate changes, like the Younger Dryas of the Early Holocene, did not seem to impact all environmental zones dramatically or to engender widespread cultural change (Meltzer and Holliday 2010).

The chronological bracketing of the Transitional Archaic period crosscuts not only shifts in the longer-term climatic trends of the Sub-Boreal and Sub Atlantic episodes, but also the oscillations that occur with differing frequencies and amplitudes within the episodes. For example, abrupt cold snaps occur ca. 2950 BP/1000 BC and 2650 BP/700 BC (see summary in Fiedel 2001:119–23). What we need are more microgeographical studies of past environments like those of Gary Coppock, John Stiteler, and Frank Vento (2011) and of Gary Stinchcomb and colleagues (2013). The impact of any change in climate in the region will be modified by a variety of variables like latitude, elevation, geology, stream networks, edaphic conditions, and preexisting vegetation. The resource potentials and carrying capacities of areas within the Middle Atlantic region differ, so that the impact of environmental change across the region would have different potential consequences for group adaptations. The relative reduction in the rate of sea level rise (cf. Horton et al. 2013; Kraft and John 1978; Nikitina et al. 2000) occurring during the Transitional Archaic period would have supported the stabilization and proliferation of plant, fish, and animal populations in the Coastal Plain of the region, providing a potential contrast with carrying capacities of more interior physiographic provinces. If we assume that the cultural behaviors used to define the Transitional Archaic are occurring in relative lockstep throughout the broader region, then causes for cultural change have to transcend contemporaneous environmental diversity and its implications for subsistence and other aspects of economy. In contrast, we might argue that, since cultural behaviors have much in common across such an environmentally diverse region, Indian peoples are responding to commonly perceived constraints or opportunities; that is, no matter what the effect of climate change on specific environments might have been, traditional ways of doing things had to be altered.

Marc Abrams and Gregory Nowacki (2008) summarize environmental and archaeological data suggesting that, at least by 3000 BP (1050 BC), the incidence of oak, chestnut, and hickory in the forests of the Northeast is a partial reflection of native peoples managing forests with fire. Of interest is their identification of two "climate-vegetation anomalies" involving the late arrival and rise of chestnut, which prefers a warm and wet climate, and the concomitant stability of hickory, which prefers warm and dry conditions (Abrams and Nowacki 2008:1124–25). "The long-term persistence of mast-dominated forests, savannas and tallgrass prairie in the eastern U.S.A. only makes sense in the context of persistent and extensive Indian burning through periods of both warming and cooling climate during the middle and later Holocene" (Abrams and Nowacki 2008:1133). Paul and Hazel Delcourt and colleagues provide a similar date for native use of fire in landscape management in the southern Appalachians (Delcourt and Delcourt 1998; Delcourt et al. 1998). The analysis of Kurt Fesenmyer and Norman Christensen (2010) implicates native peoples in the increase in the frequency of forest fires in the southern Appalachians beginning 4000 BP (2050 BC).

These observations are critical given the presumed increase in the importance of mast and other plant resources in Transitional Archaic versus Late Archaic economies. Mast certainly figures in the subsistence strategies of Late Archaic peoples. Oak and chestnut increase in the forests of the Atlantic climatic episode (8000–4500 BP/6050–2550 BC) and become dominant, reaching what may be historic levels by 5000 BP/3050 BC (Coppock, Stiteler, and Vento 2011:208). Thus, prior to the Transitional Archaic period, the potential existed for native peoples to intensify their use of mast with management strategies such as periodically burning landscapes, pruning, girdling, or removing competing tree species (Smith 2001). But, apparently, they did not. The use of fire and other landscape management strategies may be part of the reason why smaller, better-defined territories and a semisedentary trend in settlement are such distinctive features of Transitional Archaic cultures, as I will argue below.

Technology

It has been observed that during the Transitional Archaic period there is an increasing use of locally available tool stone relative to earlier periods. In some places, it may be metarhyolite or quartzite; in others, it may be argillite, chert, or jasper. One problem in characterizing trends in material use is our reliance on information from surface sites in the form of chronologically diagnostic bifaces. When we have entire chipped-stone assemblages from buried contexts, we can see that the nondiagnostic portions of the assemblage are based on other materials or reflect a mix of materials revealing an emphasis different from that derived from the diagnostics.

Major quarries of jasper, metarhyolite, and argillite display evidence of the aboriginal excavation and reexcavation of pits to retrieve raw material. Studies of jasper quarries (Anthony and Roberts 1988; Carr and McLearen 2005; Hatch 1993; Hatch and Miller

1985; Stewart and Schindler 2008) make it clear that the size and intensity of quarrying activity increases during the Late Archaic/Transitional Archaic period. Radiocarbon dates associated with quarry pit features at the Kings Quarry Site (38LH2) indicate the most intensive periods of quarry use occurred in the past 4,000 years (Carr and McLearen 2005; Stewart and Schindler 2008).

The digging and redigging of large quarry craters could imply several things about the behavior of native peoples. Larger and more intensive working of the quarries might mean that a larger group was involved in the procurement of tool stone and that labor for this activity was reorganized relative to social structures employed previously. The intensity of quarry use might also indicate higher levels of tool production to serve local needs and focused trade with groups in the broader region. Reduction in the size of exploitative or group territories, a trend typically ascribed to the Transitional Archaic period, could have resulted in people returning to the same quarries more frequently than in the past.

At Kings Quarry, R. Michael Stewart and William Schindler (2008:24, 39–45) note that heat-altered jasper artifacts are found in all excavations and in a variety of strata. Roughly 14.2% (n = 4,508) of all of the artifacts from the excavations (n = 31,783) are characterized as thermally altered. Given the general quality of the jasper at Kings Quarry, one might assume that it would benefit from heat treatment, but the evidence for intentional heat treatment is equivocal. The question remains: why do so many artifacts at Kings Quarry show signs of thermal alteration? One answer, difficult to test, is that natural fires, or fires used to clear fields by Colonial and later farmers, may be responsible for altering the artifacts long after they were discarded by prehistoric miners. This scenario seems inadequate to explain the frequency with which thermally altered artifacts appear in strata well below the existing surface and beyond the altering effects of Colonial/historic surface fires. There are various reasons, other than to improve the knapping quality of tool stone, why native miners might build fires within the active quarry zone of the site. One reason might be to maintain open areas where work repeatedly takes place. The distribution of thermally altered artifacts is patterned, and these patterns correspond with the patterning of other types of artifacts.

The appearances of stone bowls and pottery are technologically significant benchmarks, but their significance is perhaps not as transformative as typically envisioned (Stewart 2011). Neither stone bowls nor early pottery vessels appear in sufficient quantities to argue for the role of either as the premier container technology employed in cooking or storage. Fire-cracked rock, potentially employed in "hot rock" cooking in containers made of perishable materials, occurs before, during, and after the period of use of steatite bowls and early pottery. The use of rock in heat-related processing of resources seems particularly intensive during the Transitional Archaic period. This is not to say that stone bowls and early pots were not used for cooking or heat-related processing. They were, but I would argue in a more specialized way.

The social or ideological function of each type of container is difficult to determine and may be highly variable across the geographic areas of their use. Contextual data generally show stone bowls and early pots being discarded in the same types of contexts as other classes of artifacts. Steatite containers are occasionally associated with mortuary contexts (e.g., Ritchie 1959; Truncer 2004:295) at a time when mortuary features rarely contain any type of material offering. There may be differences in the cultural perceptions of the value of the different types of containers. The spatial distribution of steatite vessels and early pottery is fairly discontinuous, as has been noted (Klein 1997; Stewart 1998b), making it extremely unlikely that either type of container satisfied the domestic cooking, serving, storage, or transport needs of native peoples. In this respect, the two container technologies seem closely linked. It has been argued that steatite bowls were more highly valued because of the costs involved in procuring sufficient raw material for them and in producing them (e.g., Klein 1997). Both steatite containers and early pottery might initially represent "exotic" technologies in that they had economic *and* social or symbolic value not conveyed by the production, use, or ownership of traditional types of cooking containers (i.e., bark, wooden, or basket containers). Following Michael Russo and Gregory Heide (2004:108), these two novel and relatively rare technologies may have had both economic and social value that enhanced the power or prestige of those who possessed them.

Several technological elaborations or innovations associated with the Transitional Archaic period figure in the chapters that follow. Innovations that predate the Transitional Archaic become more widespread and are used more frequently during this period, namely, the production or use of ground-stone axes and other woodworking tools, milling equipment, stone bowls, pottery, and spearthrower weights, the use of hot rocks in cooking and resource processing, the implied production and use of dugout canoes, and the possible use of fire in managing landscapes. As noted above (Richerson, Boyd, and Bettinger 2001), innovation contributes to population growth.

Subsistence and Settlement Patterns

Expanding what we know about the range of economically useful plants being exploited through time and the relative importance of any particular food resource is critical to exploring Transitional Archaic shifts in subsistence that likely included an increasing reliance on mast and other plant foods. The growing trend toward the use of techniques to recover and identify microscopic traces of plant materials (e.g., Messner 2008, 2011; Messner and Dickau 2005; Messner, Dickau, and Harbison 2007) will be helpful, as will the wider use of flotation to recover more macrobotanical remains. We also need to begin systematically testing wetlands associated with habitation areas. Elsewhere in the Eastern Woodlands, archaeologists have demonstrated that Native Americans were planting both wild and domesticated plants, like squash, as part of tended stands in wetland habitats adjacent to settlement areas during Archaic and Woodland times (Lovis and Monaghan 2007; Monaghan, Lovis, and Egan-Bruhy 2006). This is not to say that prepared fields or gardens were not also employed. The issue here is that wetlands adjacent to Indian settlements are not typically explored for what they might reveal about the use of plants, yet they have great potential.

Nicole Waguespack (2005) points out some useful distinctions that arise from the emphasis ethnographic foraging societies place on meat versus plant foods. When meat is the mainstay of the diet, plant use is restricted to resources that do not involve a major investment of labor in procurement and processing and the creation of related tools and implements. Milling equipment and watertight containers that would be needed for processing certain types of nuts, acorns, tubers, and greens would be predictably absent or rare in artifact assemblages. The widespread evidence of plant use, the proliferation of milling equipment, the widespread occurrence of fire-altered rock implying various types of hot-rock cooking, and the production and use of stone bowls and eventually pottery that seem so characteristic of Transitional Archaic peoples across the broader Middle Atlantic region might thus be a partial reflection of rising human populations and a concomitant reduction in the availability of game over time. If we can demonstrate that mast resources are used intensively, then semisedentary types of settlements are implied, given the logistical requirements of collecting, drying, storing, and, finally, processing mast for consumption.

During the Transitional Archaic period, more people seem to be living in floodplain settings or revisiting floodplains more frequently, with the reuse of specific locations resulting in the creation of large, archaeologically visible sites. This is a trend through time that crosscuts all physiographic settings (cf. Custer 1996, 2013; Dent 1995), as the chapters in this volume make clear. Yet variability does exist. In New York portions of the Upper Susquehanna Valley, there are Late Archaic base camps situated along the river. Their settings and the location of other types of sites in the main floodplain and tributary valleys suggested to Nina Versaggi (1996:137) "a settlement system tethered to prime deer and fish aggregation areas." This "localized" use of the river valley "appears to stop abruptly at the end of the Late Archaic, and this halt lasts through the Transitional Archaic period. Snook Kill, Genesee, Susquehanna Broad[spear], and Orient diagnostics are absent on the base camps" (Versaggi 1996:137)—just the opposite of what Miller (Chapter 4) describes for Pennsylvania sections of the Susquehanna Valley.

Whatever is driving the emphasis on riverine settings and the creation of semisedentary settlements, the ecology of the situation could reinforce economic behaviors already in place, that is, the use of mast and other plant resources. Prolonged habitation at a fixed location would eventually lead to a decline in the availability of game within the foraging radius of the settlement. This in turn might lead to an increase in the importance of more sustainable plant resources, an intensification of their use, and a greater investment in storage facilities to offset subsistence risk. It could also enhance both the importance of sources of animal protein such as fish and shellfish and the intensity of their exploitation and use of related technology. For such a scenario to work, group mobility must not be a viable solution to the problem of declining game within the catchment area of a site. Factors constraining group mobility might be a combination of the effects of environmental change and population densities.

In most syntheses of regional prehistory settlement ranges or territories of the Transitional Archaic period are thought to be better defined and smaller than those of earlier times based on the regionalization of some artifact styles, patterns in tool stone use, a decrease in exotic materials discarded at quarry sites, the cyclical reuse of sites, and evidence of semisedentary settlements. Although archaeologists seem to agree on the trend of a reduction in size of settlement territories, what is behind this reduction remains at issue. Historically, the reduction has been attributed to "settling in" phenomena, such as the primary forest efficiency Joseph Caldwell (1958) finds coincident with establishment of Middle and Late Holocene environments, gradual population growth, and innovations that increase productivity. Based on their analysis of ethnographic foragers, Allen Johnson and Timothy Earle (1987:60) note that, for many foraging groups, "minimal territoriality made possible a flexibility of movement in search of food that was essential to a forager's survival." In turn, a heightened sense of territoriality is associated with the use of stable, predictable resources, with circumscribed productive environments or with groups who have improved the productivity of settings through various means. During the Transitional Archaic period, we have arguably all of these factors at work.

If we assume that mast and other plant resources in general have become a more important part of Native American economies, then we might also assume that Indian peoples are managing wild resources to some degree through transplanting, weeding, pruning, coppicing, selective replanting, and burning off landscapes (Smith 2001). As noted earlier, there is tentative evidence for an increase in deliberately set fires during this period. A heightened sense of territoriality could be related to protecting or safeguarding the results of the labor and time invested in resource management. Increases in yields as a result of resource management would continue to stimulate commitments to specific landscapes. Territories were becoming smaller not simply because of the quality and potential of Middle Holocene environments for hunter-gatherers, but also because of the technologies employed in managing the resources available in these environments. In some respects, the environmental changes attributed to the Transitional Archaic period could have circumscribed or reduced the extent of the most reliably productive environments, prompting an emphasis on river-oriented settlements from which task groups could target other settings whose productivity was contingent and variable. Peripheral environments were not abandoned—sites dating from 4500 to

2700 BP (2550 to 750 BC) are everywhere—but the ways in which they were being used changed. In such a model, population pressure need not be invoked as a factor in the reduction of settlement territories. Wholey (Chapter 6) suggests that populations were crashing during the Transitional Archaic period, in contrast to the views of Carr (Chapter 3) and Moeller (Chapter 7). But if populations were growing, it would be a further impetus for the cultural changes that we see in the archaeological record.

Society

During this period in the Middle Atlantic region, signs of increasing social complexity are seen in geographically isolated examples of burial ceremonialism at sites like Savich Farm, Red Valley, and Koens-Crispin in the New Jersey Coastal Plain (Burrow 1997; Cross 1941:81–90, 117–27; Hawkes and Linton 1916; Mounier 2003:168–74; Regensberg 1971, 1982) and in cultural systems based in Chesapeake Bay/Delmarva Peninsula areas with highly productive and predictable resources that are circumscribed (Custer 1989). It is clear that, although aspects of what could be termed "Transitional Archaic culture" are similar across a broad geographic area, the social structures in which they exist are variable. One conclusion to be drawn from this observation is that there is heightened interaction between groups regardless of their cultural differences.

Greater population densities would lead to heightened levels of interaction. L. Daniel Mouer (1990, 1991a) argues that an emphasis on riverine settings and semisedentary settlements automatically intensifies the degree of interaction between groups relative to fairly mobile settlement patterns involving a variety of environments. This is due to the spatial organization and extent of riverine versus other environments and the degree to which lines of communication between nearest neighbors in these settings do or do not cross (Mouer 1990:Figure 3a, 1991a:Figure 3). Forms of transportation and travel routes could also impact levels of interaction. The use of dugout canoes in conjunction with the refocusing of primary settlements along major waterways could be a contributing factor to greater interaction and was deemed important both in Witthoft's (1953:25) original vision of the Transitional period and in Turnbaugh's (1975:62) consideration of the dispersal of broadspears in the east. The creation of an extensive trail system akin to those of historic times (Wallace 1993) might also be important.

Exchange, as interaction between humans, and trade, as its material expression, are integral parts of any society (Oka and Kusimba 2008:340). Archaeologists have difficulties in recognizing exchange and trade that take place within communities or between related communities. We are better able to recognize exchange and trade when they involve people and goods from different geographic areas. Exchange and trade have been modeled by a number of researchers in the Middle Atlantic region (e.g., Custer 1984; Klein 1997; Lattanzi 2013; Miller 1982, and Chapter 4, this volume; Mouer 1990, 1991a; Snethkamp 1981; Stewart 1989, 1994, 2004). It is presumed that unpatterned exchange/trade predates 4500 BP in the region. But it is only between 4500 and 4000 BP (2550 and 2050 BC) that consistent and persistent patterns in the distribution of artifacts attributable to trade are seen in the archaeological record. Given the linkage between social interaction, changes in settlement patterns, and presumed population densities, it is not surprising to see consistent evidence of trade coincide with the Transitional Archaic period, regardless of the myriad purposes or functions that exchange might serve and the role that human agency and the aggrandizing behavior of individuals might play.

Following Miller (Chapter 4), the major change of the Transitional Archaic period was the operation of trade networks that led to a focus of settlement along rivers. These networks were overlaid on a hunter-gatherer adaptation that was evolving, driven primarily by population increase rather than climate change. Population increases certainly could be linked with greater levels of trade, and settlements along river systems could facilitate the operation of trade networks, but, as has been noted here and in the other chapters of this volume, there are various other reasons why river-oriented settlements became the rule. The frequent use of metarhyolite along the Susquehanna and Juniata Rivers noted by Miller and others is intriguing given the distances involved from source areas of the tool stone. I suggest that this distributional pattern is probably more a reflection of direct procurement, settlement territories that are more linear than broad and that parallel stream systems, and travel and transport made easier by the use of watercraft. It is hard to envision a people's chipped-stone technology being based so heavily on raw material that had to be acquired through trade, at least at the supposed level of sociocultural integration among the people of the time.

Anything that makes the physical or social world smaller impacts how people think about themselves. The degree of social interaction evident during the Transitional Archaic period indicates that the social world has become smaller relative to earlier times. Although heightened levels of interaction can spread common ideas over broad areas, they can also spur the heightened expression of individual or group identity that we see in microregional variations in chipped- and ground-stone technology and style, material use, and the more frequent appearance of ornaments.

Conclusion

I have introduced aspects of the Transitional Archaic period that are examined in greater detail in the other chapters of this volume, provided a snapshot of theoretical and methodological frames of reference that can be useful in thinking about the data presented in later chapters and their relationship to culture change, and taken interpretive forays into selected aspects of the technology, subsistence, settlement patterns, and society of the Transitional Archaic. I hope that some of the ideas presented by me and my colleagues will stimulate future research. Ongoing attempts to explain the changes that take place during the Transitional Archaic period will require examining the complex relationship between environmental change, population size, preexisting cultural traditions, and technological and social innovations.

Environment matters in any explanation. It is easy to imagine how climate change and its effects on the composition and structure of regional environments could initiate a variety of changes in existing Late Archaic cultures. But we need finer-grained reconstructions of ancient environments at small spatial and chronological scales to reliably understand the association of climate change with culture change. Since environments and their potentials will vary across space and time, this leaves open the possibility that heightened levels of group interaction are a major mechanism for synchronizing cultural behaviors across the range of preexisting environmental and cultural variability. For a variety of reasons, aspects of behavior and material culture resulting from a deliberate response by some groups to an environmental downturn may be picked up and imitated by others not as dramatically affected by the downturn. Thus some of the Transitional phenomena described here and in the following chapters may reflect the fact that regional populations had grown and continued to grow as a result of the natural cycles and the impact of innovations modeled by Richerson, Boyd, and Bettinger (2001), such that the frequency of social interaction reached a tipping point relative to earlier times. Evidence of exchange/trade certainly confirms heightened levels of interaction relative to earlier times.

Heightened and more regularized evidence of exchange/trade could be the default result of larger populations or the repositioning of smaller populations in certain geographic or environments such that population densities increase, that is, in riverine settings. Groups relocating to fewer productive environmental settings would increase population densities without a concomitant increase in population size. The net effect of either scenario would be elevated levels of social interaction and associated exchange/trade paralleling Mouer's (1990, 1991a, 1991b) model. If population pressure is invoked as a primary factor in the initiation of Transitional Archaic group adaptations, should we not find increasing number of sites dating to just before the appearance of broadspears, and in environmental settings that are less than ideal? A dramatic environmental downturn by its very nature could trigger population pressure and attendant processes, depending on the size of the preexisting population and the rapidity of the environmental change. More thorough regional site surveys will be critical in supporting such arguments, especially since the population curves and estimates used by researchers vary significantly (cf. Carr, Wholey, and Moeller, Chapters 3, 6, and 7).

In the end, I think that we are dealing with the "perfect storm" during the Transitional Archaic period—the coincidence of a cycle of population growth, a variety of innovations contributing to population growth, climate change reconfiguring the nature and distribution of productive environments, and increased social interaction—resulting in both elaborations of and dramatic departures from preexisting cultural traditions. I look forward to the next generation of research.

Acknowledgments

Publication of this volume was made possible by the joint efforts of Paul Raber and the Pennsylvania Archaeological Council, the Society for Pennsylvania Archaeology, and the Eastern States Archaeological Federation through its Brennan Publication Fund. I gratefully acknowledge their support.

REFERENCES

Abrams, Marc D., and Gregory J. Nowacki
2008 Native Americans as Active and Passive Promoters of Mast and Fruit Trees in the Eastern U.S.A. *Holocene* 18 (7): 1123–37.

Anderson, David G.
2001 Climate and Culture Change in Prehistoric and Early Historic Eastern North America. *Archaeology of Eastern North America* 29:143–86.

Anthony, David W., and Daniel G. Roberts
1988 *Stone Quarries and Human Occupations in the Hardyston Jasper Prehistoric District of Eastern Pennsylvania.* Report prepared for Federal Highway Administration and Pennsylvania Department of Transportation. John Milner Associates, Inc., West Chester, Pennsylvania.

Bettinger, Robert L.
1999 From Traveler to Processor: Regional Trajectories of Hunter-Gatherer Sedentism in the Inyo-Mono Region, California. In *Settlement Pattern Studies in the Americas: Fifty Years Since Viru*, edited by B. R. Billman and G. M. Feinman, 39–55. Smithsonian Institution Press, Washington, D.C.

2001 Holocene Hunter-Gatherers. In *Archaeology at the Millennium: A Sourcebook*, edited by G. M. Feinman and T. D. Price, 137–95. Kluwer Academic/Plenum Press, New York.

Bettinger, Robert L., Peter J. Richerson, and Robert Boyd
2009 Constraints on the Development of Agriculture. *Current Anthropology* 50 (5): 627–31.

Binford, Lewis R.
2001 *Constructing Frames of Reference: An Analytical Method for Archaeological Theory Building Using Hunter-Gatherer and Environmental Data Sets.* University of California Press, Berkeley.

Boyd, Robert, and Peter J. Richerson
2005 *The Origin and Evolution of Cultures.* Oxford University Press, Oxford.

Bressler, James P., Ricki Maietta, and Karen Rockey
1983 *Canfield Island Through the Ages:36LY37.* North Central Chapter No. 8, Society for Pennsylvania Archaeology and Lycoming County Historical Society, Williamsport.

Burrow, Ian
1997 The Savich Farm Site: An Archaeological Survey for Phase I of the Long Term Management Plan. *Bulletin of the Archaeological Society of New Jersey* 52:35–50.

Caldwell, Joseph
1958 *Trend and Tradition in the Prehistory of the Eastern United States.* American Anthropological Association Memoir 88. Menasha, Wisconsin.

Carbone, Victor A.

1976 *Environment and Prehistory in the Shenandoah Valley.* Ph.D. dissertation, Department of Anthropology, Catholic University of America, Washington, D.C. University Microfilms, Ann Arbor, Michigan.

1982 Environment and Society in Archaic and Woodland Times. In *Practicing Environmental Archaeology*, edited by Roger W. Moeller, 39–52. Occasional Papers 3. American Indian Archaeological Institute, Washington, Connecticut.

Carr, Kurt W., and Douglas C. McLearen

2005 Recent Testing at the Kings Jasper Quarry, Lehigh County, Pennsylvania. Paper presented at Annual Meeting of the Society for American Archaeology, Salt Lake City, Utah, April 1.

Coppock, Gary F., John Stiteler, and Frank J. Vento

2011 Assessing Intra-Watershed Paleoenvironment and Landform Development: A Case Study from South-Central Pennsylvania. *North American Archaeologist* 32 (3): 193–246.

Cross, Dorothy

1941 *Archaeology of New Jersey*, Volume 1. Archaeological Society of New Jersey and New Jersey State Museum, Trenton.

Custer, Jay F.

1984 The Paleoecology of the Late Archaic: Exchange and Adaptation. *Pennsylvania Archaeologist* 54 (3–4): 33–47.

1989 *Prehistoric Cultures of the Delmarva Peninsula: An Archaeological Study.* University of Delaware Press, Newark.

1996 *Prehistoric Cultures of Eastern Pennsylvania.* Anthropological Series 7. Pennsylvania Historical and Museum Commission, Harrisburg.

2001 *Classification Guide for Arrowheads and Spearpoints of Eastern Pennsylvania and the Central Middle Atlantic.* Pennsylvania Historical and Museum Commission, Harrisburg.

2013 Rethinking Late Archaic/Woodland Period Culture Change in the Delaware Coastal Plain. *Journal of Middle Atlantic Archaeology* 29:131–45.

Delcourt, Paul A., and Hazel R. Delcourt

1998 The Influence of Prehistoric Human-Set Fires on Oak-Chestnut Forests in the Southern Appalachians. *Castanea* 63 (3): 337–45.

Delcourt, Paul A., Hazel R. Delcourt, Cecil R. Ison, William E. Sharp, and Kristen J. Gremillion

1998 Prehistoric Human Use of Fire, the Eastern Agricultural Complex, and Appalachian Oak-Chestnut Forests: Paleoecology of Cliff Palace Pond, Kentucky. *American Antiquity* 63 (2): 263–78.

Dent, Richard J.

1995 *Chesapeake Prehistory: Old Traditions, New Directions.* Plenum Press, New York.

Dincauze, Dena F.

1970 Review of *The Miller Field Site, Warren County, New Jersey: A Study in Prehistoric Archaeology. Pennsylvania Archaeologist* 40 (3–4): 72–74.

Fesenmyer, Kurt A., and Norman L. Christensen Jr.

2010 Reconstructing Holocene Fire History in a Southern Appalachian Forest Using Soil Charcoal. *Ecology* 91 (3): 662–70.

Fiedel, Stuart J.

2001 What Happened in the Early Woodland? *Archaeology of Eastern North America* 29:101–42.

Funk, Robert E.

1976 *Recent Contributions to Hudson Valley Prehistory.* New York State Museum and Science Service Memoir 22. University of the State of New York, State Education Department, Albany.

1993 *Archaeological Investigations in the Upper Susquehanna Valley, New York State.* Persimmon Press, Buffalo, New York.

Gardner, Andrew

2009 Agency. In *Handbook of Archaeological Theories*, edited by R. A. Bentley, H. D. G. Maschner, and C. Chippindale, 95–108. AltaMira Press, Lanham, Maryland.

Hatch, James W.

1993 *Research into the Prehistoric Jasper Quarries of Bucks, Lehigh, and Berks Counties, Pennsylvania.* Report prepared for Pennsylvania Historical and Museum Commission, Harrisburg. Department of Anthropology, Pennsylvania State University, University Park.

Hatch, James W., and Patricia E. Miller

1985 Procurement, Tool Production, and Sourcing Research at the Vera Cruz Jasper Quarry in Pennsylvania. *Journal of Field Archaeology* 12:219–30.

Hawkes, E. W., and Ralph Linton

1916 *A Pre-Lenape Site in New Jersey.* Anthropological Publications of the Museum of the University of Pennsylvania 6 (3). Philadelphia.

Hayden, Brian

2001 Richman, Poorman, Beggarman, Chief: The Dynamics of Social Inequality. In *Archaeology at the Millennium: A Sourcebook*, edited by G. Feinman and T. D. Price, 231–72. Kluwer Academic/Plenum Press, New York.

Horton, Benjamin P., Simon E. Engelhart, David F. Hill, Andrew C. Kemp, Daria Nikitina, Kenneth G. Miller, and W. Richard Peltier

2013 Influence of Tidal-Range Change and Sediment Compaction on Holocene Relative Sea-Level Change in New Jersey, U.S.A. *Journal of Quaternary Science* 28 (4): 403–11.

Hummer, Chris

1991 *Biface and Ceramic Assemblage Variability in the Early Woodland: Continuity and Change at the Williamsom Site, Hunterdon County, New Jersey.* Ph.D. dissertation,

Department of Anthropology, Temple University, Philadelphia. University Microfilms, Ann Arbor, Michigan.

1994 Defining Early Woodland in the Delaware Valley: The View from the Williamson Site, Hunterdon County, New Jersey. *Journal of Middle Atlantic Archaeology* 10:141–52.

Johnson, Allen W., and Timothy Earle

1987 *The Evolution of Human Societies: From Foraging Group to Agrarian State.* Stanford University Press, Stanford, California.

Katz, Gregory M.

2000 *Archaic Period Triangular Bifaces in the Middle Atlantic Region: Technological and Functional Considerations.* M.A. thesis, Department of Anthropology, Temple University, Philadelphia.

Keeley, Lawrence H.

1995 Protoagricultural Practices Among Hunter-Gatherers: A Cross-Cultural Survey. In *Last Hunters First Farmers: New Perspectives on the Prehistoric Transition to Agriculture*, edited by T. D. Price and A. B. Gebauer, 243–72. School of American Research Press, Santa Fe, New Mexico.

Kellogg, Douglas C., and Jay F. Custer

1994 *Paleoenvironmental Studies of the State Route 1 Corridor: Contexts for Prehistoric Settlement, New Castle and Kent Counties, Delaware.* Archaeology Series 114. Delaware Department of Transportation, Dover.

Kinsey, W. Fred, III (editor)

1972 *Archeology in the Upper Delaware Valley.* Anthropological Series 2. Pennsylvania Historical and Museum Commission, Harrisburg.

Klein, Michael J.

1997 The Transition from Soapstone Bowls to Marcey Creek Ceramics in the Middle Atlantic Region: Vessel Technology, Ethnographic Data, and Regional Exchange. *Archaeology of Eastern North America* 25:143–58.

Kraft, Herbert C.

2001 *The Lenape-Delaware Indian Heritage: 10,000 BC to AD 2000.* Lenape Books, Stanhope, New Jersey.

Kraft, John C., and Chacko J. John

1978 Paleogeographic Analysis of Coastal Archaeological Settings in Delaware. *Archaeology of Eastern North America* 6:41–59.

Laland, Kevin N., and Michael J. O'Brien

2010 Niche Construction Theory and Archaeology. *Journal of Archaeological Method and Theory* 17:303–22.

Lattanzi, Gregory D.

2013 *The Value of Reciprocity: Copper, Trade, and Social Interaction in the Middle Atlantic Region of the Eastern Woodlands.* Ph.D. dissertation, Department of Anthropology, Temple University, Philadelphia. University Microfilms, Ann Arbor, Michigan.

Lovis, William, and William G. Monaghan

2007 Directly Dated *Cucurbita* from the Upper Great Lakes: Implications for Archaic and Woodland Horticulture. Paper presented at the Annual Meeting of the Society for American Archaeology, Austin, Texas.

Luckenbach, Al, Jessie Grow, and Shawn Sharpe

2010 Archaic Period Triangular Points from Pig Point, Anne Arundel County, Maryland. *Journal of Middle Atlantic Archaeology* 26:165–79.

Meltzer, David J., and Vance T. Holliday

2010 Would North American Paleoindians Have Noticed Younger Dryas Age Climate Changes? *Journal of World Prehistory* 23:1–41.

Messner, Timothy

2008 *Woodland Period People and Plant Interactions: New Insights from Starch Grain Analysis.* Ph.D. dissertation, Department of Anthropology, Temple University, Philadelphia. University Microfilms, Ann Arbor, Michigan.

2011 *Acorns and Bitter Roots: Starch Grain Research in the Prehistoric Eastern Woodlands.* University of Alabama Press, Tuscaloosa.

Messner, Timothy, and Ruth Dickau

2005 New Directions, New Interpretations: Paleoethnobotany in the Upper Delaware Valley and the Utility of Starch Grain Research in the Middle Atlantic. *Journal of Middle Atlantic Archaeology* 21:71–82.

Messner, Timothy, Ruth Dickau, and Jeff Harbison

2007 Starch Grain Analysis: Methodology and Applications in the Northeast. In *Current Northeast Paleoethnobotany*, Volume 2, edited by John Hart, 111–28. New York State Museum and Science Service Bulletin 512. University of the State of New York, State Education Department, Albany.

Miller, Patricia E.

1982 *Prehistoric Lithic Procurement: A Chemical Analysis of Eastern U.S. Jasper Sources and a Consideration of Archaeological Research Design.* M.A. thesis, Department of Anthropology, Pennsylvania State University, University Park.

Moeller, Roger W. (editor)

1990 *Experiments and Observations on the Terminal Archaic of the Middle Atlantic Region.* Archaeological Services, Bethlehem, Connecticut.

Monaghan, William G., William A. Lovis, and Kathryn C. Egan-Bruhy

2006 Earliest *Cucurbita* from the Great Lakes, Northern U.S.A. *Quaternary Research* 65 (2): 216–22.

Mouer, L. Daniel

1990 *The Archaic to Woodland Transition in the Piedmont and Coastal Plain Sections of the James River*

Valley, Virginia. Ph.D. dissertation, Department of Anthropology, University of Pittsburgh, Pittsburgh. University Microfilms, Ann Arbor, Michigan.

1991a The Formative Transition in Virginia. In *Late Archaic and Early Woodland Research in Virginia: A Synthesis*, edited by T. R. Reinhart and M. E. Hodges, 1–88. Special Publication 23. Archaeological Society of Virginia, Richmond.

1991b Concluding Remarks: Explaining the Formative Transition in Virginia. In *Late Archaic and Early Woodland Research in Virginia: A Synthesis*, edited by T. R. Reinhart and M. E. Hodges, 259–73. Special Publication 23. Archaeological Society of Virginia, Richmond.

Mounier, Alan

2003 *Looking Beneath the Surface: The Story of Archaeology in New Jersey*. Rutgers University Press, New Brunswick, New Jersey.

Nikitina, Daria L., James E. Pizzuto, Reed A. Schwimmer, and Kelvin W. Ramsey

2000 An Updated Holocene Sea-Level Curve for the Delaware Coast. *Marine Geology* 171:7–20.

Odling-Smee, F. John, Kevin N. Laland, and Marcus W. Feldman

2003 *Niche Construction: The Neglected Process in Evolution*. Monographs in Population Biology 37. Princeton University Press, Princeton, New Jersey.

Oka, Rahul, and Chapurukha M. Kusimba

2008 The Archaeology of Trading Systems, Part 1: Towards a New Trade Synthesis. *Journal of Archaeological Research* 6:339–95.

Payne, Ted M.

1990 Investigations at a Lackawaxen Generalized Hunting Settlement in the Middle Delaware River Drainage. *Bulletin of the Archaeological Society of New Jersey* 45:9–13.

Raber, Paul A., Patricia E. Miller, and Sarah M. Neusius

1998 The Archaic Period in Pennsylvania: Current Models and Future Directions. In *The Archaic Period in Pennsylvania: Hunter Gatherers of the Early and Middle Holocene Period*, edited by P. A. Raber, P. E. Miller, and S. M. Neusius, 121–37. Recent Research in Pennsylvania Archaeology 1. Pennsylvania Historical and Museum Commission, Harrisburg.

Redding, Richard W.

1988 A General Explanation of Subsistence Change: From Hunting and Gathering to Food Production. *Journal of Anthropological Archaeology* 7 (1): 56–97.

Regensburg, Richard

1971 The Savich Farm Site: A Preliminary Report. *Bulletin of the Massachusetts Archaeological Society* 32 (1–2): 20–23.

1982 The Late Archaic Period: The Savich Farm Site. In *History, Culture, and Archaeology of the Pine Barrens: Essays from the Third Pine Barrens Conference*, edited by J. W. Sinton, 101–15. Center for Environmental Research, Stockton State College, Pomona, New Jersey.

Reimer, Paula J., Edouard Bard, Alex Bayliss, J. Warren Beck, Paul G. Blackwell, Christopher Bronk Ramsey, et al.

2013 INTCAL13 and Marine13 Radiocarbon Age Calibration Curves 0–50,000 Years Cal BP. *Radiocarbon* 55 (4): 1869–87.

Richerson, Peter J., and Robert Boyd

2001 Institutional Evolution in the Holocene: The Rise of Complex Societies. In *The Origins of Human Social Institutions: Proceedings of the British Academy*, Volume 110, edited by W. G. Runciman, 197–234. Oxford University Press, Oxford.

Richerson, Peter J., Robert Boyd, and Robert L. Bettinger

2001 Was Agriculture Impossible During the Pleistocene but Mandatory During the Holocene? A Climate Hypothesis. *American Antiquity* 66 (3): 378–411.

Ritchie, William A.

1959 *The Stony Brook Site and Its Relation to Archaic and Transitional Cultures on Long Island*. New York State Museum and Science Service Bulletin 372. University of the State of New York, State Education Department, Albany.

Ritchie, William A., and Robert E. Funk

1973 *Aboriginal Settlement Patterns in the Northeast*. New York State Museum and Science Service Memoir 20. University of the State of New York, State Education Department, Albany.

Russo, Michael, and Gregory Heide

2004 The Emergence of Pottery in South Florida. In *Early Pottery: Technology, Function, Style, and Interaction in the Lower Southeast*, edited by Rebecca Saunders and Christopher Hays, 105–28. University of Alabama Press, Tuscaloosa.

Skibo, James M., and Michael B. Schiffer

2008 *People and Things: A Behavioral Approach to Material Culture*. Springer, New York.

Smith, Bruce D.

2001 Low Level Food Production. *Journal of Archaeological Research* 9 (1): 1–43.

Snethkamp, Pandora E.

1981 *Late Archaic Hunter-Gatherers in the Pennsylvania Piedmont*. Ph.D. dissertation, Department of Anthropology, State University of New York at Binghamton. University Microfilms, Ann Arbor, Michigan.

Snow, Dean R.

1980 *The Archaeology of New England*. Academic Press, New York.

Steponaitis, Laurie Cameron

1986 *Prehistoric Settlement Patterns in the Lower Patuxent Drainage, Maryland*. Ph.D. dissertation, Department of Anthropology, State University of New York at Binghamton. University Microfilms, Ann Arbor, Michigan.

Stewart, R. Michael

1980 *Prehistoric Settlement and Subsistence Patterns and the Testing of Predictive Site Location Models in the Great Valley of Maryland*. Ph.D. dissertation, Department of Anthropology, Catholic University of America, Washington, D.C. University Microfilms, Ann Arbor, Michigan.

1983 Prehistoric Settlement Patterns in the Blue Ridge Province of Maryland. In *Upland Archaeology in the East: Proceedings of a Symposium*, edited by C. Geier, M. Barber, and G. Tolley, 43–90. Forest Service Southern Region, U.S. Department of Agriculture, Roanoke, Virginia.

1984a Archaeologically Significant Characteristics of Maryland and Pennsylvania Metarhyolites, In *Prehistoric Lithic Exchange Systems in the Middle Atlantic Region*, edited by Jay F. Custer, 1–13. Monograph 3. Center for Archaeological Research, University of Delaware, Newark.

1984b South Mountain Metarhyolite: A Perspective on Prehistoric Trade and Exchange in the Middle Atlantic Region, In *Prehistoric Lithic Exchange Systems in the Middle Atlantic Region*, edited by Jay F. Custer, 14–44. Monograph 3. Center for Archaeological Research, University of Delaware, Newark.

1986 *Shady Brook Site (28Me20 and 28Me99), Data Recovery*. Trenton Complex Archaeology: Report 1. Prepared for Federal Highway Administration and New Jersey Department of Transportation, Trenton. Cultural Resource Group, Louis Berger & Associates, Inc., East Orange, New Jersey.

1987a Rhyolite Quarry and Quarry-related Sites in Maryland and Pennsylvania. *Archaeology of Eastern North America* 15:47–57.

1987b *Gropp's Lake Site (28Me100G), Data Recovery*. Trenton Complex Archaeology: Report 2. Prepared for Federal Highway Administration and New Jersey Department of Transportation, Trenton. Cultural Resource Group, Louis Berger & Associates, Inc., East Orange, New Jersey.

1989 Trade and Exchange in Middle Atlantic Region Prehistory. *Archaeology of Eastern North America* 17:47–78.

1994 Late Archaic Through Late Woodland Exchange in the Middle Atlantic Region. In *Prehistoric Exchange Systems in North America*, edited by Timothy Baugh and Jonathan Ericson, 73–98. Plenum Press, New York.

1998a Archaic Triangles at the Abbott Farm National Landmark: Typological Implications for Prehistoric Studies in the Middle Atlantic Region. Paper accompanying exhibit of Archaic-Age bifaces at Annual Meeting of the Middle Atlantic Archaeological Conference, Cape May, New Jersey. Sponsored by Archaeological Society of New Jersey and New Jersey Department of Transportation.

1998b Thoughts on the Origins of Ceramic Use and Variation. *Journal of Middle Atlantic Archaeology* 14:1–12.

2004 Changing Patterns of Native American Trade in the Middle Atlantic Region and Chesapeake Watershed: A World Systems Perspective. *North American Archaeologist* 25 (4):337–56.

2005 Some Thoughts on Fire-Altered Rock. *Bulletin of the Archaeological Society of New Jersey* 60:37–42.

2011 Stone Bowls and Early Pottery. *Journal of Middle Atlantic Archaeology* 27:147–64.

Stewart, R. Michael, and John A. Cavallo

1991 Delaware Valley Middle Archaic. *Journal of Middle Atlantic Archaeology* 7:19–42.

Stewart, R. Michael, and William Schindler III

2008 *Analysis of Artifacts from the Kings Quarry Site (36Lh2)*. Report prepared for Pennsylvania Heritage Society and Pennsylvania Historical and Museum Commission, Harrisburg. Center for Experimental Archaeology, Church Hill, Maryland.

Stinchcomb, Gary E., Timothy C. Messner, Forrest C. Williamson, Steven G. Driese, and Lee C. Nordt

2013 Climate and Human Controls on Holocene Floodplain Vegetation Changes in Eastern Pennsylvania Based on the Isotopic Composition of Soil Organic Matter. *Quaternary Research* 79 (3): 377–90.

Truncer, James

2004 Steatite Vessel Age and Occurrence in Temperate Eastern North America. *American Antiquity* 69 (3): 487–513.

Turnbaugh, William A.

1975 Toward an Explanation of the Broadpoint Dispersal in Eastern North American Prehistory. *Journal of Anthropological Research* 31 (1): 51–68.

1977 *Man, Land, and Time: The Cultural Prehistory and Demographic Patterns of North-Central Pennsylvania*. Reprinted. Originally published 1975 for Lycoming County Historical Society, Williamsport, Pennsylvania. Unigraphic, Inc., Evansville, Indiana.

Versaggi, Nina M.

1996 Prehistoric Hunter-Gatherer Settlement Models: Interpreting the Upper Susquehanna Valley. In *A Golden Chronograph for Robert E. Funk*, edited by C. Lindner and E. V. Curtin, 129–40. Occasional Publications in Northeastern Anthropology 15. Archaeological Services, Bethlehem, Connecticut.

Waguespack, Nicole
2005 The Organization of Male and Female Labor in Foraging Societies: Implications for Early Paleoindian Archaeology. *American Anthropologist* 107 (4): 666–76.

Wallace, Paul A. W.
1993 *Indian Paths of Pennsylvania*. Revised edition. Pennsylvania Historical and Museum Commission, Harrisburg.

Wholey, Heather A.
2003 *Hunter Gatherer Settlement Demography: An Estimation and Comparative Assessment for the Piedmont Virginia Archaic*. Ph.D. dissertation, Department of Anthropology, Catholic University of America, Washington, D.C. University Microfilms, Ann Arbor, Michigan.

Winterhalder, Bruce, and Douglas J. Kennett
2009 Four Neglected Concepts with a Role to Play in Explaining the Origins of Agriculture. *Current Anthropology* 50 (5): 645–48.

Witthoft, John
1953 Broad Spear Points and the Transitional Period Cultures. *Pennsylvania Archaeologist* 23 (1): 4–31.

1.

Evidence for Climate Variability During the Sub-Boreal/ Transitional Archaic Period

FACT OR FICTION?

Frank J. Vento

ABSTRACT

This chapter will focus on the responses of river systems to climate change during the Sub-Boreal climate interval or Transitional Archaic period in the Middle Atlantic region and, specifically, in Pennsylvania. This period begins at approximately 4200 BP and ends at 3000 BP. The Sub-Boreal, much like the preceding Younger Dryas (ca. 11,200 BP) and later Little Ice Age (700–400 BP) climate intervals, was a time of renewed stream channel migration and active overbank deposition. Unlike the Younger Dryas or Little Ice Age interval, however, when fluvial erosional disconformities were associated with either cold and dry or cooler and wetter climatic conditions, respectively, the Sub-Boreal interval, which coincides with the Transitional Archaic, occurred during a 1,200-year period of decreased effective precipitation associated with climatic conditions that are warmer and drier overall than those present today. The following discussion examines both archaeological and paleoenvironmental lines of evidence in the Middle Atlantic region and elsewhere for the above assertions.

Archaeological Evidence

Archaeologically, the Transitional Archaic period is defined by broadspears, which date to between approximately 4,000 and 3000 BP. Following the lead of several researchers, this period is distinguished from the Late Archaic and Early Woodland periods by the preferential use of certain, usually nonlocal lithic types, for example, metarhyolites, that were typically available in massive bedrock formations, as opposed to tabular chert or pebble sources. This period is also documented by a change to bifacial core technology, a staged biface reduction process, the caching of bifaces, curated tools, steatite bowls, large and numerous fire-cracked rock (FCR) features, the beginning of fired clay pottery, occasional burial ceremonialism, and a preference for riverine environments. Based on the current recorded site database, Transitional Archaic populations appear to have preferred encampments along larger perennial streams rather than smaller first- or second-order tributaries. Could this preference for larger perennial streams reflect the fact that, during sustained warm and dry periods, small streams would have been more affected by a lower input of water from base flow and surface runoff and thus have been less attractive to Transitional Archaic populations? As Kurt Carr has argued for at least two decades, the change from an expedient flake-and-blade technology during the Late Archaic to a biface technology during the Transitional Archaic period, concomitant with greater mobility, argues for a food economy procurement strategy that reflects environmental stress due to warmer and drier climatic conditions and lower discharges along streams in the Middle Atlantic region.

Effects of the warmer and drier climate included a decrease in the number of low-order streams, lower water volume in streams generally, a decrease in biomass on ridges, and a lowering of the water table (Graetzer 1986; Watts 1979). Evidence provided by correlations of pollen core data with pollen from surface samples of known vegetation types suggests that the overall composition of the vegetation did not change radically (Bradstreet and Davis 1975). On the other hand, changes in hydrology and decreases in productivity would likely have had some effect on the distribution of prehistoric populations. Specifically, upland areas would have become less attractive, whereas major riverine areas such as the Ohio, Delaware, and Susquehanna River floodplains and associated terraces would have been more attractive (Miller et al. 2003).

Although there is some disagreement regarding the occurrence of a Middle Holocene climatic optimum in the Northeast, there is still greater disagreement regarding the climate following 5000 BP. A number of researchers have presented evidence indicating an environment characterized by severe climatic fluctuations, including a warm and dry, or xerothermic, period between 5000 and 2600 BP (Carbone 1976; Curry and Custer 1982; Custer 1988; Vento and Rollins 1989; Vento et al. 2008). Arthur Joyce (1988) notes that researchers have presented a variety of dates within the Middle Holocene for the proposed xerothermic period. Dennis Curry and Jay Custer (1982) argue that the xerothermic corresponds to the warm and dry conditions of the Atlantic/Sub-Boreal period in the Blytt-Sernander system (Figure 1.1; described in Zeuner 1952; see also Vento et al. 2008), originally developed to describe European climatic change but frequently applied without reservation to North America. In contrast, other researchers argue that, although there were undoubted fluctuations in temperature and moisture after 5000 BP, these were no more than low-amplitude fluctuations of short duration (Beckerman 1986; Joyce 1988; Watts 1979).

Patricia Miller and colleagues (2003) have argued that the impacts on vegetation were likely minimal and the composition of the forest, as a result, was similar to the present-day forest in many respects. Custer (1984, 1988) points to a decrease in hemlock and an increase in hickory in many of the major pollen studies of the northeastern United States. Hickory, in this sense, is considered an indicator of relatively dry conditions. But, as both Jay Custer (1988) and Victor Carbone (1976) remark, the inability to identify pollen to the species level renders such an interpretation problematic. Mesic species of hickory exist (*Carya cordiformis*, *C. ovata*) and are common in the modern biota (Joyce 1988). Most xeric hickory species also grow and thrive in moist, fertile soils. The sudden and synchronous decline of hemlock across a wide range of latitudes, cited as an indicator of dry conditions, strongly supports disease rather than climatic change as the cause (Bhiry and Filion 1996; Davis 1983; Watts 1979, 1983). Likewise, pollen profiles do not show the significant increases in nonarboreal pollen, such as grasses, amaranth, and *Chenopodium*, that would suggest a major decline in overstory vegetation resulting from decreasing precipitation and increasing temperatures (Miller et al. 2003).

Carbone's (1976) quantitative analysis of data from the Shenandoah Valley is often cited to support the proposition that warm and dry conditions were present in the Middle Atlantic region during the Late Holocene. His analysis followed a methodology developed by Thompson Webb and Reid Bryson (1972), who took modern pollen samples and modern climatic data

Years B.P.	Blytt-Sernander Climatic Episodes	Pollen Zones	Forest Type	Climatic Conditions	Fluvial Conditions	Genetic Stratigraphic Horizons	Archaeological Cultural Periods	Stratigraphic Discontinuities
Present	Modern							
500	Neo-Boreal "Little Ice Age"	C-3b	Spruce-Pine Rise	Cool moist to cool dry	Alluviation	A-C	Late Woodland	
	Pacific							
1,000								
	Neo-Atlantic			Warm moist	Floodplain stability	Owasco Paleosol	Middle Woodland	Little Ice Age Disconformity 750 B.P.
1,500	Scandic	C-3a	Oak Hemlock Chestnut	Cool moist	Alluviation	Weak Bw/BC/C		
2,000								
2,500	Sub-Atlantic			Warm moist	Floodplain stability	Fox Creek Paleosol	Early Woodland	Scandic Disconformity 1750 B.P.
3,000								
3,500	Sub-Boreal	C-2	Oak Hickory	Warm dry	Severe to modest later channel migration (small tributaries) with alluviation dominant over incision along major tributaries; zonal flow and Bermuda High	Bw	Transitional Archaic	Sub Boreal
4,000								
4,500			Mid-Point Hemlock Decline			Ab (Incipient)		
5,000					Atlantic II Increased rates of vertical accretion	Bw	Late Archaic	Disconformity 4200 B.P.
5,500								
						Ab (Incipient)		
6,000				Warm and slightly moister				
6,500	Atlantic	C-1	Oak Hemlock		Atlantic I Slow continuous vertical accretion, strong soil weathering/ development of Bw, Bt Btx, Bx	Bw, Bt, Btx, Bx	Middle Archaic	
7,000								
7,500								
8,000								
						A (Incipient)		
8,500	Boreal							
9,000		B	Pine Oak	Warm dry	Zonal circulation and rapid alluviation	BC/CB/C, lamellae bands (stacked A-C horizons)		
9,500	Pre-Boreal						Early Archaic	
10,000								
					Initiation of meandering			
10,500	Younger Dryas	A-4	Spruce Pine	Cool dry	Braided	C		
11,000	Allerod							YD Disconformity 10,900 B.P.
	Intra-Allerod Cold Period (IACP)		Spruce Pine		Renewed vertical accretion, absent on low terraces due to erosion during YD			
11,500								
	Allerod					A-B horizon development		
12,000	Older Dryas	A-3/A-2						
12,500	Bolling		Spruce Parklands				Paleoindian	
13,000	Oldest Dryas							
13,500								Late Wisconsin Disconformity
14,000		T	Tundra	Warm and wet	Braided conditions	Lateral accretion/ outwash	PreClovis	
14,500								

FIGURE 1.1 Genetic/alluvial stratigraphy and climate change in Middle Atlantic Region (adapted from Vento et al. 2008).

from seventy-three sample locations in the Midwest and, using canonical correlation, calculated a set of mathematical transfer functions relating pollen frequency to climatic variables, which they then applied to three fossil pollen cores located within the same region. Carbone applied this methodology to raw data from Hack Pond, located in the Shenandoah Valley of Virginia, concluding in his 1976 study that the climate of the Shenandoah Valley involved a warm and dry period that culminated around 4350 BP (Miller et al. 2003). This period was characterized by "increased temperatures, increased desiccation and moisture stress" (Carbone 1976:106). It is not clear in Carbone's discussion when temperature and precipitation reached modern levels, although he states "the climatic shifts of the last 4,000 to 5,000 years can be better understood as perturbations of the modern pattern rather than as actual long-term shifts" (Carbone 1976:107). Problems in dating these shifts may arise from the fact that the most recent radiocarbon sample from Hack Pond was from a depth of approximately 140 centimeters and returned a date of 9520 ± 200 BP (11,262–10,251 BP or 9313–9302 BC calibrated). Although Carbone does not explicitly say so, he apparently assumes a constant rate of deposition over the last 9,000 years, an assumption that may be invalid, given what is known of variation in alluvial deposition during this period (Vento and Rollins 1989; Vento et al. 2008).

Webb and Bryson (1972) assume that climate can be considered the primary controlling factor for the composition of past vegetation within their Midwestern study region. This assumption is likely based on the proposition that other factors controlling vegetation, such as topography and soils, are constant between the modern and fossil samples. Carbone's 1976 study violates the assumption, however, in that he uses the same mathematical transfer functions developed by Webb and Bryson for the Midwest, rather than developing transfer functions from sample sites in the Shenandoah Valley, where factors such as soil and topography are radically different from those in the Midwest (Miller et al. 2003).

Noting Webb and Bryson's caution that climatic factors controlling pine in the Midwest are different from those controlling pine in the Southeast, Carbone (1976:100) reasons that, because deciduous vegetation in the two regions was similar, the pine problem is unlikely to significantly affect the overall results. However, any number of similar, but unrevealed, problems may exist as a result of applying transfer functions developed in the Midwest to the Middle Atlantic region (Miller et al. 2003).

Alluvial stratigraphy has also been cited as evidence for warm and dry conditions in the Late Holocene. Increases in overbank deposition rates have been interpreted as indicating increased runoff resulting from decreased vegetative cover. Such an interpretation is based in part on James Knox's (1983) study of the morphology of stream channels and floodplains in southwestern Wisconsin and on investigations within the Susquehanna, Ohio, and Delaware River valleys (Vento et al. 2008). Knox interprets increased alluviation prior to 6000 BP as resulting from a warm and dry period, whose climate was primarily influenced by dry westerlies. This period is well documented in the pollen profiles of the Midwest, which indicate an eastward migration of the Midwestern prairie prior to 6000 BP (King 1980). Knox (1983) theorizes that increasing rainfall and vegetation after 6000 BP would have resulted in a decrease in the magnitude and frequency of peak flows and also a decrease in overbank deposition. Knox notes that the period of greatest sediment yield during the climatic fluctuation from humid to arid to humid conditions would have occurred at the end of the warm and dry period, during which vegetation was at a minimum despite an increase in rainfall (Miller et al. 2003).

Studies of alluvial stratigraphy in the Middle Atlantic region indicate that overbank deposition was rapid during the period between approximately 5000 and 3000 BP. Frank Vento and Harold Rollins (1989) and Vento and colleagues (2008) have identified rapid vertical accretion in the Ohio, Upper and Middle Delaware, and Susquehanna Basins, consisting of sediments with Late and Transitional Archaic cultural material. Richard Scully and Richard Arnold (1981) found evidence of increasing vertical accretion in the Upper Susquehanna Basin after 4900 BP. Carbone (1976) points to the rapid deposition of culturally sterile, sandy-clay loam between 5,000 and 2,700 BP as evidence that vegetation was at a minimum due to increased temperatures and decreased rainfall (Miller et al. 2003).

Despite the significance of Knox's (1983) study for understanding the relationship between changes in the climatic optimum and changes in the stream channels and floodplain characteristics of the Midwest, the presence of similar alluvial characteristics in the Late Holocene (Sub-Boreal) of the Middle Atlantic region does not necessarily indicate that the same climatic changes were in progress. Hydrological studies show that the decrease in precipitation needed to substantially affect sediment yield and flood size is quite large. According to data gathered by Walter Langbein and Stanley Schumm (1958), a decrease in precipitation causing vegetation change from forest to grassland would result in only a 30% increase in sediment yield. Late and Transitional Archaic overbank deposition apparently increased to at least this degree, yet there is no evidence in pollen profiles of grassland vegetation during this period. Data presented by Knox (1983) indicate that changes in mean annual precipitation above 650 millimeters per annum have little effect on flood size. Modern precipitation in the Susquehanna, Delaware, and Ohio Basins is approximately 900 millimeters per annum. Thus, for decreased rainfall to affect either the sediment yield of drainage basins or the magnitude of overbank flooding, arid conditions would have been required, but, as noted above, there is no evidence of vegetation changes in the Late Holocene pollen data of the Middle Atlantic region that would indicate a change to such conditions. At most, the pollen data cited as evidence for a warm and dry period would indicate a shift in overstory forest composition involving an increase in xeric species, although, again as noted above, this interpretation of the pollen profile is subject to challenge (Miller et al. 2003).

Vento and Rollins (1989) and Vento and colleagues (2008) accept the hypothesis of a warm and dry Sub-Boreal, and they attribute rapid vertical accretion to changes in atmospheric circulation patterns. Based on Knox's (1983) discussion of the effects of zonal versus meridional circulation, Vento and colleagues (2008) and Joyce (1988) point to an increase in meridional circulation that resulted in more frequent cyclonic storms, causing more frequent overbank flooding. Patricia Miller, Frank Vento, and James Marine (2007) note that such an interpretation does not depend on an overall decrease in either precipitation, vegetation, or both to explain the increase in alluvial deposition. Although there are at present no independent supporting data for a warm and dry Sub-Boreal, the hypothesis is consistent with the pollen data, as is the hypothesis of severe climatic change (Miller et al. 2003).

Miller and colleagues (2003) further note that there is no conclusive evidence of a widespread warm and dry climate such as that hypothesized by Carbone (1976) and by Curry and Custer (1982) for the period between 5000 and 2600 BP. Rather, data suggest that modern levels of temperature and precipitation generally prevailed in both the eastern United States and the Ohio River drainage basin. Cyclonic storms, as evidenced by flood scouring and the deposition of coarse-grained material on the floodplain, likely occurred with greater frequency than in previous periods. Floodplain and terrace soils supported mesophytic species such as beech, oak, tulip tree, ash, sugar maple, and walnut. Upland soils supported forest communities dominated by chestnut, hickory, and oak (Figures 1.1–1.4). The Late Holocene forest differed from the modern forest primarily in age structure, containing trees of all ages, with a mosaic of gaps caused by falls of trees in senescence and in various stages of regeneration. These gaps gave rise to a variety of edible resources that grow best in the open, including blackberries, raspberries, and a variety of tubers (Miller et al. 2003).

In addition to the open sites previously discussed, closed rockshelter sites like Meadowcroft Rockshelter (Stratum III) and Parrish Rockshelter show higher

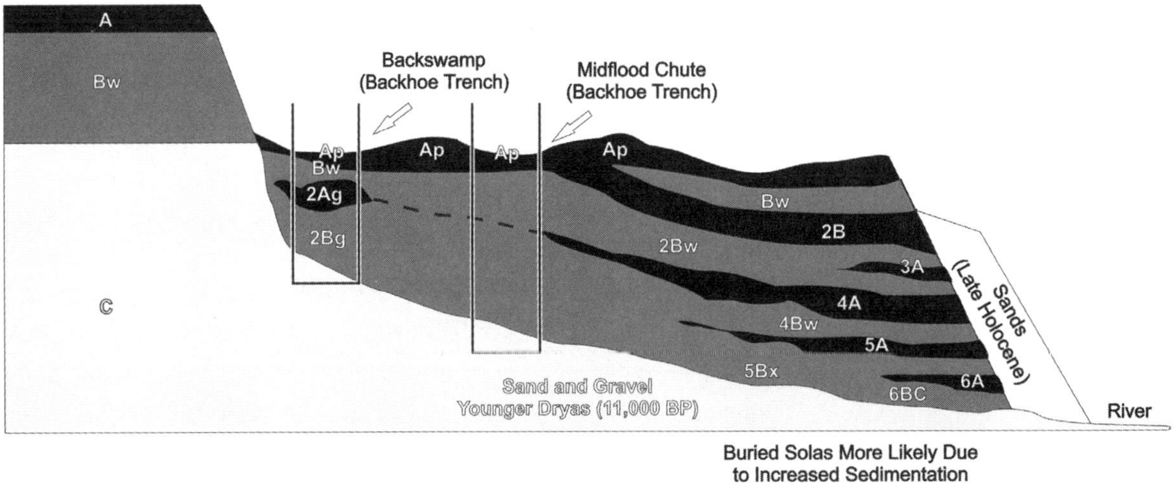

FIGURE 1.2
Idealized cross section of a terrace sequence showing stacked soil horizons. A horizons document episodes of floodplain/terrace stability; B horizons document increased rates of overbank deposition.

FIGURE 1.3
Soil development in relationship to stream order. Note increased vertical accretion during Sub-Boreal climate phase.

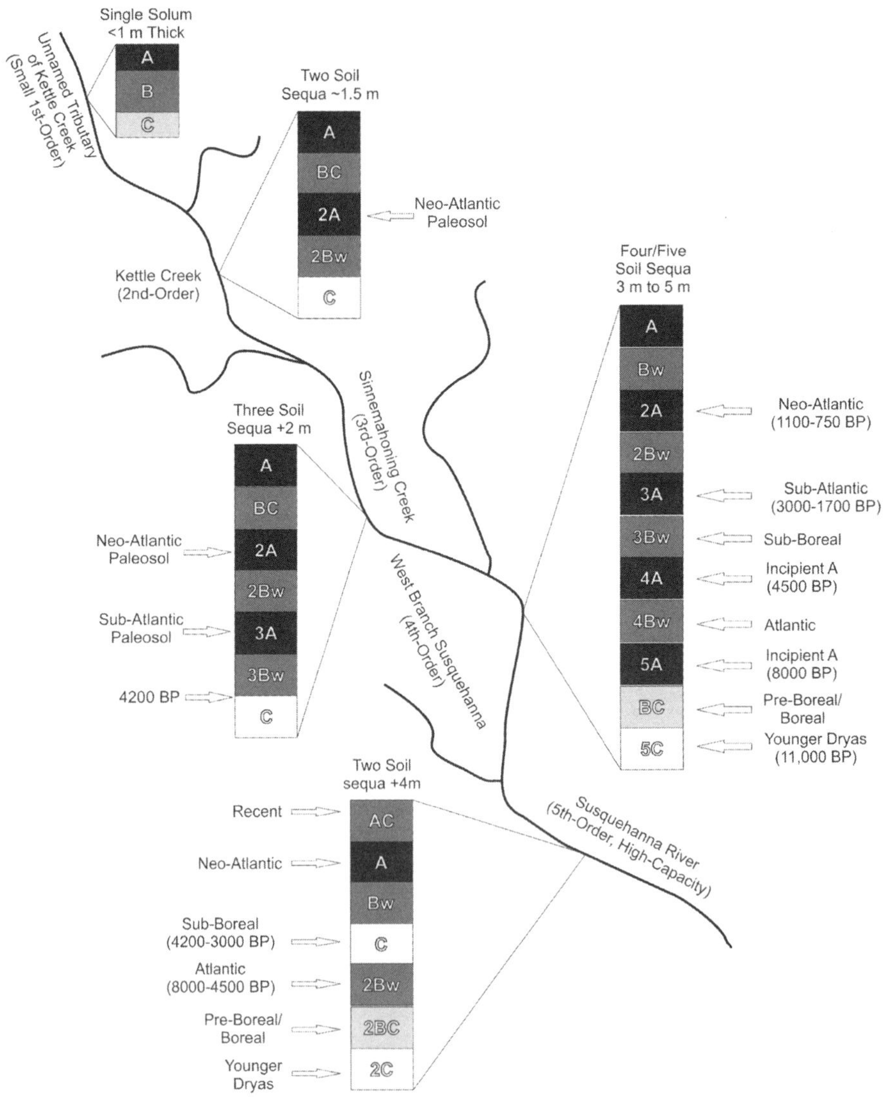

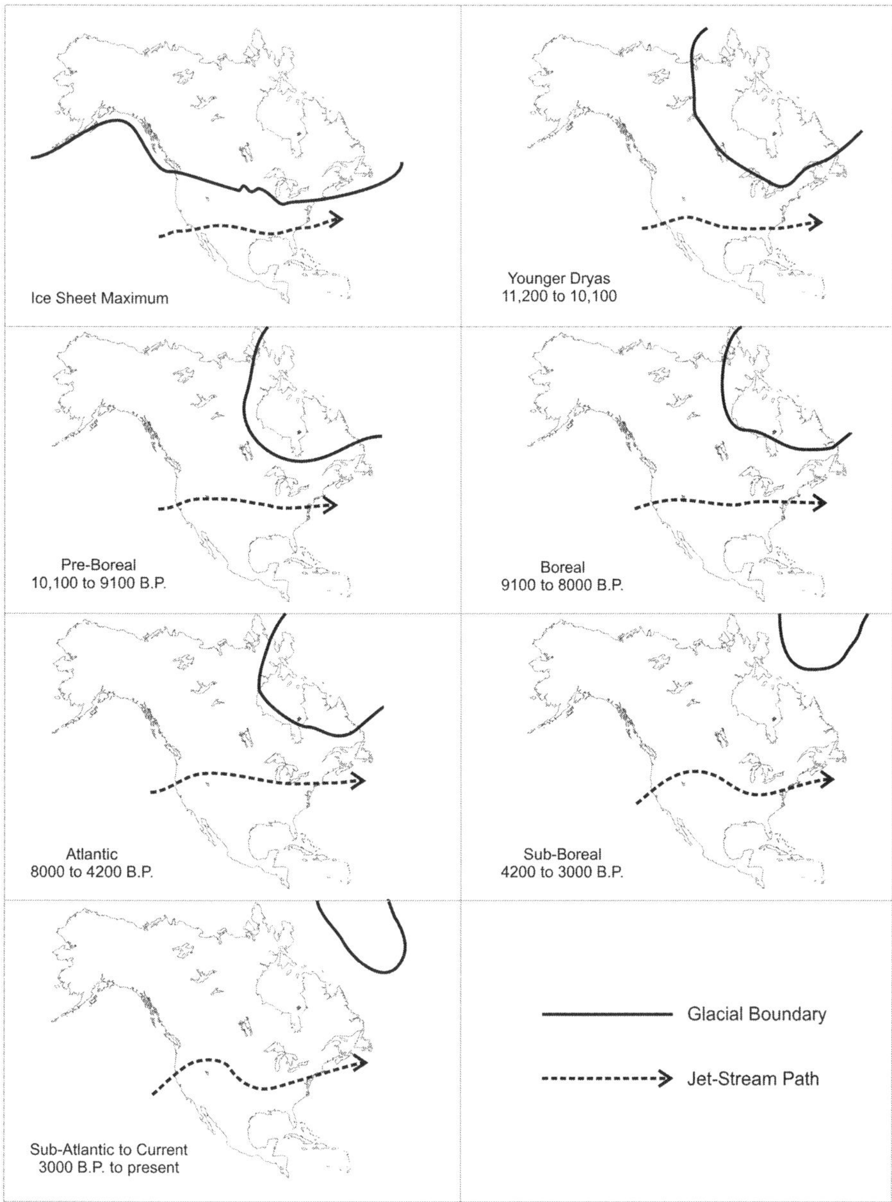

FIGURE 1.4
Ablation of Late Wisconsin ice sheet and changes in jet stream path.

rates of colluvial sedimentation associated with mass wasting processes (slope wash, creep, sheet wash) during the Transitional Archaic (Stuckenrath et al. 1982; Vento and Stahlman 2011a).

Geomorphic Fluvial Evidence

With regard to the fluvial geomorphic evidence, based on more than thirty years of personal experience in the region, I see a clear patterning in the stratigraphic record that supports my contention that rivers and streams in the region responded to these warm and drier climatic conditions by undergoing more active lateral channel migration along smaller drainage lines or more rapid vertical accretion along the major drainage lines, often reflected in the stratigraphic profiles by distinct autogenic flood events. If we briefly examine some representative sites that have a lengthy Holocene record from the Ohio, Susquehanna, and

Delaware Basins, it becomes clear that the Sub-Boreal, and thus also the Transitional Archaic culture period was one of environmental change. All of these sites occur on Late Wisconsin terraces that contain a thick Holocene package of vertical accretion and Transitional Archaic artifacts in variably thick cambic B horizons. At some sites, the cambic B horizons are immediately overlain by a surface A horizon; at others, they are capped by a cumulic A horizon that dates to the Sub-Atlantic climate interval (3000–1750 BP). The stratigraphic horizons and thickness of the Holocene soils that cap the Transitional Archaic horizons reflect variables such as channel morphology, height of the terrace above the active stream channel, valley morphology, and stream order.

The Leetsdale Site (Miller 2012) and Point State Park Site (Blades et al. 2008) on the Ohio River at Pittsburgh document rapid rates of late Middle Holocene vertical accretion. At the Leetsdale Site, the Transitional Archaic period encompasses, in places, more than 1 meter of overbank deposition in less than 1,100 years. This soil package, or defined allostratigraphic unit, in Area 1 consists of a series of nested lamellae (stacked AC/C couplets) that document a series of relatively high magnitude flood events. The rates of vertical accretion for the Sub-Boreal at the Leetsdale Site are much higher than those for deposits in the preceding Atlantic or subsequent Sub-Atlantic climatic phase. In addition, in Area 2, which is situated closer to the active river channel, the soil profiles show clear evidence for channel migration and incision of the terrace (Schuldenrein and Vento 2002).

In the upper reach of the Allegheny River near Tionesta, Pennsylvania, recent investigations (Verbka, Vento, and Shaffer 2013) at the Hunter Station Bridge Site identified more than 2.5 meters of Holocene alluvium with artifacts occurring throughout the profile. Once again, the Transitional Archaic horizons at the site include a cambic B horizon documenting continuous slow vertical accretion of the terrace.

At the Jacobs, Gould Island, and Memorial Park Sites on the North and West Branches of the Susquehanna River (Vento et al. 2008), the Sub-Boreal phase alluvial deposits form a thick cambic B horizon documenting continuous slow vertical accretion of the terrace between 4200 and 3000 BP. In the Route 11/15 corridor, extending from near Selinsgrove to Liverpool, Pennsylvania, along the main stem of the Susquehanna River, all of the excavated sites contained Transitional Archaic artifacts associated with thick cambic B horizons that, in places, were intercalated with coarse-grained autogenic flood events (C horizons) (Miller, Marine, and Vento 2007).

Soil profiles at the Smithfield Beach, Frenchtown, and Shohola Bridge Sites in the Delaware River valley document increased rates of overbank deposition during this time. At the Shohola Bridge Site, much like at Leetsdale, multiple AC/C horizons represent continuous flood deposition between very short lived episodes of stability for the period 4200 to 3000 BP (Trachtenberg et al. 2009). At the Frenchtown Site on the Middle Delaware River, the Transitional Archaic is evidenced by slow vertical accretion of the floodplain (White 2013). I contend that the higher rates of vertical accretion along the larger drainage lines, the absence of cumulic A horizons documenting long episodes of stability, and the more active lateral channel migration along smaller internal drainages all support the presence of generally warmer and drier climatic conditions favoring increased rates of surface runoff, higher sediment yield to streams, and thus also higher rates of vertical accretion.

In the Upper Delaware River valley, the Transitional Archaic period (4000–3000 BP) coincides with the late Middle Holocene (5000–3200 BP) phase (Phase IV) of reworking and aggradation (Stinchcomb et al. 2012). Following Middle Holocene (6000–5000 BP) incision, average flood deposit grain size decreases, and widespread soil formation occurs along the higher T2a alluvial terrace. Adjacent to the T2a is a lower T2b terrace that contains evidence of rapid sedimentation and multiple weakly developed buried soils. Because overbank sediment was accumulating along the lower surfaces (active floodplain), the higher, less flood-prone

T2a surface became more suitable for habitation. This T2a buried soil often holds evidence of Late and Transitional Archaic occupation. Carbon isotope composition of organic matter from Delaware River alluvial soils suggests that the Transitional Archaic period follows a shift from higher to lower C4:C3 plants, centered at 4500 BP (Stinchcomb et al. 2013). This shift may be related to major climate reorganization (the 4200 BP event and Middle to Late Holocene transition), incision and riparian development after 6000–5000 BP, or both (Stinchcomb et al. 2012).

Geomorphic evidence (not associated with fluvial geomorphology) for a 1,200-year period of warm and dry climatic conditions comes from the recent excavations at the Beech Ridge Site near Dover, Delaware (Barse and Marston 2006), where a deep, strongly weathered paleosol containing Dalton Hardaway points is overlain by a thick package of windblown sands. The late Middle Holocene component of these overlying sands is thicker and slightly coarser grained than that of sands at lower and higher levels. In fact, much of the aeolian sand package appears to have been emplaced during the late Middle Holocene. The increased rates of aeolian deflation and deposition during this time were in response to warm and dry climatic conditions. Over the years, Dennis Curry, much to his credit, has argued for aeolian deflation and subsequent burial of prehistoric sites during the Holocene on the Maryland Coastal Plain. There is now strong evidence along the entire eastern Coastal Plain for a period of late Middle Holocene aeolian deflation, proving him correct (Vento and Stahlman 2011b).

Geomorphic Evidence Outside the Middle Atlantic Region

In Georgia, David Hurst Thomas's extensive work on Late Archaic settlements on Saint Catherines Island (e.g., Bishop, Rollins, and Thomas 2011) documents a shift in settlement due to a potential marsh regression of 1.5 meters in the period 4000 to 3500 BP. Frank Vento and Patricia Stahlman (2011b), working on now-buried paleosols on Saint Catherines Island, have documented, in places, more than 3 meters of Holocene aeolian sands, with a thick portion of this package occurring during the Sub-Boreal climatic phase.

Other researchers in the region, conducting sea level and tidal channel migration studies, argue for a late Middle Holocene sea level regression or standstill at this time (e.g., Gayes et al. 1992). Timothy Chowns (2009) notes that, around 4000 BP, sea levels regressed, changing the coastal processes from tidal to wave dominated, which in turn favored tidal channel migration and spit development. Recent studies in central Florida indicate drying on the basis of a change from mangrove swamps to yellow and loblolly pines during the late Middle Holocene (e.g., Rich, Vento, and Vega 2011).

Faunal and Floral Evidence

At present in the Middle Atlantic region, there is a large set of data that documents a clear decrease in hemlock pollen as a proxy for warm and dry conditions during the period 4200 to 3000 BP. Recent pollen studies completed on cores extracted from Chesapeake Bay (Willard and Bernhardt 2004) show clear decreases in pine pollen in association with atmospheric cooling at 8000 BP and again during the Little Ice Age (700–400 BP). In the data for the period 4200 to 3000 BP, there is a large increase in pine pollen, suggesting warmer and probably drier climatic conditions. In their recent paper on pollen extracted from a deep core along Sandy Run Creek on the Georgia Coastal Plain, Heidi LaMoreaux, George Brook, and John Knox (2009) show wetter conditions than now from 4500 to 1000 BP and a sharp decrease in groundwater levels, aridity, and lower stream discharges beginning at 4500 BP. LaMoreaux, Brook, and Knox argue that this drying reflected increased winter solar radiation that raised winter temperatures, with the replacement of oak by southern pine. They further state that, with the absence of the Laurentian ice sheet, there would have been less orbitally induced seasonality, thus weakening both the polar and subtropical jet streams and opening the door for other climate change processes such as the El Niño–Southern Oscillation (ENSO). Consistent with a less stormy jet stream pattern, there was a decrease in meridional flow of moist Gulf air into eastern North America and the Upper Mississippi Valley after the Middle Holocene climatic optimum, or hypsithermal, leading to drier conditions and reduced river discharges. That said, much of the problem to date is the dearth of detailed and comprehensive archaeobotanical studies for the Transitional Archaic period in the Middle Atlantic region. If warming and drying did dominate the climate, then we should see evidence in the form of grassland expansion, an increase in pine, evidence for lower water tables, and the desiccation of swamps and bogs. Clearly, there need to be additional pollen, macrobotanical, and phytolith studies on soils that target the period 4200 to 3000 BP.

Discussion

Increased frequency of cyclonic storms after the Atlantic climatic episode (beginning as early as 6000 BP) and resultant high alluvial deposition fit with data from the Upper Ohio and Upper and Middle Susquehanna and Delaware River drainage basins. Stratigraphic evidence, in the form of coarse-grained vertical and lateral accretionary deposits, especially along the first-, second-, and third-order streams within the basins, documents the increased occurrence of large storms after 6000 BP. Similar stratigraphic evidence in the northern Midwest supports the idea of more frequent large floods after 6000 BP (Knox, McDowell, and Johnson 1981). The increased rates of overbank deposition along the major drainage lines (i.e., the Delaware and Susquehanna Rivers) and more active lateral channel migration and incision along their tributary streams precluded the development of cumulic A horizons during the Sub-Boreal climatic phase (4200–3000 BP).

Not surprisingly, the incision of the Pre-Boreal and Boreal valley-fill deposits in most areas of these basins occurred about 6000 BP, coincident with increased meridional circulation, a condition that promoted strong cyclonic storms via the lifting and mixing of warm, moist Gulf air masses by cool, dry air masses out of Canada (Grissinger, Murphey, and Little 1981; Vento and Fitzgibbons 1987). This episode of Middle Holocene incision and more frequent large floods may be responsible for the general paucity or near absence of Paleoindian, Early Archaic, and Middle Archaic sites in low-terrace contexts along most of the streams in these basins. On the other hand, there are sites along the major rivers in the Middle Atlantic region such as Leetsdale, Point State Park, Shawnee Minisink, Shawnee Island, City Island, Smithfield Beach, Cremard, Memorial Park, High Bank, Piney Island, and Canfield Island, as well as the Route 11/15 sites (Bressler, Maietta, and Rockey 1983; Hart et al. 1995; Kent 1996; Miller et al. 2003; Miller, Marine, and Vento 2007; Schuldenrein and Vento 2002; Vento and Rollins 1989; Vento et al. 1992, 2008; Kurt Carr, personal communication 2014) that clearly contain intact artifact-bearing remnants of fine-grained overbank deposits from the Late Pleistocene through the Atlantic climatic phase (see Figures 1.1–1.4).

During the period 4200 to 3000 BP, the genetic stratigraphic package on the lowermost Port Huron and Valley Heads terraces in the Ohio, Susquehanna, and Delaware Basins marks various episodes of erosion and deposition that can be attributed to atmospherically induced changes in climate. The typically thick, often mottled, cambic B horizons or C horizons of the Sub-Boreal were likely emplaced during warm and dry conditions, probably in association with meridional stabilization of the Bermuda-Azores anticyclone over eastern North America and the increased importance of warm and dry zonal flow (much as in the 1930s) that reduced vegetative cover, increased surface runoff, and promoted vertical accretion on low terraces within the basin. This situation occurs when the Bermuda-Azores high becomes particularly large and strong and retrogrades westward over the eastern portion of North America. This decreases the likelihood of precipitation while simultaneously advecting warm, dry air from the Southwest. Such conditions often occur during present-day summers.

As noted earlier, the decline of hemlock (Pollen Zone C-2) during the Sub-Boreal climatic interval (4200 to 3000 BP) supports the presence of warm and dry conditions during this time. The absence of well-developed cumulic A horizons and associated floodplain instability in the period 4200 to 3000 BP may also be attributed to these conditions. The forest of the Sub-Boreal (Pollen Zone C-2) was dominated by oak and hickory, and there is a marked reduction in pine, birch, and alder (Prentice, Bartlein, and Webb 1991:2047). A dramatic decline in hemlock that began around 5000 BP (Haas and McAndrews 2000:81) continued throughout this interval, whose cultures include those of the Late and Transitional Archaic periods (Figure 1.1). The warm and dry climate of the Sub-Boreal phase, which reduced vegetative cover and increased erosion, is associated with floodplain instability and the formation of mottled Bw horizons and C horizons along larger streams in the Middle Atlantic region (Figure 1.1; Vento and Rollins 1989; Vento et al. 1992, 2008:22).

By 3000 BP, the climate abruptly transitioned to warm and moist conditions. The Sub-Atlantic (3000–1750 BP), Scandic (1750–1200 BP), and Neo-Atlantic (1100–750 BP) climatic episodes mark a transition to warm and moist, cool and moist, and warm and moist conditions, respectively. The transition from the previous climatic episode allowed for several hundred years of floodplain stability and subsequent long-term development of A horizons. Clearly, the effects of meridional circulation, and the associated cyclonic and convectional storms, were much reduced during these climatic periods; a subsequent return to more abundant hemlock pollen from its low levels during the warm and dry Sub-Boreal indicates lowered rates of evapotranspiration and more effective precipitation.

Cooler and moister climatic phases such as the Scandic (1750–1200 BP) and Pacific (700–400 BP) effectively arrested development of A horizons as a result of frequent large floods that favored rapid vertical accretion (cambic B horizons and autogenic units of coarse-grained C horizons) on low terraces within the Middle Atlantic region. This may be a result of an increase in tropical storm (i.e., hurricane) frequency or more frequent cool-season flood events associated with more meridional flow conditions. Heavy precipitation from intensive low-pressure cells, such as those of the 1955 and 1972 tropical cyclone–induced floods, could have been rather common during these climatic phases as atmospheric flow characteristics approached those of modern times. Prior to 6000 BP, blocking effects induced by the presence of the Laurentian ice sheet would have precluded such tropically induced flood events (Vento et al. 2008). All of these data provide a strong argument for a marked change in the environment during the late Middle Holocene and especially during the Transitional Archaic period.

REFERENCES

Barse, William, and Jennifer Marston
2006 *Phase III Investigations at the Beech Ridge Site for the Crawford Carroll Avenue Project, Dover, Delaware.* Report prepared for Delaware Department of Transportation. URS Corporation, Burlington, New Jersey.

Beckerman, Ira B.
1986 *Prehistoric Settlement and Subsistence in Piedmont, North Carolina.* Ph.D. dissertation, Department of Anthropology, Pennsylvania State University, University Park. University Microfilms, Ann Arbor, Michigan.

Bhiry, Najat, and Louise Filion
1996 Mid-Holocene Hemlock Decline in Eastern North America Linked with Phytophagous Insect Activity. *Quaternary Research* 45:312–20.

Bishop, Gale A., Harold B. Rollins, and David Thomas Hurst (editors)
2011 *Geoarchaeology of St. Catherines Island, Georgia.* American Museum of Natural History, New York.

Blades, Brooke, Bruce Bevan, Frank Mikolic, and Frank J. Vento

2006 *Geoarchaeological and Geophysical Survey, Sites of Fort Duquesne and Fort Pitt, Point State Park, City of Pittsburgh, Allegheny County, Pennsylvania.* Report prepared for Pennsylvania Department of Conservation and Natural Resources, Harrisburg. A. D. Marble and Company, Inc., Conshohocken, Pennsylvania.

Bradstreet, T. E., and Ronald B. Davis

1975 Mid-Postglacial Environments with Emphasis on Maine. *Arctic Anthropology* 12 (2): 7–22.

Bressler, James, Ricki Maietta, and Karen Rockey

1983 *Canfield Island Through the Ages: 36LY37.* North Central Chapter No. 8, Society for Pennsylvania Archaeology and Lycoming County Historical Society, Williamsport.

Carbone, Victor A.

1976 *Environment and Prehistory in the Shenandoah Valley.* Ph.D. dissertation, Department of Anthropology, Catholic University of America, Washington D.C. University Microfilms, Ann Arbor, Michigan.

Chowns, Timothy M.

2011 Drainage Changes at Ossabaw, St. Catherines, and Sapelo Sounds and Their Influence on Island Morphology and Spit Building on St. Catherines Island, Georgia. In *Geoarchaeology of St. Catherines Island, Georgia*, edited by Gale A. Bishop, Harold B. Rollins, and David Hurst Thomas, Chapter 9. American Museum of Natural History, New York.

Curry, Dennis C., and Jay F. Custer

1982 Holocene Climatic Change in the Middle Atlantic Area: Preliminary Observations from Archaeological Sites. *North American Archaeologist* 3:275–85.

Custer, Jay F.

1984 *Delaware Prehistoric Archaeology.* University of Delaware Press, Newark.

1988 Late Archaic Cultural Dynamics in the Central Middle Atlantic Region. *Journal of Middle Atlantic Archaeology* 4:39–59.

Davis, Margaret B.

1983 Holocene Vegetational History of the Eastern United States. In *Late-Quaternary Environments of the United States*, Volume 2: *The Holocene*, edited by H. E. Wright Jr., 166–81. University of Minnesota Press, Minneapolis.

Gayes, P. T., D. B. Scott, E. S. Collins, and D. D. Nelson

1992 A Late Holocene Sea-Level Irregularity in South Carolina. In *Quaternary Coasts of the United States: Marine and Lacustrine Systems*, edited by C. H. Fletcher III and J. F. Wehmiller, 154–60. Society for Sedimentary Geology (SEPM) Special Publication 48. Tulsa, Oklahoma.

Graetzer, Mary Alice

1986 Settlement Patterns and Paleoclimatic Modeling: A Preliminary Study of Data from the Bald Eagle Watershed of Central Pennsylvania. Master's paper, Department of Anthropology, Pennsylvania State University, University Park.

Grissinger, E. H., J. B. Murphey, and W. C. Little

1981 Late-Quaternary Valley-Fill Deposits in North-Central Mississippi. Unpublished manuscript, U.S. Department of Agriculture, Agricultural Research Service, Oxford, Mississippi.

Haas, Jean Nicolas, and John H. McAndrews

2000 The Summer Drought Related Hemlock (*Tsuga canadensis*) Decline in Eastern North America 5,700 to 5,100 Years Ago. In *Proceedings: Symposium on Sustainable Management of Hemlock Ecosystems in Eastern North America*, edited by K. A. McManus, K. S. Shields, and D. R. Souto, 81–88. General Technical Report NE-267. U.S. Department of Agriculture, Forest Service, Northeastern Forest Experiment Station, Newtown Square, Pennsylvania.

Hart, John P., Jeffrey R. Graybill, David L. Cremeens, Michael G. Spitzer, John P. Nass, Nancy Asch Sidell, et al.

1995 *Archaeological Investigation at the Memorial Park Site (36Cn164) Clinton County, Pennsylvania.* Report prepared for U.S. Army Corps of Engineers, Baltimore District. GAI Consultants, Monroeville, Pennsylvania.

Joyce, Arthur A.

1988 Early/Middle Holocene Environments in the Middle Atlantic Region: A Revised Reconstruction. In *Holocene Human Ecology in Northeastern North America*, edited by George P. Nicholas, 185–214. Plenum Press, New York.

Kent, Barry C.

1996 Piney Island and the Archaic of Southeastern Pennsylvania. *Pennsylvania Archaeologist* 66:1–42.

King, James E.

1980 Post-Pleistocene Vegetational Changes in the Midwestern United States. In *Archaic Prehistory of the Prairie-Plains Border*, edited by A. E. Johnson, 3–11. Publications in Anthropology 12. University of Kansas, Lawrence.

Knox, James C.

1983 Responses of River Systems to Holocene Climates. In *Late-Quaternary Environments of the United States*, Volume 2: *The Holocene*, edited by H. E. Wright Jr., 26–44. University of Minnesota Press, Minneapolis.

Knox, James C., Patricia F. McDowell, and William C. Johnson

1981 Holocene Fluvial Stratigraphy and Climatic Change in the Driftless Area, Wisconsin. In *Quaternary Paleoclimate*, edited by W. C. Mahaney, 107–27. Geological Abstracts Limited, Norwich, United Kingdom.

LaMoreaux, Heidi K., George A. Brook, and John A. Knox
2009 Late Pleistocene and Holocene Environments of the Southeastern United States from the Stratigraphy and Pollen Content of a Peat Deposit on the Georgia Coastal Plain. *Palaeogeography, Palaeoclimatology, Palaeoecology* 280:300–312.

Langbein, Walter B., and Stanley A. Schumm
1958 Yield of Sediment in Relation to Mean Annual Precipitation. *Transactions of the American Geophysical Union* 39:1076–84.

Miller, Patricia E.
2012 *Archaeological Data Recovery at Site 36AL480, Leetsdale Industrial Park, Leetsdale, Pennsylvania.* Report prepared for U.S. Army Corps of Engineers, Pittsburgh District. URS Corporation, Burlington, New Jersey.

Miller, Patricia E., James T. Marine, and Frank J. Vento
2007 *Archaeological Investigations, Route11/15 Improvements, (SR 0011, Section 008), Juniata and Perry Counties, Pennsylvania*, Volume 2: *36Pe16*. Report prepared for Pennsylvania Department of Transportation, Engineering District 8-0. KCI Technologies, Inc., Mechanicsburg, Pennsylvania.

Miller, Patricia E., Frank J. Vento, James T. Marine, and Eloisa A. Pollack
2003 *Phase III Archaeological Data Recovery, Route 11/15 Improvements (SR 0011, Section 008), Juniata and Perry Counties, Pennsylvania*, Volume 3: *36Pe60*. Report prepared for Pennsylvania Department of Transportation, Engineering District 8-0, Harrisburg. KCI Technologies, Inc., Mechanicsburg, Pennsylvania.

Prentice, I. Colin, Patrick J. Bartlein, and Thomson Webb III
1991 Vegetation and Climate Change in Eastern North America Since the Last Glacial Maximum. *Ecology* 72 (6): 2038–56.

Rich, Frederick J., Frank J, Vento, and Anthony Vega
2011 Evolution of Late Pleistocene–Holocene Climates and Environments of St. Catherines Island and the Georgia Bight. In *Geoarchaeology of St. Catherines Island, Georgia*, edited by Gale A. Bishop, Harold B. Rollins, and David Hurst Thomas, Chapter 2. American Museum of Natural History, New York.

Schuldenrein, Joseph, and Frank J. Vento
2002 *Interim Geomorphology Report for Archaeological Site 36AL480, Area 3 South, Leetsdale Industrial Park, Leetsdale, Allegheny County, Pennsylvania*. Report prepared for Greenhorne and O'Mara, Inc., and U.S. Army Corps of Engineers, Pittsburgh District, Contract DACW 59-01-T-0028. Geoarchaeology Research Associates, Inc., Yonkers, New York.

Scully, Richard W., and Richard W. Arnold
1981 Holocene Alluvial Stratigraphy in the Upper Susquehanna River Basin, New York. *Quaternary Research* 15:327–44.

Stinchcomb, Gary E., Steven G. Driese, Lee C. Nordt, and Peter M. Allen
2012 A Mid to Late Holocene History of Floodplain and Terrace Reworking Along the Middle Delaware River Valley, U.S.A. *Geomorphology* 169–170:123–41.

Stinchcomb, Gary E., Timothy C. Messner, Forrest C. Williamson, Steven G. Driese, and Lee C. Nordt
2013 Climatic and Human Controls on Holocene Vegetation Changes in Eastern Pennsylvania Based on the Isotopic Composition of Soil Organic Carbon. *Quaternary Research* 79:377–90.

Stuckenrath, Robert, James M. Adovasio, Jack Donahue, and Ronald C. Carlisle
1982 The Stratigraphy, Cultural Features and Chronology at Meadowcroft Rockshelter, Washington County, Pennsylvania. In *Meadowcroft: Collected Papers on the Archaeology of Meadowcroft Rockshelter and the Cross Creek Drainage*, edited by R. C. Carlisle and J. M. Adovasio. Department of Anthropology, University of Pittsburgh, Pittsburgh.

Trachtenberg, Samuel, Kenneth Basalik, Frank J. Vento, Phillip La Porta, Linda Scott Cummings, and Joseph Schuldenrein
2009 *Shohola-Barryville Bridge Replacement Project (S.R. 0434, Section 470), Shohola Township, Pike County, Pennsylvania, and the Hamlet of Barrysville, Sullivan County, New York; Archaeological Investigation, Volume 1*. Report prepared for the United States Department of Transportation, Federal Highways Administration and the Pennsylvania Department of Transportation. Cultural Heritage Research Services, Inc. North Wales, Pennsylvania.

Vento, Frank J., and Philip T. Fitzgibbons
1987 *Archaeological and Geoarchaeological Investigations in the Cowanesque River Valley*. Report prepared for U.S. Army Corps of Engineers, Baltimore District. Vendel Environmental, Pittsburgh.

Vento, Frank J., and Harold B. Rollins
1989 *Genetic Stratigraphy, Climate Change, and Deep Burial of Archaeological Sites in the Susquehanna River Drainage Basin*. Report prepared for Pennsylvania Historical and Museum Commission, Harrisburg. Quaternary Research Institute, Clarion University of Pennsylvania, Clarion.

Vento, Frank J., Harold B. Rollins, R. Michael Stewart, Paul A. Raber, and William Johnson
1992 *Genetic Stratigraphy, Climate Change, and Deep Burial of Archaeological Sites in the Susquehanna, Ohio, and Delaware River Basins*. Report prepared for Pennsylvania Historical and Museum Commission, Harrisburg. Quaternary Research Institute, Clarion University of Pennsylvania, Clarion.

Vento, Frank J., Harold B. Rollins, Anthony Vega, James M. Adovasio, Patricia Stahlman, David B. Madsen, and Jeffrey S. Illingworth

2008 Development of a Late Pleistocene–Holocene Genetic Stratigraphic Framework for the Mid-Atlantic Region: Implications in Archaeology. Paper presented at 73rd Annual Meeting of the Society for American Archaeology, Vancouver, British Columbia, March 26–30.

Vento, Frank J., and Patricia Stahlman

2011a *Geoarchaeological and Archaeological Investigations at Parrish Rockshelter (36Fo106), Forest County, Pennsylvania.* Report prepared for the Allegheny National Forest, Marienville Ranger District. Clarion University of Pennsylvania.

2011b Development of a Late Pleistocene–Holocene Genetic Stratigraphic Framework for St. Catherines Island: Archaeological Implications. In *Geoarchaeology of St. Catherines Island, Georgia*, edited by Gale A. Bishop, Harold B. Rollins, and David Hurst Thomas, Chapter 4. American Museum of Natural History, New York.

Verbka, Joseph M., Frank J. Vento, and Scott Shaffer

2013 *Phase I and II Archaeological Investigations for S.R. 0062, Section B01, Hunter Station Bridge over the Allegheny River Project, Tionesta Township, Forest County, Pennsylvania.* Unpublished report prepared for Pennsylvania Department of Transportation, Harrisburg.

Watts, W. A.

1979 Late Quaternary Vegetation of Central Appalachia and the New Jersey Coastal Plain. *Ecological Monographs* 49 (4): 427–69.

1983 Vegetational History of the Eastern United States 25,000 to 10,000 Years Ago. In *Late-Quaternary Environments of the United States*, Volume 1: *The Late Pleistocene*, edited by S. C. Porter, 294–310. University of Minnesota Press, Minneapolis.

Webb, Thompson, III, and Reid A. Bryson

1972 Late- and Postglacial Climatic Change in the Northern Midwest, U.S.A.: Quantitative Estimates Derived from Fossil Pollen Spectra by Multivariate Statistical Analysis. *Quaternary Research* 2:70–115.

White, Sharon D.

2013 *Stage III Archaeological Data Recovery, Site 28-Hu-18, Frenchtown Wastewater Treatment Plant Upgrade Project, Frenchtown Borough, Hunterdon County, New Jersey.* Report on file, New Jersey Historic Preservation Office, Trenton, New Jersey.

Willard, Debra A., and Christopher E. Bernhardt

2004 Pollen Stratigraphy and Land-Use Change, Pocomoke Sound. In *Pocomoke Sound Sedimentary and Ecosystem History*, edited by T. M. Cronin, Chapter 7. U.S. Geological Survey Open-File Report OFR-2004-1350.

Zeuner, Frederick E.

1952 *Dating the Past: An Introduction to Geochronology.* Methuen & Company, Limited, London.

2.

The End of the Late Archaic Period in the Upper Susquehanna Valley of Pennsylvania

LAMOKA AND ITS VARIANTS

Robert D. Wall

ABSTRACT

The final cultures of the Late Archaic period in the Upper Susquehanna Valley that immediately precede those of the Transitional Archaic period are described, and their ties to Lamoka and the Narrow-Stemmed Point tradition are examined. Finds at Late Archaic sites in this region that manifest these ties are summarized, as is the evidence they provide regarding final Late Archaic economy and society.

The purpose of this chapter is to describe what are chronologically the most recent Late Archaic cultures of the Upper Susquehanna Valley of Pennsylvania, that is, cultures that immediately precede those of the period known as the "Terminal Archaic" or "Transitional Archaic." For this purpose, the latter two terms are synonymous since both refer to cultures that are at the interface between the Archaic and Woodland periods. The Upper Susquehanna Valley includes the region upstream from the confluence of the North and West Branches of the Susquehanna River. Archaeological evidence of these cultures, based on finds of diagnostic artifacts in good contexts include, for example, Lamoka, Vestal, Bare Island, and Brewerton artifacts, which date from ca. 5950 to 2950 BP or 4000 to 1000 BC (Funk 1988:156).

Regional manifestations of the Late Archaic are primarily identified by their characteristic artifact types, such as ground-stone tools and point types (Custer 1996; Stewart 1995, 2003). It is acknowledged that point typologies can be quite complex, given the frequent co-occurrence of types in the same context. For example, large-stemmed points are not just Late Archaic in age, but may be found in later Terminal Archaic contexts (Custer 1996, Stewart 1995). Furthermore, regional variability in artifact types over time and space makes the system of point classification somewhat complex and nebulous.

Supporting data are often elusive or inconsistent. Certainly, there was a broad Eastern Woodlands hunting and gathering adaptation in the Archaic period, with numerous subregional variants that followed a variety of area-specific adaptive strategies and cultural traditions. As more substantial data become available, these broadly defined cultures may eventually be more clearly defined. Until such time, it may be more appropriate to focus on what defines more specific cultural phenomena such as Lamoka, Vestal, Bare Island, and other Late Archaic manifestations.

Earlier Late Archaic cultural sequences of Laurentian affiliation and its cognates extend back to the end of the Middle Archaic period. Diagnostic artifacts related to this sequence include, for example, Otter Creek projectile points and later Brewerton forms (Funk 1988). Otter Creek points distinguish the early or proto-Laurentian cultures. Evidence from the McCulley Site (Funk and Hoagland 1972), for example, in the Upper North Branch of the Susquehanna River shows a late fall occupation, with the recovery of animal-bone points, Otter Creek points, butchering tools, and evidence of fishing activities (Turnbaugh 1977:116).

Generally, the Brewerton occupations, marked by several types of Brewerton points, gouges, and chopping tools, range from about 4700 to 3950 BP or 2750 to 2000 BC (Turnbaugh 1977). Archaeological investigations at Site 36PE61 on the Susquehanna River near Liverpool, Pennsylvania, showed radiocarbon-dated Brewerton occupations at 5590 ± 80 BP (Taylor et al. 1996:152–56; 6563–6268 BP or 4614–4319 BC calibrated), though later data recovery excavations also produced more recent dates closer to 3950 BP or 2000 BC (Miller et al. 2008).

An earlier Brewerton or proto-Brewerton occupation has been recorded at the Mansfield Bridge Site in Tioga County (Wall et al. 2003). Chronologically equivalent to the Neville occupation in the Northeast, it is the most substantial component represented at the Mansfield Bridge Site and was radiocarbon dated to ca. 7350–7050 BP or 5400–5100 BC, substantially earlier than the Brewerton phase described above and within range of the Middle Archaic components revealed at the Neville Site in New Hampshire (Dincauze 1976). A contemporaneous occupation at the Memorial Park Site marked by finds of Neville points was radiocarbon dated by five bulk soil samples to ca. 7090–6720 BP or 5140–4770 BC (Hart et al. 1995:511). In contrast to the limited exposure of the Memorial Park Site occupation, the component excavated at Mansfield Bridge contained a number of hearth features, some isolated and others in clusters, distributed over a broad area. All of the hearths and their associated artifacts appear to be short-term events, a common pattern in the Late Archaic period.

The ground-stone tool types more typically represented on northern Laurentian sites are less frequent on Pennsylvania sites, where projectile point styles define affiliations more than anything else. What we tend to see from most Late Archaic sites in the Upper Susquehanna Valley of Pennsylvania is a hearth or two, a few stemmed or large notched points in B horizons, or a surface collection consisting of a variety of stemmed points and associated workshop debris, including the kind of raw materials (e.g., rhyolite and quartzite) commonly used by Late Archaic peoples. What we would like to see but rarely do is evidence of structures, activity areas of varied functions, preserved remains of bone and other perishable technology, a better-preserved inventory of charred botanical remains, and faunal remains that show what people hunted, netted, or trapped. What we more commonly see on these sites are lithics and fire-cracked rock (FCR) features and, more rarely, pit features and middens. The lack of storage features on Late Archaic sites may indicate a more transitory and perhaps broad-spectrum type of adaptation. This may have involved hunting and the constant gathering of selected plants during their seasonal availability by relatively mobile populations. During the winter, a greater emphasis on hunting and fishing and the use of stored foods such as nuts and acorns may have provided sufficient sustenance until the spring.

In this regard, William Gardner (1987:48) noted that the most common site type represented in the Archaic period in much of the Middle Atlantic region is the transient camp or station, which would have been utilized for specialized resource procurement. It is assumed that such sites would have tied into base camps both nearby and some distance away, depending on the type of resource exploited, and that some procurement sites in the uplands should evidence, for example, relatively high frequencies of nutting stones and ground-stone artifacts (Gardner 1987:67). This assumption is based primarily on the presence of larger, Late Archaic floodplain sites with extensive platform hearths and workshop debris, compared to the more sparsely occupied upland sites containing a few points and a scatter of debitage. This settlement pattern appears to have been well established in most drainage basins of the Middle Atlantic region, including the Susquehanna Basin, by the end of the Late Archaic period, ca. 3950 BP or 2000 BC. Although substantiated as more typical of Transitional Archaic sites in the region, the same pattern is found in at least the final millennium of the Late Archaic, where evidence of Lamoka occupations such as those at Allenwood (36UN82) underlies similar platform hearths in the Terminal Archaic strata (Wall 1995, 2000). Variations in this pattern in the Upper Susquehanna Valley, for example, may have included broader hunting and foraging ranges and fewer base camps (Versaggi 1996:137).

For the Upper Susquehanna Valley, Bruce Rippeteau (1977) notes that, after 5950 BP or 4000 BC, there is evidence indicating a rapid spread of hunter-gatherer populations, which may relate to the growing dominance of deciduous forests in the east with the associated mast and small game. This development would have had an influence on shifts in technology geared to the exploitation of a wider range of cyclical and seasonally available food resources.

For other regions of the Eastern Woodlands during the Late Archaic, Russell Stafford (1991) has found that nut masts, especially hickory, were intensively exploited, and extractive camps were most likely established where high yields were available. Nancy Asch, Richard Ford, and David Asch (1972:29) note that, for small populations dependent on wild foods, concentration on the procurement of hickory nuts is more efficient than the exploitation of other wild plant food resources. Once gathered, such mast may have been transported to larger base camps for further processing. Nuts may also have been regularly collected during upland forays undertaken for other purposes, for example, hunting or procurement of lithic raw material. Collected nuts of various kinds may have been consistently stored for winter consumption, hence their ubiquitous representation on many Archaic sites. These are just some of the factors that may have played important roles in the development of the Late Archaic subsistence settlement pattern in the Eastern Woodlands, a pattern that most likely intensified in the latter portion of the Late Archaic period, as evidenced by larger sites of longer duration and by the onset of the Narrow-Stemmed Point tradition.

Because the discussion that follows focuses primarily on the period just prior to the Terminal Archaic, there is a greater emphasis on Lamoka and its cognates in the Narrow-Stemmed Point tradition. Where specific components have not been identified, more general statements about Late Archaic cultures are made for comparative purposes only. Except where noted, all calibrated radiocarbon dates are new to this chapter and employ the Calib 7.0 program.

The Late Late Archaic Period, or Lamoka and the Narrow-Stemmed Point Tradition

The Narrow-Stemmed Point tradition developed during the latter part of the Middle Holocene dry climatic episode, a trend that was definitely in place by ca. 6,000 BP, based on regional lake level and pollen data, and that lasted until between 5,000 and 3,000 BP (Knox 1983; Webb et al. 1993:454; Wendland and Bryson 1974). The initial development of the Narrow-Stemmed Point tradition corresponds to the onset of the warm and dry conditions of the Sub-Boreal climatic episode (4200–3000 BP), a period of active channel migration and floodplain accretion along with a marked absence of developing A horizons. In the Upper Susquehanna Valley, the dry climatic pattern and resulting vertical accretion of floodplain deposits occurred between 4700 and 3000 BP (Knox 1983:34). The overall effect of these dry climatic conditions on, for example, Lamoka settlement patterns, is uncertain but may have resulted in more intensive use of more productive riverine and lakeshore environments.

Although defined as "Laurentian" by Robert Funk (1988), based on the presence of some Laurentian-type artifacts such as gouges and bannerstones, Lamoka is more clearly part of the Narrow-Stemmed Point tradition that follows the Laurentian sequence. It has its roots in the Brewerton phase and is followed by the Terminal Archaic Broadspear tradition. Bare Island points are contemporaneous with Lamoka, as are Wading River points and, in the Upper Delaware Valley, Lackawaxen points (Kinsey 1972). Points at all of these Narrow-Stemmed Point tradition sites are followed in sequence by broadspears (Funk et al. 1993:156).

Bare Island and Lackawaxen points normally have long, narrow triangular blade forms with well-defined shoulders and symmetrical edges. Their stems are usually thick and rectangular with straight sides. Lackawaxen stemmed points have been radiocarbon dated between 5180 and 3660 BP or between 3230 and 1710 BC in the Upper Delaware Valley (Kinsey 1959, 1972:410–1211; Kraft 1975:29–31), and Bare Island points have been dated to ca. 4150 BP or 2200 BC (Funk 1965; Ritchie 1971:14–15, Plate 2, Nos. 3, 6). Bare Island points are also found in stratified contexts at the Higgins Site (Ebright 1992) and at Site 18ST659 in southern Maryland, where Bare Island points were manufactured by splitting quartz and quartzite cobbles to produce staged bifaces and long, narrow flake blanks for stemmed projectile points. The flake blanks have bladelike dimensions but are much thicker, having been produced by hard hammer percussion. This reduction phenomenon was most likely common in narrow-stemmed point assemblages throughout Coastal Plain and nearby Piedmont environments of the Middle Atlantic region, including Pennsylvania.

The Lamoka chronology in the Upper Susquehanna drainage basin of New York covers the time span 2500–1900 BC (uncalibrated; Funk et al. 1993). The Lamoka Lake Site itself has consistently produced radiocarbon dates of ca. 4450 BP or 2500 BC (Ritchie 1980:42–43). Funk and colleagues place Vestal after Lamoka and feel there is no overlap, stating that Vestal is "rooted in the preceding Lamoka occupation" (Funk et al. 1993:223). Vestal points are broad bladed and notched and perhaps the immediate forerunners to the Broadspear tradition, though recent work by Laurie Miroff, Jeremy Wilson, and Nina Versaggi (2008) at the Castle Gardens Site suggests these points may be contemporaneous with Lamoka and may perhaps have served a different function in Lamoka tool kits. Versaggi and colleagues (2001) note that there could be more basic differences between Lamoka and Vestal that transcend simple projectile point morphology. In fact, there were very likely the same kinds of complexity and diversity that we see in more contemporary hunter-gatherer populations (Versaggi et al. 2001:123). Differences in tool classes between Lamoka and Vestal, based on recovered assemblages from the Hallstead Park Site, showed clear distinctions even at the subsistence level (Versaggi et al. 2001).

Beyond point types, Susquehanna Valley Lamoka sites are characterized by material remains that include charred botanicals such as acorns, beechnuts, butternuts, hazelnuts, walnuts, and hickory nuts (Funk et al. 1993:266; Miroff, Wilson, and Versaggi 2008). Faunal remains are extremely rare, however, except from the Lamoka Lake Site, where deer were very important, along with bear, medium-sized and small mammals, birds, turtles, and some fish. At almost every other Lamoka site, including Pennsylvania sites, little identifiable faunal material is preserved. The evidence from Lamoka Lake exemplifies a broad-spectrum adaptation that includes intensive fishing activities, indicated by the recovery of approximately 8,000 netsinkers. The hunting, gathering, and food-processing equipment comprises numerous projectile points, bifacial knives, pitted stones, pestles, and mortars, showing the overall importance of hunting as well as fishing (Funk et al. 1993:266). It also appears that subsistence priorities changed seasonally, contingent on availability of certain key game species such as deer, passenger pigeon, fish, and squirrel (Versaggi et al. 2001:126).

Lamoka settlement patterns show year-round occupation of valley floors, with seasonal use of the uplands (Funk et al. 1993:285). Larger camps and small habitation sites were present on or near riverbank loci of the Susquehanna River and its larger tributaries. In Pennsylvania, this type of site would include Allenwood (36UN82; Wall 1995, 2000). Upland areas were likely an important component of the settlement system, included by Versaggi (1987) as part of the "whole valley system," whereby various task-specific activities such as quarrying, gathering seasonally available food resources, and performing single tasks in upland localities were an essential part of the overall subsistence pattern.

Community pattern data for Lamoka in the Upper Susquehanna Valley are scant or nonexistent. Farther west, a number of small-house patterns were revealed by William Ritchie's follow-up excavations in 1962 at Lamoka Lake (Ritchie 1980:72–73). The hearths associated with the houses were ash- and charcoal-laden basins. The data from Lamoka Lake imply short-term use over perhaps many years, which explains the patterns of structure overlap and reuse. Interior hearths appear to be linear and central to the structures (Ritchie 1980:76). Lamoka phase burials were found below middens at the Lamoka Lake Site (Funk et al. 1993:285). No comparable community pattern or human burial data have been reported from any Pennsylvania Lamoka sites.

The Lamoka Lake Site represents a more or less ideal situation with regard to preservation of features and associated assemblages. Other New York Upper Susquehanna Valley sites such as Kuhr Number 2, Englebert, Fortin Locus 1, and Mattice Number 2, contained Lamoka occupations that are comparable to Pennsylvania sites and lack the more elaborate features and structures of the Lamoka Lake Site. For example, Kuhr Number 2 has a radiocarbon-dated Lamoka component at 3850 BP or 1900 BC with living floors including a scatter of fire-reddened soil, fire-cracked rock, and calcined bone (Funk et al. 1993). The Englebert Site has a Lamoka component radiocarbon dated to 3850 BP or 1900 BC and Fortin Locus 1 has a Lamoka component dated to 3750 BP or 1800 BC with hearths, associated Lamoka points, and other tools, and relatively empty areas between hearths (Funk et al. 1993). This may suggest short-term occupations that were hearth focused but left little debris outside of the hearth ring of activities. Many Lamoka sites, including Fortin Locus 1, contain evidence of fishing as an important means of subsistence; netsinkers were recovered from three distinct Lamoka occupations at the Fortin Site (Funk and Rippeteau 1977:20–21). The occupations range from ca. 4185 to 3880 BP, slightly older than the occupation range at the Allenwood Site (36UN82). Finally, the Mattice Number 2 Site, with its dense cluster of hearths, FCR scatters, and associated Lamoka points and tools, was radiocarbon dated to 3870 BP or 1720 BC.

Pennsylvania Upper Susquehanna Lamoka Sites

Lamoka settlement patterning in the Upper Susquehanna Valley of Pennsylvania also indicates an increased riverine focus, with specialized but diffuse exploitation of the uplands including many ephemeral locations. Surface site data from the West Branch Valley of the Susquehanna (Turnbaugh 1977) also show an increase in site size at this time, perhaps suggesting the gradual focus of subsistence strategies on locally abundant food resources such as shellfish and fish spawns. This is evidenced by the recovery of a number of netsinkers from the Lamoka component at sites such as Allenwood (36UN82; Wall 2000). West Branch Valley sites appear to have been mostly seasonal occupations (Turnbaugh 1977), whereas, in the Upper Susquehanna Valley of New York, intensively occupied Lamoka sites were present on floodplains in the fall and into the winter, judging from finds of charred nuts from autumn harvests and the general lack of netsinkers (Funk and Rippeteau 1977:19)

Evidence from surface collections of Lamoka sites in the West Branch Valley shows greater use of local lithic resources. Onondaga cherts appear to be derived mostly from local cobble sources (Turnbaugh 1977). Lamoka sites in the West Branch Valley are located at or near the mouths of tributary streams entering the Susquehanna River. In the uplands, hunting camps such as the Site 36LY160 rock shelter demonstrate frequent use of such areas for hunting and gathering. Lamoka points were recovered from the shelter, but pits, hearths, or other features were lacking (Turnbaugh 1974). Adzes recovered were not beveled but are similar to some at the Lamoka Lake Site. In the surrounding area, finds of Lamoka points in remote upland settings indicate that many sites were simply short-term hunting and gathering camps. Even some of the Susquehanna River floodplain sites such as West Water Street (Custer, Watson, and Bailey 1994) and Allenwood Bridge (36NB3; Miller 1992) evidence relatively short term occupations. At West Water Street, the Late Archaic assemblage suggests late-stage biface reduction, perhaps retooling the hunting assemblage. At Allenwood Bridge, the Late Archaic occupation is represented by mostly fire-related basins dating to ca. 3450–3350 BP or 1500–1400 BC (Miller 1992). This was probably a short-term camp represented by low densities of tools and hearths. In Stratum VI at the East Bank Site, radiocarbon-dated contexts associated with both Lamoka and Brewerton points date to ca. 3600 BP (East et al. 2002:III-16). In general, Lamoka occupations in the Susquehanna Valley range from 3950 to 2950 BP (East et al. 2002:I-31).

There has also been some work by James Bressler, Ricki Maietta, and Karen Rockey (1983) at the Canfield Island Site (36LY37) in Williamsport, where a sequence of occupations date from the Late Archaic (including Lamoka) through the Late Woodland period. In some of the smaller drainage basins of the Upper Susquehanna, small, single-component Lamoka sites such as 36SQ109, along Wyalusing Creek, have produced Lamoka hearth features, including small basins and fire-cracked rock clusters (Breetzke 1998). The Wyalusing Creek Site (36SQ109) is a single-component Lamoka occupation consisting of ca. 1,500 lithic artifacts in the context of ten features (Figure 2.1). Calibrated radiocarbon dates range from 2190 to 1890 BP or from 2920 to 2325 BC (Breetzke 1998; calibration in original publication). The

FIGURE 2.1 Lamoka points from Wyalusing Creek Site (36SQ109). Credit: Rob Tucher.

site is interpreted as a short-term hunting, fishing, and nut-harvesting site. The Wiser Site (36CE442), another autumn nut-harvesting site in the Bald Eagle Creek valley was radiocarbon dated to a comparable time frame of 4060 ± 70 BP (4744–4416 BP or 2795–2467 BC calibrated) and 3910 ± 60 BP (4447–4216 BP or 2498–2267 BC calibrated), with narrow- and broad-stemmed points in the same assemblage (East et al. 2002:I-31).

Similar finds also come from buried Late Archaic sites in the North Branch Valley of the Susquehanna. At the Jacobs Site (36LU90), a short-term occupation was radiocarbon dated to 3880 BP, and another Late Archaic occupation was recorded just beneath this stratum. All of the features comprised by the occupations appear to be hearth related. The Skvarek Site (36LU132) has earlier Late Archaic (Vosburg, Brewerton, and Otter Creek) occupations with a later radiocarbon-dated Lackawaxen component producing a few tools and debitage in a feature context dated to 4160 ± 70 BP (Miller 1994; 4848–4520 BP or 2899–2571 BC calibrated). Lackawaxen is roughly contemporaneous with Lamoka. Finally, a Lamoka horizon dating to 3900 BP was recorded at the Gould Island Site within the context of an incipient A horizon at about 200 centimeters below surface (Vento and Rollins 1989). The Late Archaic occupation, found in the lower Bb2 and Bb2a soils from 130 to 175 centimeters below surface, was dated to 4070–3750 BP (Weed and Wenstrom 1992).

In the North Branch Valley, there is some evidence of stratified Lamoka and Brewerton occupations near the Mifflinville Site (Wall, Stewart, and Koldehoff 1990; Jacoby et al. 1999). The site contained both Lamoka and Bare Island points in feature contexts. The Allenwood (36UN82) and Mifflinville (36CO17) Sites are described below as examples of more substantial Lamoka occupations in the Upper Susquehanna Valley of Pennsylvania.

Allenwood Site, Lamoka Occupation

Situated within Holocene deposits capping a Pleistocene (Valley Heads) terrace of the Susquehanna River (Wall 1995, 2000), the Allenwood Site (36UN82) represents buried and stratified deposits dating from the Middle Archaic to the Late Woodland period, that is, from ca. 6950 to 450 BP or from 5000 BC to AD 1500. The horizontal extent of these buried deposits across the floodplain is uncertain, although it is believed that they are substantial in this section of floodplain. The earliest component appears to be sparsely represented evidenced by the recovery of a single bifurcate projectile point. A Brewerton point was found at approximately the same stratigraphic position. Major components at the site include Lamoka, Terminal Archaic, and Clemson Island. Block excavations, totaling 84 square meters, were made below the base of the deepest cultural components.

The Lamoka occupation at Allenwood, dating from ca. 3900 to 3600 BP and representing one of the more intensively occupied living surfaces revealed on the site, includes a dense concentration of fifteen hearth features such as fire-reddened stains, fire pits with fire-cracked rock, more diffuse scatters of FCR, and charcoal smears (Figures 2.2–2.4). Most of the hearth features seem to be a result of single or short-term events, though some of the more diffuse scatters, such as Feature 27, appear to have been reused several times. The Lamoka component seems to have been an intensive but short-term occupation. There are likely components from a number of related or contemporaneous occupations buried in an intact state throughout this section of floodplain.

One of the Lamoka features (Feature 30), a large circular stain (85 by 90 cm) surrounded by reddened soils and charcoal concentrations, contained food refuse (e.g., walnut or hickory nutshells and acorn fragments) and a netsinker. Another hearth feature consisted of fire-cracked rock scatter containing charcoal, hickory nuts, and walnuts and another netsinker. More complex hearth features consisting of FCR concentrations, likely representing separate-use events, were recorded in the center of the block excavations and also contained netsinkers and charred nut remains. Flotation samples recovered additional nut

FIGURE 2.2
Feature 27, Lamoka component, Allenwood Site (36UN82; scale bar: 50 cm). Credit: Henry Holt.

FIGURE 2.3
Feature 29, Lamoka component, Allenwood Site (36UN82; scale bars: 50 cm and 30 cm). Credit: Henry Holt.

FIGURE 2.4
Feature 48, Lamoka Component, Allenwood Site (36UN82; scale bars: 50 cm and 20 cm). Credit: Henry Holt.

remains, acorns, and cherry seeds. Other hearths, both large and quite compact small features, contained similar remains, and all appear to be closely related to food processing on the site. Debitage associated with the features includes local cherts and nonlocal metarhyolites.

Subsistence evidence from the Allenwood Site includes some botanical remains such as hickory nuts, walnuts, acorns, and hazelnuts. Pitted stones and anvils may have provided working surfaces for processing plant foods. No faunal material was recovered, but evidence of fishing is based on the recovery of netsinkers. Hunting equipment includes a number of projectile points. Though little or no use-wear shows on these items, it is assumed that they served as butchering tools, along with a complement of flake tools.

Defining the community pattern for the Lamoka living floor at Allenwood is a matter of sorting out the hearth clusters in some kind of logical order to see any discernible spatial relationships. At the west end of the site block, a cluster of three features was recorded, all relatively shallow stains with charcoal, some fire-reddened soils, and fire-cracked rock. The small size of the features indicates use over a short duration at each one, perhaps during the course of successive visits to the site. Very little in the way of finished tools was recovered from this area.

In the center of the block, a larger concentration of features varying in size and shape was encountered. Feature 27, dating to ca. 3850 BP, may have been periodically reused by successive occupants of the site. Fire-cracked rock was scattered over a large area, but the feature contained within its boundaries several discrete, single-episode hearths. Feature 29 exhibited a similar pattern of individual hearths, but separate hearths were less apparent. Along the edge of Feature 29, several small hearth areas were recorded, all having the appearance of single-event hearths.

Other areas of the block revealed small hearths with dense concentrations of fire-cracked rock, ash deposits, and burned soils that also appeared to be single-event features. Dates from several of the features were consistent with the dates for the Lamoka occupation overall. Distributions of artifacts around features did not occur in obvious clusters, but no area of the Lamoka component lacked some kind of stone tool associations, including both chipped-stone and cobble tools, although the extreme west end of the block (farthest from the river) contained fewer net-sinkers than the rest of the block.

Ritchie (1932:50) defines Lamoka points as small, percussion-chipped bifaces with narrow blades and stemmed or side-notched bases, usually left thick and unfinished; the Lamoka points recovered from Allenwood fit this description well (Figures 2.5 and 2.6). Another artifact type usually associated with Lamoka sites and present in the Allenwood assemblage is the beveled adze (Figure 2.7; Ritchie 1980:67). Usually made from fine-grained igneous material, beveled adzes are believed to have been used for dugout boat construction (Ritchie 1944:296).

The Lamoka assemblage at Allenwood shows all stages of bifacial reduction, with more finished points recovered than staged bifaces, which are almost exclusively made from Shriver chert. The projectile points appear to have been used principally as weapons, which would support a hunting camp function for the site. The lack of obvious use-wear on the points and other bifaces is consistent with the idea of a short-term hunting-fishing station where weapons, fishing equipment, and expedient flake tools form the primary components of the tool kit. The presence of a variety of flake tools (e.g., large retouched flakes, spokeshave edges, flakes with graver spurs, and crudely fashioned celts from retouched metasedimentary flakes) provides some support for this idea.

Retooling on the site is evident but not a major activity. For instance, a small collection of Shriver chert bifaces and biface fragments indicates some use of local materials for replenishing hunting-related tools and perhaps butchering implements by those camped in that location. The presence of block cortex on early- and middle-stage biface forms of Shriver chert shows that the Lamoka inhabitants of the site had some knowledge of local outcrop sources. Other raw materials are represented (e.g., rhyolite, jasper, quartzite, argillite, metasedimentary material, and miscellaneous cherts), but only to a minor degree. Rhyolite use

FIGURE 2.5
Lamoka points from Allenwood Site (36UN82).
Credit: Rob Tucher.

FIGURE 2.6
More Lamoka points from Allenwood Site (36UN82). Credit: Rob Tucher.

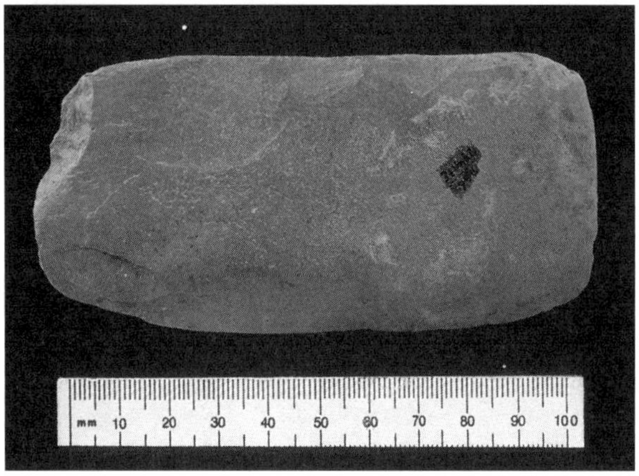

FIGURE 2.7
Beveled adze from Allenwood Site (36UN82). Credit: Rob Tucher.

is certainly much less emphasized when compared to later Terminal Archaic groups since only eighty rhyolite flakes were found in all Lamoka levels combined. As with the Terminal Archaic and later components, the rhyolite appears to have been brought to the site in a more or less finished form. The metasedimentary material represented in the assemblage most likely relates to the acquisition of cobbles for the manufacture of netsinkers and other cobble tools.

Mifflinville Site

The Lamoka and contemporaneous (e.g., Bare Island) occupations at the Mifflinville Site (36CO17) consist of a few hearths and tool-manufacturing areas nearby (Jacoby et al. 1999). These hearth features were found to be associated with Lamoka points, cores, netsinkers, debitage, and fire-cracked rock. In one area, bifaces were mapped within four concentrations of biface reduction flakes, along with projectile points and staged bifaces. A small hearth was recorded nearby. Around the edge of the hearth, biface sections, cores, and a mano indicate both workshop activities and food processing. No samples from the hearth features were radiocarbon dated.

The remaining living floor exposed in this Lamoka component consisted of a few small hearths and chipping clusters that included cores and staged biface fragments. Some rhyolite use was evident here, as it was in the Lamoka component of the Allenwood Site (36UN82), in spite of the abundance of local Shriver chert. This may indicate the very beginning of the intensive use of rhyolite as a preferred raw material, a trend that is readily apparent in the Terminal Archaic cultures that follow. Netsinkers are also well represented in the component, as they are at many other Lamoka sites. The intensive fishing activity is further supported by protein residue data indicating the use of trout, catfish, and American eel (Jacoby et al. 1999). The intensification of riverine activities such as fishing may reflect a trend toward settlement along major rivers influenced by the dry climatic conditions of the middle postglacial xerothermic. This settlement shift may have established the basis for the intensive Terminal Archaic use of riverbank environs at Mifflinville and many other sites along the Susquehanna River.

Other evidence from Late Archaic occupations at Mifflinville includes boiler dump features, large platform hearths, burned soils, and smaller hearths, as well as a few pit features. The pattern of hearth distribution shows that the site was likely reoccupied a number of times by small groups of hunter-gatherers during the last few millennia of the Late Archaic period and into the Terminal Archaic. Diversity in the tool assemblages recorded in near-hearth locations evidences fishing, core reduction, biface manufacturing, hunting, and the processing of food.

Memorial Park Site

Located in Lock Haven, Clinton County, Pennsylvania, just above the confluence of Bald Eagle Creek with the West Branch of the Susquehanna River, the Memorial Park Site (36CN164) is a large (3.5 ha or 8.3 ac) multicomponent site that includes identified Clemson Island, Middle Woodland, Late Archaic, and perhaps earlier occupations within 4 to 5 meters of alluvial deposits (Hart et al. 1995). Goodwin and Associates found evidence of six buried soils in its Phase II work on the site (Neuman 1989), classifying the buried soils as separate analytical units that include buried A horizons intercalated with cambic B horizons. For example, Soil 2 contains the base of a partially plow disturbed Clemson Island component, an intact earlier Clemson Island occupation (buried A horizon), and the upper portion of a Middle Woodland occupation (B horizon). Soil 3 contains a Middle Woodland component (buried A horizon) and a Terminal/Late Archaic component in the lower B horizon. Soil 4 contains a Late Archaic component within a buried A horizon, and additional Late Archaic materials within the underlying B horizon. Soil 5, the upper portion of which dates to approximately 4400 BP or 2450 BC, contains lithic artifacts within buried A horizon and underlying B horizon contexts. The upper portion of Soil 6, a buried A horizon, is the deepest cultural component recorded on the site to date. Data recovery excavations were completed by GAI, Inc., with supplemental geomorphological investigations conducted by Joseph Schuldenrein and Frank Vento (1993; Cremeens and Hart 2009).

The Laurentian Archaic components at Memorial Park consist of an Early Laurentian component (6350–5790 BP or 4400–3840 BC), a Vergennes-like complex (6250–5650 BP or 4300–3700 BC), and a Late Laurentian component (5200–4900 BP or 3250–2950 BC). The Late Laurentian component is marked by Beekman triangles and by Brewerton, Otter Creek, and Vosburg points. Activities represented include biface thinning and tool maintenance, with both local and nonlocal (e.g., jasper) raw materials used. Tool manufacturing is indicated by large amounts of debitage in the occupations (Hart et al. 1995:513). Likely used repeatedly as a base camp, the site is represented by a wide range of activities. Base camps were used as localities from which forays into surrounding uplands were staged (Hart et al. 1995:513). Aside from the obvious focus on hunting (147 bifaces), subsistence evidence includes hickory nuts, butternuts, and pepo gourds, the last being the earliest find in the Susquehanna Basin (Hart et al. 1995:514; Hart and Sidell 1997).

The final Late Archaic component at Memorial Park, the Piedmont Archaic component (4455–3950 BP) dates consistently with other Narrow-Stemmed Point tradition sites in the broader region. The occupation is marked by recoveries of Bare Island and Lamoka points within an array of about thirteen fire-related features. Subsistence data from this component include hickory nuts and walnuts, and workshop activities include late-stage biface production and resharpening as well as resource extraction (Hart et al. 1995:515; Hart and Sidell 1997).

Conclusions

Many of the Lamoka and other contemporaneous Late Archaic sites noted above evidence the systematic use and reuse of riverine and large-stream environs over a number of years. Most of the high-order stream-associated sites tend to be short-term occupations, even those which are used repeatedly. Such camps would have provided staging areas for exploiting the surrounding terrain for usable plant and animal food resources, taking into account seasonal factors and localized fluctuations in resource abundance and predictability. Briefly occupied upland sites and rock shelters, evidenced by much smaller numbers of projectile points, tools, and debitage than those at the more extensive floodplain staging areas, were also diverse in their usage. The material remains of the larger staging areas and base camps along high-order streams and rivers often include numerous reused hearth areas (e.g., at the Allenwood Site) from intermittent visits. Hearth features are typically formed in bowl-shaped depressions, such as those recorded at the Lamoka Lake Site, at other smaller camps in New York, such as those at the Bent Site (Ritchie 1932; Ritchie and Funk 1973), and at many of the Upper Susquehanna Pennsylvania sites.

Discarded netsinkers and tools from fishing equipment maintenance and tool kit replenishment were also evident at a number of sites. At Allenwood, for example, concentrations of netsinkers may have been the result of leaving a fishnet behind during a short-term fishing activity. It is unlikely that damaged larger nets would have been carried from site to site; rather, they would have been left behind and repaired upon return.

Larger staging areas and base camps would likely have been at strategic locations such as major stream confluences, where periodic gatherings for communal hunts, trade, and social interaction could take place. There is little evidence of such sites in the Upper Susquehanna Valley, but it is logical to assume they would have existed in the vicinity of major confluences.

The Lamoka occupation at sites such as Allenwood may have been part of a network of temporary encampments made along the river and in selected upland localities to take advantage of local subsistence resources and to replenish raw materials such as lithics. Some (e.g., Cavallo 1987; Custer 1988; Stewart 1989) have suggested that the same pathways were consistently used to connect seasonal base camps in the network during the final years of the Late Archaic and into the Terminal Archaic. These camps and pathways may have been used to exploit specific subsistence resources (e.g., fishing during spawning periods) and to procure raw materials from well-known outcrop sources for replenishing tool kits. Specialized procurement sites known for consistently and predictably yielding much-sought-after food resources would have been routinely revisited. This may have included good fishing sites such as Allenwood (36UN82) or Mifflinville (36CO17) or areas near spawning streams.

Hearth-focused activity areas appear to dominate occupations throughout the drainage basins of the Susquehanna and nearby rivers during the latter part of the Late Archaic period. In fact, this type of community pattern was prevalent throughout the Eastern Woodlands. Most Archaic sites tend to lack structural features such as dwellings, at least those of a type that can be easily recognized in the archaeological record. Perhaps the kinds of structures that were used at this time left little or no trace. On the other hand, hearths, defined by fire-cracked rock clusters and burned earth, are well represented, although it is impossible to determine whether such hearths represent the interior of structures or simply a focal point for activities within a broader community setting.

The incidence of subsistence evidence is inconsistent from site to site. More common is evidence of tool use and resharpening debris related to food processing and consumption. Much less common are faunal and botanical remains from Late Archaic sites. At the Mifflinville and Allenwood Sites, for example, foods consumed adjacent to hearths included walnuts and hickory nuts. Among the food-processing tools were flake tools, scrapers, manos, and steatite containers. Hickory nuts and walnuts were also recovered from Late Archaic features at the Memorial Park Site. Rarer finds such as pepo gourds from Memorial Park indicate that most plant foods are not well preserved in Late Archaic contexts and that we are likely seeing only a fraction of what was actually used.

Another fact evident in Lamoka and related Narrow-Stemmed Point tradition sites in the Upper Susquehanna Valley is the incipient use of nonlocal raw materials such as rhyolite and jasper, materials evident in Lamoka components but not in the high frequencies seen in Terminal Archaic assemblages. R. Michael Stewart (1984, 1989) notes that exchange networks in the region by this time may have been well established, using rhyolite and distributing it widely at great distances from its source. There is a notable increase in the use of rhyolite in later Terminal Archaic occupations at both Mifflinville and Allenwood. On the other hand, its incipient use in the few millennia prior to this suggests the initial formation of regional exchange networks or perhaps a much broader range of seasonal rounds to extract raw materials such as rhyolite in transportable form. Rhyolite cores, for example, are not common in Late Archaic assemblages. It is more likely that large flakes and quarry blanks of rhyolite were transported from quarry sources. The result was probably, as Stewart (1989:65–66) suggests, the emergence of ritualized intergroup exchange within a broader established pattern of subsistence pursuits, either group to group in a chain-like pattern, or as part of a broader, more complex, network.

This pattern of regional exchange is also evident in nearby drainage basins such as that of the Potomac River (Wall 1992). At Site 18AG168, for example, Late Archaic occupations are represented by diagnostic Lamoka and contemporaneous Buffalo stemmed points, and rhyolite usage is quite evident. Although even more apparent in the Broadspear occupation, where rhyolite workshop areas were recorded, such usage has its beginning toward the end of the Late Archaic period. A detailed collections analysis on the use of rhyolite in the Upper Potomac Valley in the Late Archaic shows that about 10% of Late and Terminal Archaic diagnostics are made from rhyolite and most are broadspears (Wall 1992:5).

Steatite, as well, was moved from primary sources near the mouth of the Susquehanna River to populations in the North and West Branch Valleys; it is evident as finished artifacts at a number of Upper Susquehanna Valley sites during the Late Archaic period. Evidence for this movement of steatite far from its natural source area is present at sites such as Allenwood (36UN82; Wall 1995), Mifflinville (36CO17), Gould Island (36LU105), Kettle Creek (36CN165 and 36CN199; Petraglia, Knepper, and Risetto 1998), Jacobs (36LU90; Weed and Wenstrom 1992), and Skvarek (36LU132; Miller 1998). Like rhyolite, steatite became even more common during the Terminal Archaic period, when large soapstone vessels were manufactured.

Stability in riverine settlements by the Terminal Archaic period is suggested by sites such as Allenwood and Mifflinville, where large platform hearth features are predominant. This may represent either periodic group aggregation or more consistent (or at least frequent) use of these settings, enhancing a previously established pattern of settlement. In other words, earlier Late Archaic peoples may have initiated the use of routinely occupied base camps. As routines became established, the more productive sites may have been used increasingly to maximize subsistence resources and minimize the distance to other valued raw materials. The result may have been more streamlined rounds of settlement in which fewer sites were used for longer periods of time or more frequently.

REFERENCES

Asch, Nancy B., Richard I. Ford, and David L. Asch
1972 *Paleoethnobotany of the Koster Site: The Archaic Horizons.* Illinois Valley Archaeological Program Research Papers, Volume 6. Reports of Investigations 24. Illinois State Museum, Springfield.

Breetzke, David (editor)
1998 *Phase III Data Recovery Investigations for the Wyalusing Creek Bridge Replacement Project, S.R. 0706, Rushville, Rush Township, Susquehanna County, Pennsylvania.* Report prepared for Federal Highway Administration and Pennsylvania Department of Transportation, Engineering District 4-0. Cultural Resource Group, Louis Berger & Associates, Inc., East Orange, New Jersey.

Bressler, James P., Ricki Maietta, and Karen Rockey
1983 *Canfield Island Through the Ages: 36LY37.* North Central Chapter No. 8, Society for Pennsylvania Archaeology and Lycoming County Historical Society, Williamsport.

Cavallo, John A.
1987 *Area B (28Me1-B), Data Recovery.* Trenton Complex Archaeology: Report 8. Prepared for Federal Highway Administration and New Jersey Department of Transportation, Bureau of Environmental Analysis, Trenton. Cultural Resource Group, Louis Berger & Associates, Inc., East Orange, New Jersey.

Cremeens, David L., and John P. Hart
2009 Holocene Alluvial Geomorphology of the Memorial Park Site (36CN164), West Branch of the Susquehanna River, Pennsylvania. *Archaeology of Eastern North America* 37:47–64.

Custer, Jay F.
1988 Late Archaic Cultural Dynamics in the Central Middle Atlantic Region. *Journal of Middle Atlantic Archaeology* 4:39–59.

1996 *Prehistoric Cultures of Eastern Pennsylvania.* Anthropological Series 7. Pennsylvania Historical and Museum Commission, Harrisburg.

Custer, Jay F., Scott C. Watson, and Daniel N. Bailey
1994 *Data Recovery Investigations at the West Water Street Site, 36CN175, Lock Haven, Clinton County, Pennsylvania.* Report prepared for U.S. Army Corps of Engineers, Baltimore District. KFS Historic Preservation Group, Philadelphia.

Dincauze, Dena
1976 *The Neville Site: 8000 Years at Amoskeag.* Peabody Museum Monographs 4. Peabody Museum of Archaeology and Ethnology, Harvard University, Cambridge, Massachusetts.

East, Thomas C., Christopher T. Espenshade, Margaret G. Sams, Jessica Smoker, Matthew G. Hyland, Patricia H. Baker, and Bryan C. Henderson
2002 *Phase I/II/III Archaeological Investigations, Northumberland and Union Counties, S.R. 0080, Section 52D, Bridge Expansion and Highway Improvement Project.* Report prepared for Federal Highway Administration and Pennsylvania Department of Transportation, Engineering District 3-0. Skelly and Loy, Inc., Monroeville and Harrisburg, Pennsylvania.

Ebright, Carol
1992 *Early Native American Prehistory on the Maryland Western Shore: Archeological Investigations at the Higgins Site.* Archeological Report 1, Maryland State Highway Administration, Project Planning Division, Environmental Evaluation Section, Baltimore [Maryland Geological Survey, Division of Archeology File Report 250].

Funk, Robert E.
1965 The Archaic of the Hudson Valley: New Evidence and New Interpretations. *Pennsylvania Archaeologist* 35:3–4:139–60.

1988 The Laurentian Concept: A Review. *Archaeology of Eastern North America* 16:1–42.

Funk, Robert E., Robert J. Dineen, Charles E. Gillette, Franklin J. Hesse, James T. Kirkland, Donald M. Lewis, et al.
1993 *Archaeological Investigations in the Upper Susquehanna Valley, New York State.* Two volumes. Monographs in Archaeology. Persimmon Press, Buffalo, New York.

Funk, Robert E., and H. Hoagland
1972 An Archaic Camp Site in the Upper Susquehanna Drainage. *New York State Archaeological Association* 54:11–22.

Funk, Robert E., and Bruce E. Rippeteau
1977 *Adaptation, Continuity and Change in Upper Susquehanna Valley Prehistory.* Occasional Publications in Northeastern Anthropology 3. George's Mills, New Hampshire.

Gardner, William M.
1987 Comparison of Ridge and Valley, Blue Ridge, Piedmont, and Coastal Plain Archaic Period Site Distribution: An Idealized Transect (Preliminary Model). *Journal of Middle Atlantic Archaeology* 3:49–80.

Hart, John P., Jeffrey R. Graybill, David L. Cremeens, Michael G. Spitzer, John P. Nass, Nancy Asch Sidell, et al.
1995 *Archaeological Investigations at the Memorial Park Site (36CN164) Clinton County, Pennsylvania.* Report prepared for U.S. Army Corps of Engineers, Baltimore District. GAI Consultants, Inc., Monroeville, Pennsylvania.

Hart, John P., and Nancy Asch Sidell
1997 Additional Evidence for Early Cucurbit Use in the Northern Eastern Woodlands East of the Allegheny Front. *American Antiquity* 62 (3): 523–37.

Jacoby, Robert, Robert Wall, Rhea Rogers, and John Killeen
1999 *Phase III Archaeological Investigations of Site 36Co17 and Site 36Co18 for the Mifflinville Bridge Replacement, SR 2028, Mifflinville, Pennsylvania.* Report prepared for Pennsylvania Department of Transportation Engineering District 3-0, Montoursville, Pennsylvania. Cultural Resource Group, Louis Berger & Associates, Inc., East Orange, New Jersey.

Kinsey, W. Fred, III
1959 Recent Excavations on Bare Island in Pennsylvania: The Kent-Hally Site. *Pennsylvania Archaeologist* 29:109–33.

Kinsey, W. Fred, III (editor)
1972 *Archeology in the Upper Delaware Valley.* Anthropological Series 2. Pennsylvania Historical and Museum Commission, Harrisburg.

Knox, James C.
1983 Responses of River Systems to Holocene Climates. In *Late-Quaternary Environments of the United States,* Volume 2: *The Holocene,* edited by H. E. Wright Jr., 26–41. University of Minnesota Press, Minneapolis.

Kraft, Herbert C.

1975 *The Archaeology of the Tocks Island Area.* Archaeological Research Center, Seton Hall University Museum, South Orange, New Jersey.

Miller, Patricia E.

1992 *Archaeological Data Recovery, Site 36Nb3, S.R. 0044, Section 004, Northumberland and Union Counties, Pennsylvania.* Report prepared for Pennsylvania Department of Transportation, Engineering District 3-0, Montoursville. Archaeological and Historical Consultants, Inc., Centre Hall, Pennsylvania.

1994 *Archaeological Data Recovery: The Skvarek Site (Site 36LU132). Proposed Shickshinny/Mocanaqua Bridge Replacement (S.R. 0239), Salem and Conyngham Townships, Luzerne County, Pennsylvania.* Report prepared for Luzerne County Commissioners and Pennsylvania Department of Transportation, Engineering District 4-0, Wilkes-Barre. Archaeological and Historical Consultants, Inc., Centre Hall, Pennsylvania.

1998 Lithic Projectile Point Technology and Raw Material Use in the Susquehanna River Valley. In *The Archaic Period in Pennsylvania: Hunter-Gatherers of the Early and Middle Holocene Period*, edited by Paul A. Raber, Patricia E. Miller, and Sarah M. Neusius, 91–119. Recent Research in Pennsylvania Archaeology 1. Pennsylvania Historical and Museum Commission, Harrisburg.

Miller, Patricia E., James T. Marine, Sharon White, and Frank J. Vento

2008 *Archaeological Investigations, Route 11/15 Improvements (SR 0011, Section 008) Juniata and Perry Counties, Pennsylvania*, Volume 6: *Synthesis.* Report prepared for Pennsylvania Department of Transportation, Engineering District 8-0, Harrisburg. KCI Technologies, Inc., Mechanicsburg, Pennsylvania.

Miroff, Laurie E., Jeremy J. Wilson, and Nina M. Versaggi

2008 Reconsidering Culture-Historic Taxa in the Late Archaic. *North American Archaeologist* 29:2:157–77.

Neuman, Thomas N.

1989 *Phase II Intensive Survey, Historic and Prehistoric Archeological Investigations at Lock Haven, Clinton County, Pennsylvania.* Report prepared for U.S. Army Corps of Engineers, Baltimore District. Contract DACW 31-87-R-0010. R. Christopher Goodwin and Associates, Inc., Frederick, Maryland.

Petraglia, Michael, Dennis Knepper, and John Rissetto

1998 The Nature of Prehistoric Activities on Kettle Creek, an Upland Tributary of the West Branch of the Susquehanna. *Journal of Middle Atlantic Archaeology* 14:13–38.

Rippeteau, Bruce E.

1977 New Data and Models for 8,000 Years of Archaic Societies and Their Environments in the Upper Susquehanna Valley of New York State. In *Amerinds and Their Paleoenvironments in Northeastern North America*, edited by W. S. Newman and B. Salwen, 392–99. Annals of the New York Academy of Sciences 288. New York.

Ritchie, William A.

1932 *The Lamoka Lake Site.* Researches and Transactions of the New York State Archeological Association 7 (4). Rochester.

1944 *The Pre-Iroquoian Occupations of New York.* Memoir 1. Rochester Museum of Arts and Sciences, Rochester, New York.

1971 *A Typology and Nomenclature for New York Projectile Points.* New York State Museum and Science Service Bulletin 384. University of the State of New York, State Education Department, Albany.

1980 *The Archaeology of New York State.* Revised edition. Harbor Hill Books, Harrison, New York.

Ritchie, William A., and Robert Funk

1973 *Aboriginal Settlement Patterns in the Northeast.* New York State Museum and Science Service Memoir 20. University of the State of New York, State Education Department, Albany.

Schuldenrein, Joseph, and Frank J. Vento

1993 *Geoarchaeological Investigations at the Memorial Park Site (36CN164), Pennsylvania.* Unpublished report prepared for U.S. Army Corps of Engineers, Baltimore District.

Stafford, C. Russell

1991 Archaic Period Logistical Foraging Strategies in West-Central Illinois. *Midcontinental Journal of Archaeology* 16 (2): 212–46.

Stewart, R. Michael

1984 South Mountain (Meta) Rhyolite: A Perspective on Prehistoric Trade and Exchange in the Middle Atlantic Region. In *Prehistoric Lithic Exchange Systems in the Middle Atlantic Region*, edited by Jay F. Custer, 14–44. Monograph 3. Center for Archaeological Research, University of Delaware, Newark.

1989 Trade and Exchange in Middle Atlantic Region Prehistory. *Archaeology of Eastern North America* 17:47–78.

1995 The Status of Woodland Prehistory in the Middle Atlantic Region. *Archaeology of Eastern North America* 23:177–206.

2003 A Regional Perspective on Early and Middle Woodland Prehistory in Pennsylvania. In *Foragers and Farmers of the Early and Middle Woodland Periods in Pennsylvania*, edited by Paul A. Raber and Verna L. Cowin, 1–33. Recent Research in Pennsylvania Archaeology 3. Pennsylvania Historical and Museum Commission, Harrisburg.

Taylor, Randy K., Robert Wall, Alison Helms, and Brad Koldehoff

1996 *Phase I and II Archaeological Investigations Along S.R.0011 Section 002, Perry and Juniata Counties, Pennsylvania.* Report prepared for Pennsylvania

Department of Transportation, Engineering District 3-0, Montoursville. Cultural Resource Group, Louis Berger & Associates, Inc., East Orange, New Jersey.

Turnbaugh, William A.

1974 A Lamoka Component in North Central Pennsylvania. *Man in the Northeast* 8:3–21.

1977 *Man, Land, and Time: The Cultural Prehistory and Demographic Patterns of North-Central Pennsylvania.* Reprinted. Originally published 1975 for Lycoming County Historical Society, Williamsport, Pennsylvania. Unigraphic, Inc., Evansville, Illinois.

Vento, Frank J., and Harold B. Rollins

1989 *Development of a Late Pleistocene-Holocene Genetic Stratigraphic Framework as It Relates to Atmospheric Circulation and Climate Change in the Upper and Central Susquehanna River Drainage Basin.* Report prepared for Bureau for Historic Preservation, Pennsylvania Historical and Museum Commission, Harrisburg. Clarion University of Pennsylvania, Clarion.

Versaggi, Nina M.

1987 *Hunter-Gatherer Settlement Models and the Archaeological Record: A Test Case from the Upper Susquehanna Valley of New York.* Ph.D. dissertation, Department of Anthropology, State University of New York at Binghamton. University Microfilms, Ann Arbor, Michigan.

1996 Prehistoric Hunter-Gatherer Settlement Models: Interpreting the Upper Susquehanna Valley. In *A Golden Chronograph for Robert E. Funk*, edited by C. Lindner and E. V. Curtin, 129–40. Occasional Publications in Northeastern Anthropology 15. Archaeological Services, Bethlehem, Connecticut.

Versaggi, Nina M., LouAnn Wurst, T. Cregg Madrigal, and Andrea Lain

2001 Adding Complexity to Late Archaic Research in the Northeastern Appalachians. In *Archaeology of the Appalachian Highlands*, edited by L. P. Sullivan and S. C. Prezzano, 121–33. University of Tennessee Press, Knoxville.

Wall, Robert D.

1992 Lithic Resource Utilization in Western Maryland Prehistory. *Journal of Middle Atlantic Archaeology* 8:1–9.

1995 *Allenwood Federal Correctional Complex Sanitary Water Treatment Facility, Gregg Township, Union County, Pennsylvania, Phase III Data Recovery Investigations.* Report prepared for U.S. Department of Justice, Federal Bureau of Prisons, Washington, D.C. Cultural Resource Group, Louis Berger & Associates, Inc., Washington, D.C.

2000 A Buried Lamoka Occupation in Stratified Contexts, West Branch Valley of the Susquehanna River, Pennsylvania. *Pennsylvania Archaeologist* 70 (1): 1–44.

Wall, Robert D., R. Michael Stewart, and Brad Koldehoff

1990 *Phase II Archaeological Investigations for the Mifflinville Bridge Replacement Project, L.R. 2028, Section 004, Columbia County, Pennsylvania.* Report prepared for Modjeski and Masters, Inc., and Pennsylvania Department of Transportation, Harrisburg. Cultural Resource Group, Louis Berger & Associates, Inc., East Orange, New Jersey.

Wall, Robert D., Rick Vernay, Delland Gould, and Hope E. Luhman

2003 *Hunters to Horticulturalists: The Archaeology of the Mansfield Bridge Site, SR 6015, Section D52, Tioga County, Pennsylvania.* Report prepared for Gannett Fleming, Inc., and Pennsylvania Department of Transportation, Engineering District 3-0, Montoursville. Cultural Resource Group, Louis Berger & Associates, Inc., East Orange, New Jersey.

Webb, Thompson, III, Patrick Bartlein, Sandy Harrison, and Katherine Anderson

1993 Vegetation, Lake Levels, and Climate in Eastern North America for the Past 18,000 Years. In *Global Climates Since the Last Glacial Maximum*, edited by H. E. Wright Jr., J. E. Kutzbach, T. Webb III, W. F. Ruddiman, F. A. Street-Perrott, and P. J. Bartlein, 415–67. University of Minnesota Press, Minneapolis.

Weed, Carol S., and William P. Wenstrom (editors)

1992 *Cultural Resources Investigations of 36LU90 (Jacobs Site) and 36LU105 (Gould Island Site), Luzerne County, Pennsylvania.* Report prepared for Transcontinental Gas Pipe Line Corporation, Houston, Texas. Panamerican Consultants, Tuscaloosa, Alabama.

Wendland, Wayne, and Reid A. Bryson

1974 Dating Climatic Episodes of the Holocene. *Quaternary Research* 4 (1): 9–24.

3.

The Evolution of Cultural Adaptations During the Transitional Period in the Delaware and Susquehanna River Valleys in Pennsylvania

Kurt W. Carr

ABSTRACT

In examining the evolution of Transitional adaptive strategy in Native American cultures of the Susquehanna and Delaware drainage basins, I will argue that artifacts and features of the Transitional period represent a more intensive exploitation of the environment than those of the Late Archaic in response to increasing population pressure, aggravated by a slight change in the climate. Broad-bladed bifaces in standardized shapes, lithic exchange systems, steatite bowls, and burial ceremonialism reflect an increasingly structured social system that solidified social networks and functioned to reduce subsistence risks when resources were limited. Social groups who employed this strategy were more successful than those who did not.

The purpose of this chapter is to review a model of the development, evolution, and disappearance of the artifact and feature assemblages that define the Transitional period. Most aspects of this model were developed during the 1980s and 1990s in the cultural ecological approach to the Middle Atlantic region common during those years. The model was inspired, first and foremost, by William Gardner (1987), but significant contributions were made by Victor Carbone (1976), John Cavallo (1996), Jay Custer (1984), Kenneth Sassaman (1999), R. Michael Stewart (1989), and James Truncer (2004). Much of what is presented below is a brief summary of their research, which, I hope, does justice to their work.

Many of the issues debated twenty-five years ago have not been resolved and continue to blur or complicate our understanding of the Transitional period. Some of the complications may reflect the limitations of the archaeological record or of an overly simplified model. It is now clear that our characterization of this period must be more complex, encompassing more than simply broadspears in jasper or metarhyolite, steatite bowls, and sites located on floodplains.

I assume that culture is an adaptive strategy used by humans to exploit the environment, using Lewis Binford's (1965:205) definition: "Culture is an extrasomatic adaptive system that is employed in the integration of a society with its environment and with other cultural systems." In this chapter, an explicitly evolutionary and processual approach to the analysis of the Transitional period will be taken; the defining artifacts, features, and community or settlement patterns of the time from approximately 4300 to 2700 BP will be viewed as the material remains of an adaptive strategy. Human societies "internally and historically, generate variation which interacts with and is selected by aspects of the environment" (Shennan 1996:x). Given the existing database—and the complicated chronology, scant subsistence data, and very few large-scale, fine-grained excavations with which to interpret social organization—a processual approach results in a reasonably productive model, one that can serve as a baseline for future investigation, including postprocessual studies.

Groups of humans who develop a combination of technology, social organization, settlement systems, and cultural traditions that can consistently extract sufficient calories from the environment to reproduce new offspring represent a successful adaptation in the Darwinian sense: the traits that represent successful strategies for exploiting the environment (both natural and cultural) are selected. The successful strategies that are reflected in material remains can be documented in the archaeological record by increases in specific feature or artifact types, in community or settlement patterns, or in site distributions.

The processual approach should not be confused with optimal foraging theory. Humans make choices that sometimes do not result in a successful adaptation either in the short term or over long periods of time. Most frequently in the prehistoric world of temperate climate foragers, cultural adaptations evolved slowly as the environment (both cultural and natural) changed. People adjusted their adaptive strategies to exploit this change. Some individuals, families, and groups made unsuccessful adjustments that did not extract sufficient calories from the environment to reproduce and to raise the next generation. These adaptive strategies are difficult to identify in the archaeological record because they did not exist for very long. Long-term changes in adaptive strategy, such as the Paleoindian/Early Archaic change, for example, are commonly recognized and well documented. In archaeological terms, artifacts, features, and community or settlement patterns reflect these adaptations. As these components change, I assume the adaptive strategy is also changing.

Settlement systems are frequently used to document changes in how societies exploited the environment. The exploitation or abandonment of new ecological zones is used as an indicator of changes in adaptive strategy. Custer (1996), Stewart (1987), and Robert Wall and colleagues (1996) have discussed broad changes in settlement systems during the Late Archaic, Transitional, and Early Woodland periods, but it has been difficult to document specific changes over these time periods. There seem to be changes in the size of sites, but does this represent occupation by a few large groups or by many small groups? More large-scale excavations and finer-grained intrasite mapping are needed to make this determination. In addition, throughout these time periods, there seems to be a focus on the use of floodplain resources. The specific locations on the floodplain may change, but the ecological implications of these changes are not obvious, an issue Joseph Blondino examines in Chapter 5. The present chapter will focus on distinctive artifacts and features of the period from approximately 4300 to 2700 BP to identify changes in adaptive strategy.

Throughout the Archaic period, from the Pre-Boreal to the Boreal to the Atlantic climatic episode, there were gradual changes in the natural environment. Archaeologists have also detailed changes in the cultural environment throughout this time, primarily in the realm of material culture and technology. One can imagine a variety of nontechnological cultural changes, for example, in religion, language, and music that are not as easily identified in the archaeological record. As noted by Herbert Maschner and Steven Mithen (1996:7), it can be assumed that "societies are always in a state of readjustment, experimentation, and change because certain individuals within the society will be attempting to manipulate it to his/her own ends." We can speculate on the specific manifestations of individual or group behavior, but, during this time period, it is difficult to develop testable hypotheses concerning this behavior.

Some of these changes are neutral with regard to adaptive strategy. Some are difficult to identify in the archaeological record. Relative population density is one cultural factor that can be estimated from archaeological data for the Archaic period. By all accounts (e.g., Fiedel 2001; Reeve 1992; Steponaitis 1980; Wholey 2009), human populations were increasing throughout the Early, Middle, and Late Archaic periods in the Middle Atlantic region. These changes in the natural and cultural environment required incremental adjustments to the adaptive strategy. With sudden changes in the environment, the adaptive strategy could also change suddenly. It is proposed that increasing population density, aggravated by a slight change in climate, is the source for much of the cultural change that constitutes the archaeological record of the Transitional period. Such change represents an early example of adaptive strategy changing quickly in response to increasing population density in the Middle Atlantic region.

The definition of the Transitional period (the time between ca. 4300 and 2700 BP) has been controversial since it was proposed by John Witthoft (1949, 1953), who visualized this time as a period of transition between the Archaic foraging pattern and the Woodland horticultural pattern. Witthoft argued that Transitional culture was a "canoe traveling culture, exploiting fish, waterfowl and large game" (Witthoft 1953:25). William Ritchie (1969:150) felt this was a stage of culture connecting the Late Archaic and Early Woodland periods. Ritchie agreed with the use of the term "Transitional," and both authors interpreted this as a distinct stage of cultural development, as did W. Fred Kinsey (1972: 347), who found that this time period was different from the Late Archaic period. With the advantage over Ritchie of having additional radiometric dates, Kinsey asserted that the changes during this period occurred quickly, although, arguing that all cultures are in transition, he rejected the use of the term "Transitional." He further argued that the time period, which he believed did not deserve a specific designation, represented "a single rapidly expanding tradition that differentiated into several related phases" (Kinsey 1972:347). Referring to an undergraduate manuscript by Charles Hunter (1970), Kinsey (1972:347) agreed with Hunter that the several phases of the period reconverge at the end of the Broadspear phase to form the Fishtail or Orient phase.

William Turnbaugh (1975:137) preferred the term "Terminal Archaic" and saw the "progression of narrow stemmed points as abruptly terminated by the appearance of characteristic broad projectiles." Custer (1996:163) described this and the Early and Middle Woodland periods with the term "formative," reflecting "societies slowly transformed from relatively mobile hunters and gathers to the sedentary villagers of the succeeding Late Woodland chronological period." He viewed Witthoft's Transitional period as a complex (actually, two complexes: the "Poplar Island complex" and the "Delaware Valley Archaic complex") in a larger cultural transformation from one cultural adaptation to another.

Presentations on the Transitional period were common at the Middle Atlantic Archaeological Conference meetings and in journal publications in the mid- to late 1980s and early 1990s (e.g., Cavallo and Kondrup 1986; Custer 1984; Moeller 1990; Stewart 1989; Truncer 1990). Many people preferred the term "Terminal Archaic," but, as Patricia Miller (2009) recently argued, this time is certainly not the end of anything. I would agree with Kinsey (1972:345) that all cultures are in transition, but I argue that the archaeology of this time period is different from the archaeology of periods both before and after: it is neither Archaic nor Woodland in character. It would also seem that cultural change at the beginning and end of the Transitional period occurred more quickly than before or after.

Archaeological Manifestations of the Transitional Period

This chapter focuses on the Delaware and Susquehanna River valleys of Pennsylvania; the details of its model probably do not apply to other drainage basins of the Middle Atlantic region. This presentation covers the time from approximately 4300 to 2700 BP, from the end of the Late Archaic period into the Early Woodland. For reasons that will be explained below, the Fishtail phase is considered part of the Transitional period.

Cultural adaptations during this time in this region can be identified by a cluster of traits that evolve over a period of approximately 1,600 years. Following the lead of several authors (Cresson 1990; Custer 1984, 1996; Kinsey 1972; Ritchie 1969; Sassaman 1999; Stewart 1989; Truncer 2004; Turnbaugh 1975; Wall et al. 1996; Witthoft 1953), this period is distinguished from the Late Archaic and Early Woodland periods (excluding the Fishtail phase) by the following:

1. The use of distinctive broad-bladed biface forms. They begin as contracting-stemmed bifaces (Snook Kill, Koens-Crispin, and Lehigh), evolve into expanding-stemmed forms (Susquehanna and Perkiomen), and end with Fishtail forms.
2. The preferential use of certain usually nonlocal lithic types. These were generally available from massive bedrock formations as opposed to tabular chert or pebble sources.
3. A change to a bifacial core technology and a staged biface reduction process for some tools.
4. A curated tool technology.
5. Large and numerous fire-cracked rock features.
6. The caching of bifaces.
7. The use of steatite vessels.
8. The beginning of fired-clay pottery.
9. Occasional burial ceremonialism.
10. The location of sites closer to water sources, notably wetlands.

These traits seem to coalesce in eastern Pennsylvania over a 400-year period between 4300 and 3900 BP, as observed at a number of sites in the Delaware and Susquehanna Valleys. They disappear by approximately 2700 BP, although it should be noted that not all of the traits are necessary to identify an occupation from this period. Radiocarbon dates or diagnostic artifact types such as broadspears, fishtail points, steatite bowls, or steatite-tempered pottery are used here to identify sites dating to this time period.

The main excavations considered (Figure 3.1; Table 3.1) include (1) those in the Upper Delaware Valley

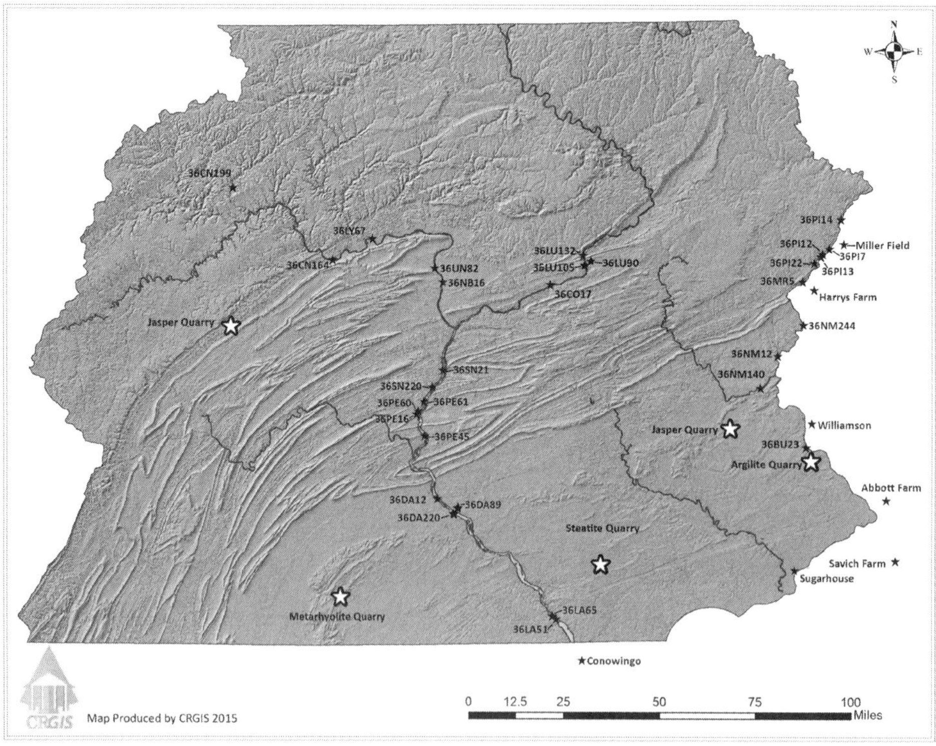

FIGURE 3.1
Map of sites referenced in text.

TABLE 3.1 Sites referenced in text and Figure 3.1

State	Site Number	Site Name
Pennsylvania	36BU23	Lower Blacks Eddy
	36CO17	Mifflinville
	36CN164	Memorial Park
	36CN199	Kettle Creek East
	36DA12	City Island
	36DA89	Calver Island
	36DA220	
	36LA51	Bare Island
	36LA65	Piney Island
	36LU90	Jacobs
	36LU105	Gould Island
	36LU132	Skvarek
	36LY37	Canfield Island
	36MR5	Smithfield Beach
	36NB16	East Bank
	36NM12	Sandts Eddy
	36NM140	Oberly Island
	36NM244	Driftstone
	36PE16	Wallis
	36PE45	Girtys Notch
	36PE60	P-11
	36PE61	P-12
	36PH137	Sugarhouse
	36PI07	Brodhead-Heller
	36PI12	Egypt Mills
	36PI13a	Faucett
	36PI14	Zimmerman
	36PI22	Peters-Albrecht
	36SN21	
	36SN220	MHF-1
	36UN82	Allenwood
New Jersey		Abbott Farm
		Miller Field
		Harrys Farm
		Savich Farm
		Williamson
Maryland		Conowingo

conducted for the Tocks Island Reservoir Project (Kinsey 1972); (2) those in the Middle Delaware Valley at the Abbott Farm Complex conducted for highway improvements (Cavallo 1996, Stewart 1987, Wall et al. 1996); (3) a water system project in the Lower Delaware Valley (Schuldenrein et al. 1991); (4) several highway and bridge projects on the main stem of the Susquehanna River (Miller, Vento, and Marine 2007a, 2007b, 2009); (5) a gas pipeline project on the North Branch of the Susquehanna (Weed and Wenstrom 1992); and (6) various projects on the North and West Branches of the Susquehanna (Bressler, Maietta, and Rockey 1983; Jacoby et al. 1999; Miller 1995; Wall 2000). All radiocarbon dates, with laboratory numbers, are presented uncorrected and calibrated in Table 3.2.

Chronology and Diagnostic Bifaces

The most conspicuous and temporally diagnostic chipped-stone tools of the Transitional period are a group of broad-bladed bifaces (commonly known as "broadspears") and related fishtail biface types. The broad-bladed varieties first appear in the Late Archaic period in the southeastern United States in the form of the Savannah River type (Custer 1996:177; Kinsey 1972:359). Patricia Miller, Frank Vento, and James Marine (2007b:84) identified Savannah River types at 3900 BP on Calver Island in the Lower Susquehanna Valley. At stratified sites in eastern Pennsylvania, broad-bladed bifaces are found just above strata exclusively containing (1) stemmed Lackawaxen types, such as those at the Faucett, Brodhead-Heller, Egypt Mills (Kinsey 1972), and Lower Blacks Eddy Sites (Schuldenrein et al. 1991); (2) Barry Kent's (1996) type E (a narrow straight-stemmed form) such as found at the Piney Island, City Island, and Calver Island Sites (Miller, Vento and Marine 2007b); (3) narrow-stemmed points (Turnbaugh 1975:137); or (4) Lamoka types such as found at the Allenwood Site (36UN82; Wall 2000).

Broad-bladed bifaces are added to these Late Archaic forms at about 4300 BP with the appearance of Snook Kill, Koens-Crispin, and Lehigh types (Turnbaugh 1975:139). Although Koens-Crispin and Snook Kill bifaces are usually considered the earliest of the broadspears, dating to between approximately 4000 and 3800 BP according to Noel Justice (1987:160), Stewart (1987:VII-16) recorded a date for Koens-Crispin bifaces of 4370 + 100 BP at the Gropps Lake Site associated with the Trenton Complex. Joseph Schuldenrein and colleagues (1991:33) reported a date

TABLE 3.2 Radiocarbon dates by artifact type or subsistence resource

Artifact Type/ Plant Specimen	Site Number	Site Name	Date in Years BP	Calibrated Dates	Laboratory Number	Reference
Koens-Crispin	36BU23	Lower Blacks Eddy	3520 ± 100	4084–3567 BP or 2135–1618 BC	Beta-24905	Schuldenrein et al. 1991
	36BU23	Lower Blacks Eddy	3610 ± 150	4300–3567 BP or 2351–1618 BC	Beta-19320	Schuldenrein et al. 1991
		Savich Farm	3640 ± 67	4151–3824 BP or 2202–1875 BC	P-1780	Burrow 1997
		Miller Field	3670 ± 120	4300–3695 BP or 2351–1746 BC	Y-2587	Kraft 1970
		Savich Farm	3931 ± 65	4527–4218 BP or 2578–2269 BC	P-1781	Burrow 1997
	Isolated Find	Coney Creek	3940 ± ?		N/A	Walter and Merritts 2008
	36BU23	Lower Blacks Eddy	4020 ± 180	4893–3979 BP or 2944–2030 BC	Beta-19318	Schuldenrein et al. 1991
		Gropps Lake	4370 ± 100	5307–4811 BP or 3358–2862 BC	Beta-11775	Stewart 1987
		Savich Farm	4416 ± 57	5084–4859 BP or 3135–2910 BC	P-1782	Burrow 1997
Lehigh	44LD15	Catoctin Creek	3460 ± 100	3976–3477 BP or 2027–1528 BC	Beta-11801	Inashima 2008
	36PI22	Peters-Albrecht	3670 ± 100	4293–3704 BP or 2344–1755 BC	Y-1826	Kinsey 1972
	36NM244	Driftstone	3740 ± 70	4159–3982 BP or 2348–1943 BC	Beta-131311	Blondino 2008
Susquehanna	36DA12	City Island	3250 ± 90	3623–3322 BP or 1744–1373 BC	Beta-107413	Carr, Chapter 3, this volume
	36CO17	Mifflinville	3430 ± 140	4008–3376 BP or 2059–1427 BC	Beta-84323	Jacoby et al. 1999
	36PI7	Brodhead-Heller	3570 ± 100	4101–3612 BP or 2152–1663 BC	Y-2340	Kinsey 1972
	36CN199	Kettle Creek East	3580 ± 100	4151–3631 BP or 2202–1682 BC	Beta-65777	Inashima 2008
	36PI14	Zimmerman	3600 ± 80	4098–3693 BP or 2149–1744 BC	Y-2344	Kinsey 1972
	36CO17	Mifflinville	3630 ± 120	4295–3632 BP or 2346–1683 BC	Beta-84325	Jacoby et al. 1999
		Miller Field	3670 ± 120	4300–3695 BP or 2351–1746 BC	Y-2587	Kraft 1970
	26CO17	Mifflinville	3900 ± 80	4527–4090 BP or 2578–2141 BC	Beta-84321	Jacoby et al. 1999

(continued)

TABLE 3.2 *(continued)*

Artifact Type/ Plant Specimen	Site Number	Site Name	Date in Years BP	Calibrated Dates	Laboratory Number	Reference
Perkiomen	36PI13a	Faucett	3450 ± 120	3992–3445 BP or 2043–1496 BC	Y-2478	Kinsey 1972
	36PE61	P-12	3490 ± 40	3866–3682 BP or 1917–1733 BC	Beta-180534	Miller, Vento, and Marine 2009
	36PI7	Brodhead-Heller	3570 ± 100	4101–3612 BP or 2152–1663 BC	Y-2340	Kinsey and McNett 1972
		Miller Field	3590 ± 100	4156–3632 BP or 2207–1683 BC	Y-2588	Kraft 1970
		Miller Field	3670 ± 120	4300–3695 BP or 2351–1746 BC	Y-2587	Kraft 1970
Fishtail	36PI13a	Faucett	2760 ± 100	3159–2729 BP or 1210–780 BC	Y-2477	Kinsey 1972
	28ME1-B	Abbott Farm Area B	2870 ± 200	3483–2675 BP or 1534–726 BC	Beta-11797	Cavallo 1996
	36NM244	Driftstone	2920 ± 30	3160–2969 BP or 1211–1020 BC	UGAMS-02948	Blondino 2008
	36NM244	Driftstone	3070 ± 80	3452–3057 BP or 1503–1108 BC	Beta-43899	Blondino 2008
	28ME1–B	Abbott Farm Area B	3080 ± 180	3648–2842 BP or 1699–893 BC	Beta-11790	Cavallo 1996
	36PI7	Brodhead-Heller	3120 ± 120	3594–2993 BP or 1645–1044 BC	Y-2339	Kinsey and McNett 1972
		Miller Field	3170 ± 120	3646–3065 BP or 1697–1116 BC	Y-2589	Kraft 1970
	36PI14	Zimmerman	3230 ± 120	3726–3158 BP or 1777–1209 BC	Y-2343	Kinsey 1972
Steatite Vessels	36MR5	Smithfield Beach	2710 ± 150	3180–2420 BP or 1231–471 BC	Beta-15568	Fischler and Mueller 1988
	36LA51	(Upper) Bare Island	2950 ± 50	3245–2957 BP or 1296–1008 BC	Beta-116286	Inashima 2008
	36DA0162	McCormicks Island	3190 ± 50	3514–3333 BP or 1565–1384 BC	Beta-116287	Inashima 2008
	36PI14	Zimmerman	3230 ± 129	3732–3143 BP or 1783–1194 BC	Y-2343	Kinsey 1972
Cucurbits (squash)	36CN164	Memorial Park	5404 ± 552	7337–4950 BP or 5388–3001 BC	AA-19129	Hart and Sidell 1997
	36CN164	Memorial Park	2625 ± 45	2852–2703 BP or 903–754 BC	AA-19128	Hart and Sidell 1997
	36SN21		3780 ± 60	4300–3981 BP or 2351–2032 BC	Beta-61311	Miller 1995
Chenopodium	36DA89	Calver Island	3980 ± 40	4530–4348 BP or 2581–2399 BC	Beta-222274	Miller, Vento, and Marine 2007a

Note: Dates calibrated with Calib 7.0.

of 4020 + 180 BP associated with the Koens-Crispin type at the Lower Blacks Eddy Site, although there are also two later dates. At the Savich Farm Site, the dates for Koens-Crispin bifaces range between 4416 + 57 BP, 3931 + 65 BP, and 3640 + 67 BP (Burrow 1997:39). A single date for the Lehigh type in the region, 3670 + 100 BP, is reported by Kinsey (1972) from the Peters-Albrecht Site in the Upper Delaware Valley. On Calver Island in the Lower Susquehanna Valley, however, Koens-Crispin bifaces are found later, between 3500 and 3300 BP (Miller, Vento, and Marine 2007a:84). The dates from the sites in the Delaware Valley appear to be slightly older than those in the Susquehanna Valley, although, considering the small number of datings, the disparity may be the result of sampling error. Snook Kill, Koens-Crispin, and Lehigh types will here be taken to define the Early Broadspear phase, with a date range of approximately 4300 to 3700 BP.

Perkiomen and Susquehanna biface types appear by 3700 BP (Turnbaugh 1975:141–42). Kinsey (1972) reports a series of dates for the Perkiomen type ranging from 3670 + 120 BP at the Miller Field Site to 3450 + 120 BP at the Faucett Site. Miller, Vento, and Marine (2009:45) recovered a Perkiomen broadspear at Site 36PE61 from a feature radiocarbon dated to 3490 + 40 BP. At the Mifflinville Site on the North Branch of the Susquehanna River, there are three dates for Susquehanna broadspears of 3430 + 140 BP, 3630 + 120 BP (Beta-84325), and 3900 + 80 BP (Jacoby et al. 1999), the last date being 200 years older than other dates for broadspears of this type. On Calver Island, all but one Susquehanna broadspear were found in the occupations dating between 3300 and 3000 BP (Miller, Vento, and Marine 2007b:91). On City Island, a Susquehanna broadspear was found associated with a fire-cracked rock hearth dated to 3250 + 90 BP. The dates at Calver Island and City Island are slightly later than those from farther upriver in the Susquehanna Valley and especially those in the Delaware Valley. Broadspears of these types will be used to define the Late Broadspear phase, with a date range of approximately 3700 to 3200 BP.

Jay Custer and David Bachman (1985) were among the first to argue that narrow-stemmed points were part of the Broadspear artifact assemblage. According to Miller (1998:112), narrow-stemmed bifaces continued to be used in the Susquehanna Valley throughout the Broadspear phase (ca. 4300–3200 BP); at some sites, they outnumber broad-bladed bifaces. Miller, Vento, and Marine (2007b: 96) found that there were twice as many stemmed points as broadspears in the Transitional levels on Calver Island. Stewart (1987) and Wall and colleagues (1996:154) describe similar findings at the Trenton Complex, in the Middle Delaware Valley. And according to Peter Siegel, Robert Kingsley, and Tod Benedict (2001), Oberly Island, on the Lower Lehigh River, was also dominated by stemmed points throughout the Late Archaic and (based on radiocarbon dates) Transitional periods. In addition, Miller, Vento, and Marine (2007b:89) found triangles in Transitional contexts at the Wallis Site and Site 36PE60, whereas, in the Upper Delaware Valley, Kinsey (1972) reports that Transitional components at the Brodhead-Heller and Faucett Sites mainly contain broad-bladed bifaces dating from 3600 BP. Although the evidence is mounting that broadspears and narrow-stemmed bifaces were both being used during this time period, I argue here that the technological advantages and cultural meaning of broadspears are more significant than those of the narrow-stemmed forms. Therefore, it is appropriate that occupations be characterized by broadspears rather than by the narrow-stemmed forms. In addition, the broad-bladed bifaces are diagnostic for this time period, whereas the narrow-stemmed forms have little chronological distinctiveness.

Although bioturbation and poor excavation techniques have been cited as the reason broadspears and stemmed projectile points are found in the same occupation, Custer (1991, 1996:176–77) argues that the consistent association and contemporaneity of broadspears and narrow-stemmed bifaces can no longer be questioned, noting (Custer 1996:177) that broadspears "are fairly good indicators of occupations spanning the

2500–1500 BC time period. However, their absence in an assemblage does not preclude the possibility that it may date also to this time interval." An alternative explanation is that bioturbation was especially violent during this period, although this seems less likely.

By 3100 BP, the broad-bladed forms begin to disappear, although, according to Wall and colleagues (1996:154), there is an overlap with fishtail points and Susquehanna broadspear types. Many of the characteristics of the Transitional period continue after 3000 BP (traditionally the Early Woodland period) associated with Orient (and Dry Brook) fishtail bifaces. Here I argue that these Fishtail forms are clearly part of a Fishtail phase of the Transitional adaptive strategy. There is continuity in biface types, lithic technology, lithic preferences, fire-cracked rock features, and the use of steatite containers. Fishtail projectile points are traditionally included in the Early Woodland period (Kinsey 1972) simply because they are associated with ceramics. Here I treat them as indicating a phase within the Transitional period. At the Abbott Farm Area B Site, Cavallo (1996:81–82) reports dates of 2870 + 200 BP and 3080 + 180 BP. Kinsey (1972:433) reports a date of 2760 + 100 BP from the Faucett Site, 3120 + 120 BP from Brodhead-Heller, 3170 + 120 BP from Miller Field, and 3230 + 120 BP from the Zimmerman Site. At the Driftstone Site in the Upper Delaware Valley, Blondino (2008, and chapter 5, this volume) reports dates of 3070 + 80 BP and 2920 + 30 BP. Miller, Vento, and Marine (2007a:80) recovered fishtail points associated with dates of 2610 BP and 2830 BP. This would suggest a date range for this Fishtail phase of approximately 3100 to 2700 BP (Fiedel 2001; Kinsey 1972; Ritchie 1969).

As argued by Roger Moeller (Chapter 7), the chronology of broad-bladed bifaces is not as precise as some (myself included) would like it to be, but there are sufficient numbers of Broadspear components radiometrically and stratigraphically dated to support the Early Broadspear, Late Broadspear, and Fishtail phases proposed in this chapter. The chronological or cultural relationships between Snook Kill, Koens-Crispin, Lehigh, Susquehanna, and Perkiomen types have not been conclusively defined. The meaning of these different types will be discussed further below, but there are probably both functional and cultural factors involved. It would be convenient if these types had specific temporal or geographical limits. Susquehanna and Perkiomen bifaces are generally found in different drainage basins, but not always. It is clear that additional radiometric dates for these biface types are important for documenting their relationships.

The Environment

The Middle and Late Archaic periods are associated with the warm and moist Atlantic climatic episode, which lasts almost 4,000 years; in the eastern United States, the climatic conditions of this episode probably represent an optimum period for a general foraging adaptation (Klein 1997; Wholey 2009:4). The beginning of the Transitional period nearly corresponds to the beginning of the warm and dry Sub-Boreal climatic episode at 4500 BP, reflected in the geomorphology of sites such as Gould Island, Jacobs, Allenwood, Calver Island, City Island, and Lower Blacks Eddy, where broad-bladed bifaces are found in a B horizon either overlying a Late Archaic A horizon containing stemmed points or just below an A horizon containing fishtail points, as documented in detail by Vento and colleagues (2008; Vento, chapter 1, this volume). There is a discontinuity between Late Archaic and Transitional components representing more active vertical sediment accretion and an increase in particle size. This widespread pattern suggests increased flooding, characteristic of the warm and dry Sub-Boreal, with less precipitation leading to less vegetation and thus also to more frequent overbanking. Stuart Fiedel (2001:123) stresses that this is a time of a "radically fluctuating" climate, causing unpredictable changes in flora and fauna. The co-occurrence of this climatic event with the Broadspear phase of the Transitional period is clear; I would agree that the shift in climate results in a less predictable environment.

The Fishtail phase corresponds to the onset of the Sub-Atlantic climatic episode and a return to warm and moist conditions. It is argued here that, by 2700 BP, Transitional hunter-gatherers were faced with a new set of environmental and cultural conditions, and a new adaptive strategy began to emerge.

As noted by Miller (2009), the environmental reconstruction for the Sub-Boreal is debatable. Vento and colleagues (2008; Vento, Chapter 1, this volume) argue convincingly that geomorphological evidence demonstrates the change to a warm and dry climate, an argument supported by research in other regions (Vento 2009). Miller (Chapter 4) counters that there is little evidence of change reflected in pollen or in macrobotanical or faunal remains; although I agree, I would also point out that the database of such evidence is practically nonexistent for the Middle Atlantic region.

Lithic Preferences, Lithic Technology, and the Tool Kit

The preferential use of certain lithic types for the production of broad-bladed bifaces has long been recognized as a characteristic of the Transitional period (Bergman et al. 1992; Kent, Smith, and McCann 1971:93–94; Kinsey 1972; Ritchie 1969; Stewart 1989; Turnbaugh 1975; Witthoft 1953). There is a shift from the preferential use and curation of distinctive lithic types during the Paleoindian/Early Archaic period to the exclusive use of a variety of local lithic sources during the Middle and Late Archaic periods. This is commonly felt to represent the exploitation of smaller territories by Middle and Late Archaic groups. Robert Kingsley, James Robertson, and Daniel Roberts (1990:138), in their overview of the Schuylkill River valley, argue that the absence of artifacts in certain locally available lithic types such as jasper also suggests more restricted territoriality during the Late Archaic.

In eastern Pennsylvania, Late Archaic groups used many different lithic types that are found in abundance and in a variety of package forms. In the Upper Susquehanna and Delaware Valleys (the Appalachian Plateau and Ridge and Valley provinces), cherts are commonly used during the Archaic period, and tabular cherts are frequently found in Ordovician or Devonian formations. Quartzite in bedrock and cobbles is used in both the Ridge and Valley and the Piedmont province, and argillite, quite commonly in the Delaware Valley. Quartz and hornfels are also commonly used in the Piedmont province during the Late Archaic.

During the Transitional period, there is a shift away from local materials for most broad-bladed bifaces and curated tools. This seems to occur in phases. Initially, Snook Kill and Koens-Crispin bifaces are commonly found in a limited number of lithic materials such as quartzite, argillite, and chert. Kingsley, Robertson, and Roberts (1990:178) found that early broadspears (specifically, Koens-Crispin types) in the Schuylkill Valley are made from quartzite and argillite. In the Delaware Valley, Wall and colleagues (1996) found these early types to be made from argillite, whereas, in the Susquehanna Valley, Miller, Vento, and Marine (2007a:79) found them to be made of chert, argillite, slate, and metarhyolite. Quartz, a common tool stone during the Late Archaic, decreases significantly in the Early Broadspear component on Calver Island. In the Upper Delaware Valley, Perkiomen occupations become dominated by jasper tools and debitage between 3500 and 3400 BP (Kinsey 1972:180. 204, 217). In the Middle Delaware Valley at Abbott Farm, argillite is used throughout the Late Archaic and Transitional periods. In the Susquehanna Valley, from approximately 3900 to 3500 BP, the percentage of metarhyolite debitage increases, but it is not until after 3400 BP that it becomes the most common tool stone at many sites (Miller, Vento, and Marine 2007a:80). At Calver Island, it becomes the prevailing tool stone only after 3300 BP. Jasper is the most common tool stone for Fishtail occupations in the Upper Delaware

Valley (Kinsey 1972), and metarhyolite, the most common for Fishtail occupations in the Susquehanna Valley (Miller, Vento, and Marine 2007a:80).

Based on the above, lithic preferences over this period follow a general pattern in both the Susquehanna and Delaware drainage basins. During the Late Archaic period, local lithic material types of a wide variety are used. During the Early Broadspear phase, bifaces and curated tools are of argillite, chert, and quartzite, whereas the debitage is of a limited range of local lithic types. During the Late Broadspear phase, jasper is the prevailing tool stone for Perkiomen occupations, although, in the Susquehanna Valley, metarhyolite does not become the main tool stone for Susquehanna Broadspear occupations until after 3400 BP. This pattern of a focus on jasper in the Upper Delaware Valley, argillite in the Middle and Lower Delaware Valleys, and metarhyolite in the Susquehanna Valley continues until the end of the Fishtail phase. Although broadspears are frequently made in a preferred lithic material type, Miller (chapter 4) notes that it is rare that more than 50% of an assemblage including the debitage is in the same material. As we will see, other biface types are in use during this time period, frequently in local lithic types. There are clear lithic preferences during the Transitional period, although local lithic materials continue to be used throughout this time. It is tempting to suggest that the dichotomy of local versus nonlocal lithic preferences has a functional or social explanation.

Beginning in the Early Woodland period, after 2700 BP, there is a return to the use of a variety of local lithic materials (Kinsey 1972:366; McLearen 1991:113; Miller 1998:111; Raber 2008:38; Robertson and Kingsley 1994:94), but lithic preferences continue after the Fishtail phase. The bifaces of the Meadowood phase in the Upper Delaware and Upper Susquehanna Valleys are usually in Onondaga chert. Hellgrammite bifaces are found in the Coastal Plain of these two valleys, often in jasper in the Delaware Valley and metarhyolite in the Susquehanna Valley (Hummer 1991, 1994).

There were both technological and cultural advantages in choosing jasper, metarhyolite, or argillite as the preferred lithic type. The large formations of these materials, compared to those of many cherts in the region, facilitated the production of broad-bladed blanks and bifaces. Although its impurities and voids make it somewhat unpredictable, Hardyston jasper can be available in very large micro-cryptocrystalline blocks and is a preferred tool stone throughout prehistory. Lockatong argillite and Catoctin metarhyolite, though lacking the micro-cryptocrystalline structure of jasper, are quite homogeneous and available in large deposits, thus facilitating the knapping of large, thin flakes for the production of broadspears. But the technological characteristics of these lithic types are only part of the reason they are used in broadspear production. The relatively unlimited supply of these raw materials facilitated their use in a trade and exchange system. The movement of jasper and metarhyolite in the Delaware and Susquehanna drainage basins, in particular, suggests increased social communication in the region not reflected in the archaeological record during the Middle and Late Archaic periods.

Moreover, it has long been recognized that the Transitional period is characterized by a change in lithic technology. Jack Cresson (1990), Jay Custer (1996), Barry Kent (1999), and James Truncer (1990) have described the distinctive bifacial technology used in the production of broad-bladed bifaces. Beginning with the Middle Archaic, there is a shift from the Paleoindian/Early Archaic pattern emphasizing bifacial cores to the use of a variety of informal core types (Carr, Bergman, and Haag 2010). Christopher Bergman and colleagues (1986) documented this change at the Sandts Eddy Site, for example. The Late Archaic technology used with the Lamoka or Bare Island phases involved technological systems that simply converted flakes from informal/opportunistic cores into bifaces and expedient flake tools. In contrast, the Transitional period is characterized by distinctive broad-bladed projectile points/knives that were produced using bifacial cores and a staged biface reduction sequence (Cresson 1990). The so-called biface thinning flakes that increase in frequency during the Late Archaic and early Transitional periods reflect a move to bifacial cores and bifacial reduction.

At the Lower Blacks Eddy Site (36BU23), Schuldenrein and colleagues (1991) found Lackawaxen biface types made in argillite, dating to before, during, and after the Transitional period and produced through staged bifacial reduction in the same features, presumably used by the same groups. Argillite is available in very large deposits that facilitate the use of bifacial cores. Other narrow-stemmed point types associated with the Broadspear tradition in other lithic types, however, may not have required staged biface reduction. More research on the production of these bifaces types needs to be conducted.

Bifacial drills, pins, scrapers, and awls in standardized shapes are also associated with the Transitional period (Truncer 1990:12; Witthoft 1953). These tools, along with broad-bladed bifaces, are part of a curated technology, as opposed to an expedient technology, so characteristic of the Middle and Late Archaic periods. The function of broadspears continues to be debated. In edge wear studies, Jay Custer and Glenn Mellin (1986) and Custer (2001:37) argued for their use as knives, but Truncer (1990:33) demonstrated with experimental work their use also as projectile points. Recently, Miller, Vento, and Marine (2007b:91), in their microwear analysis of stemmed points and broadspears collected from the Calver Island Site, found that all these were multifunctional, serving as projectile points, knives, and scrapers. In contrast, fishtail points collected from this site functioned only as projectile points (Miller, Vento, and Marine 2007b:91). That said, multipurpose bifaces, hafted scrapers, awls, and drills clearly mark a curated technology, contrasting with expedient Late Archaic or Middle Woodland technological organization.

Based on an overview by Stewart (1989:54–56), the caching of bifaces increases during the Transitional period. Kingsley, Robertson, and Roberts (1990:178) identified one argillite biface cache (probably Koens-Crispin) and one jasper broadspear cache from the Schuylkill Valley. Elinor Fehr and colleagues (1971:43–44) report five caches of broadspears, mainly in jasper but also in chert, chalcedony, and argillite, from the Sandts Eddy Site on the Delaware River associated with the Late Broadspear and Fishtail phases. Large flakes could be produced at the quarry from bedrock formations for the mass production of large broad-bladed biface preforms. Cresson (1990) has identified both a large and a small blank form in caches from this period; caches of the small form suggest its possible use in a trade and exchange system. Several adze or celt caches have been identified by Kinsey (1972) in the Upper Delaware Valley, and a rather spectacular example was recovered from City Island in the Susquehanna Valley (Figure 3.2; Myers, Dorney, and Friedman 1995).

Binford (1980) argues that a curated technology and the caching of bifaces suggest increased residential mobility. William Parry (1994) also argues for increased mobility based on a staged biface reduction sequence. Although it is unclear whether there is an increase in residential mobility during this period, that tool stone for bifaces and steatite for containers are moving long distances demonstrates at least some increased mobility. Based on observations by Stewart (1989), lithics seem to be

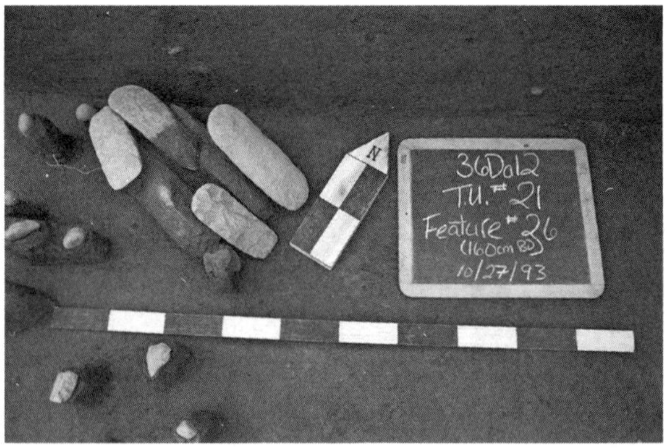

FIGURE 3.2
Axe and adze cache from City Island Site, Dauphin County (scale bar: 100 cm).

moving in standardized shapes, and it is believed that much of this is the result of trade. Miller (1998) notes an increase in jasper along the North Branch of the Susquehanna River, suggesting trade with the Delaware Valley and increased communication between the two drainage basins. Regardless of the degree of actual residential mobility, the movement of lithic material, steatite vessels, and bifaces in standardized shapes suggests greater social interaction throughout the region.

As an alternative explanation to increased residential mobility, Kurt Carr, Christopher Bergman, and Crista Haag (2010) have suggested a technological basis for the use of bifaces and bifacial cores: a biface simply has more mass than a generalized expedient flake tool and can be modified for the circumstances at hand. Based on experimental work (Eren, Greenspan, and Sampson 2008), it has been shown that bifacial cores are an efficient use of tool stone in that they minimize weight and maximize the number of tool blanks. A bifacial technology and a curated tool assemblage represent a more flexible technology, facilitating adjustments in the tool kit to an unpredictable environment, specifically, to a decrease in predictable food resources brought on by the warm and dry Sub-Boreal. I would emphasize the technological advantages of bifacial tools over the increased residential mobility of Transitional groups.

According to Lewis Binford (1962:219) and James Deetz (1967:45), artifacts have technomic, sociotechnic, and ideotechnic meaning. It has been proposed that biface types are symbols that reflect group identity; Louis Brennan (1967) characterizes this concept as the "Coe Axiom." Although the reality of this proposal can be debated (Custer 2001:76–81), there are certain time periods when biface types seem to have a stronger sociotechnic or ideotechnic meaning. Some biface types are chronologically specific and morphologically distinctive. For example, the Paleoindian period with its fluted bifaces, the Early Archaic period with its notched and serrated bifaces, and the early Middle Archaic with its bifurcate bifaces are all examples of times in the Middle Atlantic region when there was a limited variety of projectile point types and limited intratype variation, compared to other times. These may represent times when there were shared ideas covering broad regions on the appropriate shape of projectile points. Although technological factors may have contributed to the making of these shapes or types, sociotechnic and ideotechnic factors were probably more important. It is argued here that in some cultural settings, biface types and tool types reflect shared cultural values and indicate increased social communication between bands.

In the Middle Atlantic region, after the Bifurcate phase and into the Late Archaic period, biface types seem to vary greatly in shape (Miller 1998). The rules of production seem to allow for a great deal of variation for the Lamoka, Lackawaxen, Poplar Island, Bare Island, or Kent's type E bifaces. The variety of identified styles seems to be only partly affected by the variety of lithic material types used during this time (Kent 1996). In addition to intratype differences, there also seem to be regional differences, with the Lamoka type concentrated in the north on the Appalachian Plateau and the Lackawaxen type and Kent's type E more common in the Lower Susquehanna and Lower Delaware Valleys. These types clearly persist over long periods of time (Custer 2001).

In contrast, broadspears clearly exemplify bifaces with strong sociotechnic or ideotechnic meaning. The distribution of Susquehanna and Perkiomen broadspear types found throughout the Middle Atlantic region is an indication of shared values over a wide area and probably also of an increase in social communication within the region. It is generally believed (e.g., Custer 1996:192; Kinsey 1972:353; Witthoft 1953:12, 19) that Susquehanna broadspears are concentrated in the Susquehanna Valley, and Perkiomen broadspears, in the Delaware Valley. Although there are examples of Perkiomen bifaces in the Susquehanna Valley (Miller, Vento, and Marine 2007a:69, 84) and Susquehanna bifaces in the Delaware, these, according to Kinsey (1972), are rare.

TABLE 3.3 Number of sites by artifact type in Delaware and Susquehanna drainage basins

	Delaware			Susquehanna			
Artifact Type	Number of Sites	% of Sites by Type	Density of Sites per 100 km²	Number of Sites	% of Sites by Type	Density of Sites per 100 km²	Total Sites by Type
Broadspear	137	28	0.82	355	72	0.71	492
Koens-Crispin	81	24	0.48	256	76	0.51	337
Lehigh/Snook Kill	56	29	0.33	138	71	0.28	194
Perkiomen	143	43	0.85	193	57	0.39	336
Susquehanna	52	16	0.31	277	84	0.56	329
Fishtail	144	39	0.86	229	61	0.46	373
Steatite Vessels	17	11	0.10	141	89	0.28	158
Transitional Sites	352	30	3.00	826	70	7.03	1,178

Drawing on the Pennsylvania Archaeological Site Survey (PASS) files, Table 3.3 lists the total number of sites (not number of bifaces) for each of these drainage basins by component. There are nearly 200 examples of Perkiomen broadspears in the Susquehanna Valley or Susquehanna broadspears in the Delaware. Interestingly, the density of Perkiomen broadspears is very high in the Delaware Valley (0.85 sites/100 km²) compared to the Susquehanna (0.39 sites/100 km²), whereas the difference in density of Susquehanna broadspears is not as great in the two drainage basins. It is also notable that fishtail points are found at nearly twice the density in the Delaware Valley as they are in the Susquehanna. Moreover, steatite bowls are found at nearly three times the density in the Susquehanna Valley as they are in the Delaware. This may simply be the result of sampling error or inaccurate data in the site files. In Kinsey's (1972:353) discussion of Susquehanna broadspears in the Upper Delaware Valley, he notes that, even though Susquehanna bifaces can be found in the Upper Delaware, they are far outnumbered by Perkiomen bifaces.

If the generalization is true (i.e., that these two biface types are generally restricted to separate drainage basins), the differential distribution of these two types could have social implications. If there is any relationship between biface style and social organization, these two types suggest a more structured social organization—one with more rules than a simple bilateral band. Assuming that males make these bifaces, the distinction suggests a social organization that creates two groups of males. A simple hypothesis is that the distribution is the result of a patrilocal postmarriage residence rule since males did not frequently move their residence between these two drainage basins. There are certainly other explanations, but these symbolic artifacts suggest a more structured social organization than that during the Middle or Late Archaic period. Although this hypothesis is not easily tested, it is significant that the social distinction was being made during the Transitional period but not during either the Late Archaic or the Early Woodland period in artifacts commonly recovered from archaeological sites—another indication of important social differences between these time periods.

Fire-Cracked Rock Features

Large fire-cracked rock features also characterize the sites of the Transitional period (Turnbaugh 1975:142; Kinsey 1972:346; Wall et al. 1996:167), although, as with all of the Transitional traits listed above, these features are not found on all sites from this period. They seem to be particularly common at riverine sites; they are found with stemmed components of the Late Archaic period, such as at the City Island Site, with those of the Lamoka phase, such as at the

Allenwood Site (Wall 2000), although there they are usually not as common or as large. As documented by Kinsey (1972) in the Upper Delaware Valley, by Robertson and Kingsley (1994) in the Lower Delaware Valley, and by Miller, Vento, and Marine (2007a) in the Susquehanna Valley, fire-cracked rock features become larger and more extensive at sites associated with Susquehanna and Perkiomen bifaces. During the Fishtail phase, they become very common and very large, such as at the Brodhead-Heller and Peters-Albrecht Sites in the Upper Delaware Valley (Kinsey 1972:203, 309) or at the Trenton Complex in the Middle Delaware Valley (Wall et al. 1996). But they are usually rare during phases of the later Early Woodland period, such as the Meadowood and Hellgrammite phases, especially at sites situated in the Susquehanna drainage basin above Conowingo, Maryland, or in the Delaware drainage basin north of Easton, Pennsylvania. In this region, fire-cracked rock features decrease in frequency by Middle Woodland times. It is interesting that the Hellgrammite component at the Williamson Site, in the Middle Delaware Valley, is associated with extensive fire-cracked rock features (Hummer 1991). In the Lower Delaware and on to the Coastal Plain, however, large fire-cracked rock features continue well into the Woodland period (Custer 1996:235).

Even though a great deal of research has been done on these features, their function is still unclear (Wall et al. 1996:167–77). Kinsey (1972:205) proposed they were used for the drying of fish, but others have suggested they were used for the roasting of meats or the rendering of nuts for oil. There is also good evidence that they were used for stone boiling or steaming (Cavallo and Kondrup 1986; Stewart 1998; Turnbaugh 1975:161; Wall et al. 1996:166). More recently, Blondino (2009) has documented a correlation between sites of the Fishtail phase in the Upper Delaware Valley and floodplain wetlands. He argues (Chapter 5) that some of these features could be bake ovens, used for processing starchy foods such as roots harvested from the adjacent wetlands.

Documented at numerous, mostly riverine sites from this period, these features seem to represent the mass processing of some type of food, whatever their specific functions. In the Susquehanna and Delaware drainage basins, these features begin in the Late Archaic, increase in size during the Late Broadspear phase, become very large during the Fishtail phase, and nearly disappear during the later Early Woodland period. It is assumed here that large fire-cracked rock features represent an intensification of the exploitation of the environment. Unfortunately, the lack of organics has not supported that assumption. Social activities significant to the adaptation almost certainly took place around these features, but the data to define these activities are lacking.

Steatite Vessels

The age and function of steatite vessels have been intensively analyzed by Kenneth Sassaman (1999), Gary Shaffer (2008), and James Truncer (2004). Sassaman (1999:86, 2006:151) reports that steatite bowls mainly date to between 3700 and 2400 BP. Truncer (2004:51; 2006) argues that they date over a much longer time, beginning at 4900 BP. Sassaman (2006) and Truncer (2006) have both studied the chronology of steatite in detail, but they clearly differ in what they believe are valid dates. Considering the differences, there is a need for additional radiometric dating, especially using residue obtained directly from the steatite shards. In the Susquehanna and Delaware drainage basins, the dates seem to range between 3500 and 2700 BP.

Of significance in the discussion between Sassaman and Truncer is the question of the chronological relationship between steatite vessels and fired-clay ceramics. In the Southeast, ceramics are clearly older (Sassaman 1993). The dating is less clear in the Middle Atlantic region. Although broadspears and ceramics were found together at the Calver Island Site and Site 36DA220, and steatite was found with ceramics at Calver Island, Miller, Vento, and Marine

(2007b:85) believe that this is due to bioturbation and that the ceramics at Calver Island are later than steatite or the broadspears. In their reviews of the data in the Susquehanna Valley, R. Michael Stewart (2009) and Thomas East and colleagues (2001) argue that steatite and ceramics overlap for several hundred years. Stewart (2011) cites the chronological overlap as evidence that they had different functions. Sassaman (1999) cites the overlap as evidence that there was a shift from male control of steatite to female control of ceramics. The direct dating of steatite and ceramics is critical to resolving this issue.

Steatite vessels have been interpreted as both technological innovations and ideological symbols. Custer (1984:38) has discussed the functional advantages of these vessels in food processing. It is generally agreed that steatite vessels are more durable and more efficient in transferring heat than ceramic ones (Truncer 2004:75–78). They retain heat longer but ceramic vessels heat more quickly (Stewart 2011). Because there is obviously a greater cost in acquiring steatite than clay (Stewart 2011), Klein (1997) and Sassaman (1999) have emphasized the ideological function of steatite vessels. Although I would agree with Custer (1984) and Truncer (2004) that the very largest bowls, many gallons in size, represent an increase in technological efficiency and an intensification of the exploitation of the environment, I would also agree with Klein (1997) and Stewart (1998) that the small bowls are less efficient and more likely play a significant social role in these societies. Like broadspears and lithic exchange, steatite bowls (at least small specimens) probably contributed to solidifying social networks that functioned to reduce risks when resources were limited.

As described by Shaffer (2008:16), designs on these vessels are rare. Notching on rims and lugs is the most common decoration; incised parallel lines or triangles are less common. The incising of steatite required some effort and almost certainly suggests symbolic meaning. A more structured social organization is being reflected in the decorations on these artifacts. More so than projectile points, as Shaffer (2008:18) notes, designs on steatite vessels almost certainly communicated information to other groups that facilitated interactions. This is another indicator of increased communication motivated by a need for social cooperation.

Subsistence

People during the Transitional period in the Susquehanna and Delaware Basins practiced a general foraging subsistence pattern. Based on similarities in tool types and site locations, their food sources were similar to those of the Late Archaic period. In terms of basic tool types, the tool kit used during the Transitional period was similar to the Late Archaic tool kit in many ways. Adzes, axes, bannerstones, grinding stones, and netsinkers are commonly found on sites from both time periods. And microwear analysis conducted on flaked-stone tools from the Late Archaic period through the Fishtail phase on Calver Island, for example (Miller, Vento, and Marine 2007b), appears to show the same range of activities. As discussed above, however, it is the flaked-stone technology and lithic preferences of the two times that were very different.

The analysis of plant residues and the direct dating of food remains (both residues and seeds) have begun to improve our understanding of the prehistoric diet in general, and specifically that of the Late Archaic through Early Woodland periods, but these studies are just beginning and more need to be completed, using museum collections whenever possible. That said, a pattern is beginning to emerge: people during the Transitional period (1) used a broader range of plant foods that were available in large quantities but that had increased collection costs and (2) practiced a foraging subsistence pattern but supplemented their diet with domesticated plants.

John Hart and Nancy Sidell (1997:524–525) briefly review the data for the use of domesticates beginning in the Late Archaic period in the Northeast.

They document *Cucurbita pepo* rind fragments at the Memorial Park Site on the West Branch of the Susquehanna dating to 5404 + 552 and 2625 + 45 BP. Cucurbits were also recovered at Site 36SN21 on the main branch, dating to 3780 + 60 BP (Miller 1995). Hart and Sidell (1997:533) argue that domesticated plants, in the form of the Eastern Agricultural Complex species (*Chenopodium*, knotweed, little barley), were already a regular part of the diet, possibly by Late Archaic times and certainly by Early Woodland times. In addition, they suggest that maize agriculture was not suddenly adopted during the Late Woodland period east of the Allegheny Front but was added to an existing subsistence pattern that included a variety of domesticated plants.

Several projects employing fine-grained collection techniques (e.g., Miller, Vento, and Marine 2007b, 2009) have recently been completed in the Susquehanna Valley. On Calver Island, Miller, Vento, and Marine (2007a; Miller, chapter 4, this volume) have been able to document a variety of plant foods recovered through water screening and extensive residue analysis of steatite and ceramic bowl fragments. To briefly summarize, Late Archaic features contained hickory nut and black walnut fragments along with a low frequency of acorn fragments. For the Early Broadspear phase, hickory nut, black walnut, and acorn fragments were recovered from nearly all features. Miller, Vento, and Marine (2007a:75, 73, 2007b:88, 84) believe that *Chenopodium* seeds dated to 3980 + 40 BP may have been domesticated, based on their morphology; they note that *Chenopodium* (along with little barley and knotweed) is part of the Eastern Agricultural Complex in the Midwest and suggest that other seed plants may have been used, concurring with Hart and Sidell (1997), and they argue that seeds have higher procurement and processing costs than nuts or berries. The use of *Chenopodium* is consistent with smaller foraging areas, greater sedentism, and larger group size, which appear consistent with a reduced variety of lithics and increased number of contemporaneous features at Transitional sites.

The Late Broadspear diet included black walnuts, hickory nuts, little barley, wild rye grass, and an increase in acorns. Miller, Vento, and Marine (2007b:89) also report such an increase at the Wallis Site and Site 36PE60. They argue that black walnuts and hickory nuts were insufficient to support the group; thus seeds and a different variety of acorns were added to the diet. Residues from steatite bowls yielded starches from tubers of the lily family (Miller, Vento, and Marine 2007b:89). These data support Blondino's (2009) argument for the exploitation of starchy root plants in wetland areas (see also chapter 5, this volume). Truncer (2004:103) and Miller, Vento, and Marine (2007b) stress that steatite bowls allowed for the more intensive processing of acorns; red oak acorns, specifically, require repeated boiling to remove the tannins, as opposed to white oak acorns, commonly used during the Late Archaic, which do not.

For the Fishtail phase, hickory nut, walnut, and acorn fragments were present, and grass and tuber residues were recovered from steatite bowls (Miller, Vento, and Marine 2007a:78). Squash residue was recovered from the Memorial Park, Wallis, and Girtys Notch Sites, dating to this time period. Because, however, only a few sites from the Fishtail phase and Early Woodland period have been tested using residue analysis or flotation recovery, these results may not be representative of all sites.

As a response to the increase in human population and the less productive environment of the Sub-Boreal climatic episode, one option for the people of the Transitional period was to extract more calories from the habitat. The evidence is mounting to support the proposition that, during the Transitional period, there was an increase in the number of plant foods that were being exploited, such as seeds and tubers. These required more processing time and therefore an increase in work effort. Transitional groups were intensifying their exploitation of the environment. The groups who exploited these foods were more successful than those who did not. Despite the increased cost of acquiring steatite, the use of portable cooking containers allowed for the exploitation of a wider variety of plant foods (especially red oak acorns and tubers). Finally, there is evidence from the Susquehanna drainage basin that domesticated plants of the Eastern Agricultural Complex were added to the subsistence system. This also increased work effort and probably required some changes in social organization. On the other hand, the evidence for domesticates is minimal, and there is clearly a need to systematically use more refined archaeological collection methods to increase our sample of dietary remains from all time periods.

Site Locations

Kinsey (1972:346) characterized the Transitional period as having a "riverine efficiency," meaning that sites from this time period are most frequently found in riverine settings. In contrast, several authors, including Witthoft (1953), have noted that Transitional sites are also found along small streams in nonriverine settings. James Truncer (1990:33) and Herbert Kraft (1990:78) have observed that diagnostic projectile points from the Late Archaic and Transitional periods are found on the same sites and are located in the same ecological zones, although this observation was not quantified by either author.

There are many examples of broadspears found in upland settings or along low-order streams in eastern Pennsylvania. With the PASS files, sites can be classified by general topographic settings. In Figure 3.3, riverine sites are defined as those located on floodplains or terraces of second-order or larger streams; the percentages of riverine compared to upland sites are given by time period in the Susquehanna and Delaware drainage basins. Riverine and upland sites from the Transitional and Late Archaic periods have similar distributions. Early Woodland sites characterized by Meadowood and Hellgrammite bifaces show an increased use of riverine environments. Sites with steatite show the strongest preference for riverine settings for the Transitional period, although sites from the Paleoindian period show the strongest preference for these settings overall.

There is anecdotal information that suggests intrasite changes in the location of Late Archaic compared to Transitional components. Patricia Jehle and Kurt Carr (1983) conducted site surveys in nonriverine settings of southeastern Pennsylvania. Based on the testing of fewer than ten sites, one of their tentative conclusions was that on multicomponent sites, the broadspears were frequently concentrated away from concentrations of Late Archaic points and closer to the source of water. Jehle and Carr suggest that,

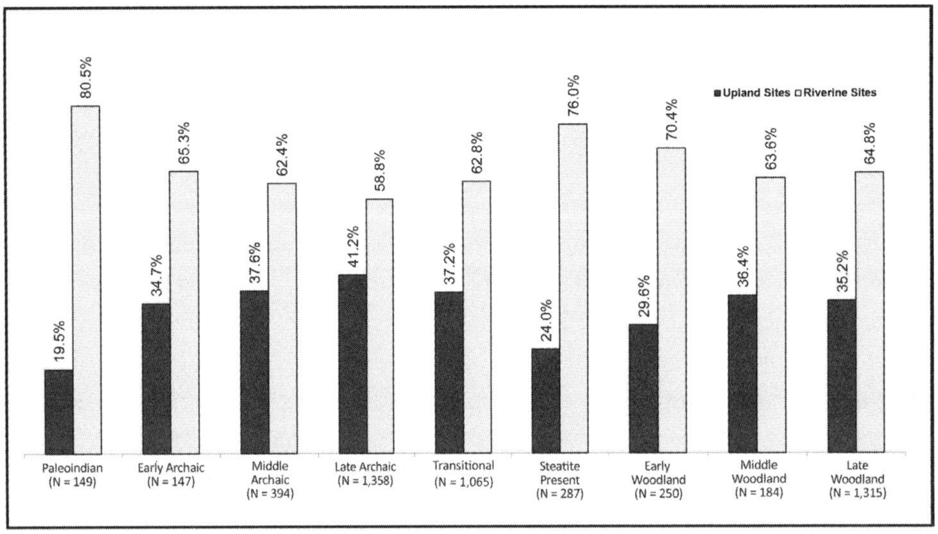

FIGURE 3.3 Comparison of riverine and upland sites by time period in Susquehanna, Potomac, and Delaware drainage basins in Pennsylvania.

with the decrease in precipitation during the Sub-Boreal, the microecology of the sites changed during the Broadspear occupation, and therefore the specific focus/orientation of the occupation also changed.

More recently, Dorothy Merritts (Walter and Merritts 2008), a geomorphologist at Franklin and Marshall College, inadvertently documented a Transitional site in a wetland. While examining Late Woodland and Early Contact environments in the Piedmont of Pennsylvania and Maryland, she and her team recorded a metarhyolite Koens-Crispin broadspear, recovered from along Chickies Creek, Lancaster County, and radiocarbon-dated the hydric soils surrounding it to 3960 BP. It is assumed that people were not actually living in a wetland but that the soils returned to hydric conditions at the end of the Transitional period, corresponding to the Sub-Atlantic warm and moist episode. This find supports the argument that Broadspear occupations are frequently found closer to wetlands than other Late Archaic occupations are.

PASS site file data such as average distance to nearest stream, second-nearest stream, or stream confluence (Figure 3.4) and nearest stream order, second-nearest stream order, or confluence order (Figure 3.5) illustrate that the locations of Late Archaic,

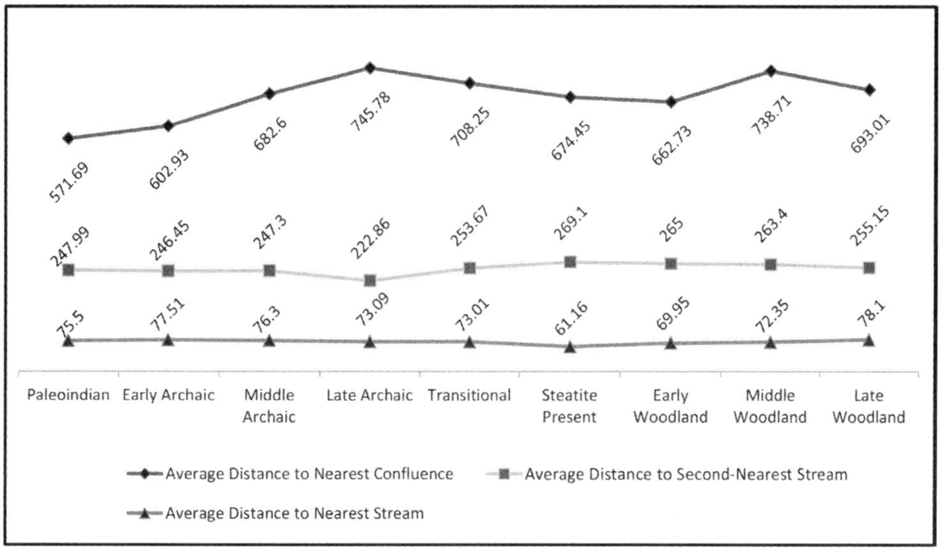

FIGURE 3.4 Distance in meters to nearest stream, second-nearest stream, and nearest perennial stream confluence for sites by time period in Susquehanna, Potomac, and Delaware drainage basins in Pennsylvania.

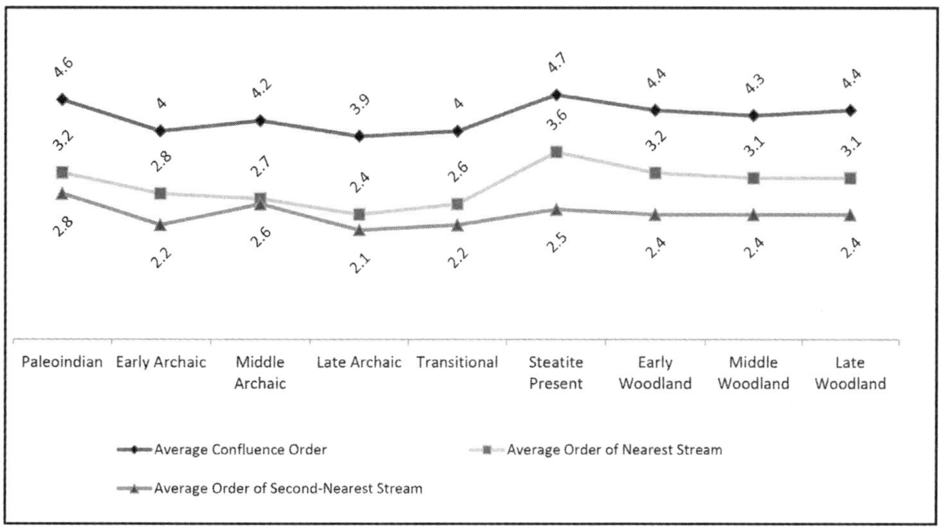

FIGURE 3.5 Order of nearest stream, second-nearest stream, and nearest perennial stream confluence for sites by time period in Susquehanna, Potomac, and Delaware drainage basins in Pennsylvania.

Transitional, or Early Woodland sites are similar in eastern Pennsylvania. Although Transitional sites that produced steatite are more often associated with higher-order streams than Archaic and Woodland sites are, more Paleoindian sites seem to be situated close to water and high-order streams than sites of all other time periods.

Miller, Vento, and Marine (2007a:80–81) examined a number of Late Archaic, Broadspear, and Fishtail occupations or components at sites in the Susquehanna Valley (Calver Island, Memorial Park, Skvarek, Wallis, Girtys Notch, 36PE60, and 36PE61) and defined the different functional types of these sites based on features, artifact types, and artifact numbers. For the Late Archaic period, both short- and long-term base camps were identified. In contrast, for the Broadspear phase, all the occupations seem to represent long-term base camps. Although the geomorphology of the Fishtail occupations is more complicated, these also seem to be long-term camps. This suggests that riverine camps were occupied by larger groups and for longer periods of time during the Transitional than during the Late Archaic period, which is certainly consistent with the use of domesticated plants. On the other hand, as noted by Miller, Vento, and Marine (2007a:83), in contrast to surrounding regions, post mold patterns have not been recorded on any of these sites, which, contrary to Binford (1980) and Parry (1994), is not consistent with increased residential mobility associated with a curated technology.

Population

Heather Wholey (2009) has reviewed the role of population density and population pressure in cultural change. Population pressure is experienced when populations approach or overshoot their carrying capacity (Wholey 2009:2). Potential responses to population pressure "include territorial competition, greater technological efficiency, shifts in extractive strategy, changes in social organization or population movements" (Wholey 2009:3). During the Transitional period, several of these changes can be inferred from the archaeological record. I argue here that population pressure is the major factor in cultural change during the Transitional period.

I assume that human population density was increasing in the Delaware and Susquehanna drainage basins between Paleoindian and Late Archaic times. There is no unequivocal evidence to the contrary. Examining projectile point frequencies in Virginia and Maryland as reflections of population change, Stuart Reeve (1992:126) and Laurie Steponaitis (1980) found an increase throughout the Archaic period, followed by a decrease during the Transitional and Early Woodland periods. Based on projectile point type frequencies and components, Fiedel (2001:110–12) reported a significant decline in population during the Early Woodland period, with an increase through the Middle Woodland. Although there is some debate about both the reality of this reported significant drop in the Early Woodland human population and the assumption that numbers of projectile points reflect any relationship to real human population numbers, these issues will not be addressed here, and the artifact or component numbers will simply be presented.

Figure 3.6 is a plot of the average number of archaeological sites per hundred years based on data from the PASS files for the Susquehanna, Delaware, and Potomac drainage basins within Pennsylvania. These numbers are presented in Figure 3.6 per hundred calendar years and in Figure 3.7 per hundred radiocarbon years. Each of the points on the graph represents the average number of sites containing certain diagnostic projectile points or, when appropriate, pottery types, rather than the number of points or point types themselves. Tables 3.4 and 3.5 present the data that form the basis for Figures 3.6 and 3.7. The tables include the dates and number of sites for each time period. The Paleoindian period is defined by the number of sites with fluted points; the Early Archaic period, by the number of sites with Kirk, Palmer, Thebes, or Charleston projectile points; and the Middle Archaic period, by the number of sites with MacCorkle, St. Albans, and LeCroy bifurcate points. Later Middle Archaic types such as Neville, Stanley, or Otter Creek points are so poorly recorded in the site files that their numbers are not reliable. The Late Archaic period is defined by projectile points of the Brewerton, Piedmont, and Lamoka traditions; the Transitional period, by broadspears and steatite bowls. The Early Woodland period is defined by fishtail projectile points, by steatite-tempered and flat-bottomed, grit-tempered pottery (although, in this chapter, these artifact types are considered part of the Transitional period), by Meadowood and Hellgrammite projectile points, and by Vinette I and modified Vinette I pottery; the Middle Woodland period, by Fox Creek points and Middle Woodland pottery types; and the Late Woodland period, by Late Woodland pottery types and triangular projectile points. The number of sites represented by each of these biface and pottery types is divided by the duration of the period in years and multiplied by 100 to determine the number of sites per hundred-year interval.

As the graph in Figure 3.6 shows, there is a continuous increase in numbers of sites per hundred-year interval from the Bifurcate period up through the Transitional period. I think the decrease in the number of sites during the Early and Middle Woodland periods is artificial and reflects our inability to identify diagnostic projectile points and pottery from this time. Moeller (2009) has also made this argument and

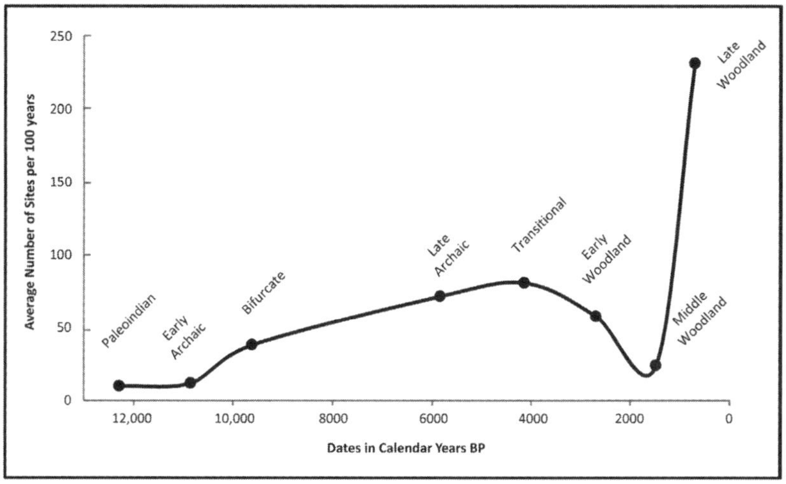

FIGURE 3.6
Population curve based on numbers of sites per time period in calendar years BP.

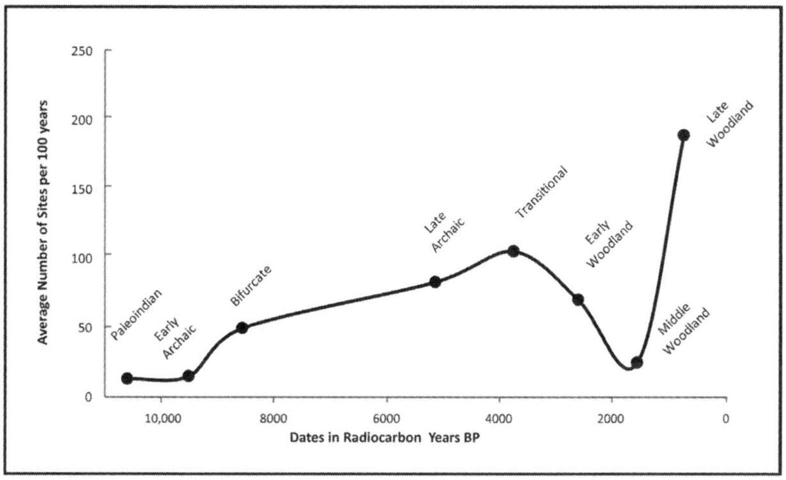

FIGURE 3.7
Population curve based on numbers of sites per time period in radiocarbon years BP.

especially cites the poor quality of the pottery that contributes to the underrepresentation of this period.

Based on numbers of sites, the graph in Figure 3.6 also shows a steady increase in Native American populations since Paleoindian times, a period of 8,000 years. The Sub-Boreal represents a fluctuating warm and dry climate during the Transitional period that resulted in a less productive and less predictable environment in terms of food resources. Late Archaic populations were faced with the problem of recovering fewer calories from the environment using the Late Archaic adaptive strategy. They were beginning to exceed the carrying capacity of the Susquehanna and Delaware drainage basins using that particular strategy, which resulted in population pressure. During the Sub-Boreal climatic episode, the availability or predictability of food resources decreased. It is assumed that population pressure has an effect on technology, and therefore it is not surprising that we see an increase in technological efficiency (as indicated by the flexibility of bifacial technology, by fire-cracked rock features, and by steatite cooking containers) and a shift in extractive strategy (to more different types of plant foods and possibly domesticates) and in social organization (to trade and exchange, increased social communication, and burial ceremonialism) as a response to increasing population pressure.

As noted by Wholey (2009:6), the curve plotted in Figure 3.6 "is a population trajectory rather than a computation of actual numbers of people living at any given time." Admittedly, this is not an accurate population curve for the region. And, as noted above (Custer 2001:76–81, Miller 1998; Wall et al. 1996:154), the Late Archaic biface types used in this analysis

TABLE 3.4 Number of sites by time period in calendar years BP

Time Period	Calendar Dates BP	Midpoint BP	Duration in Years	Number of Sites	Sites per 100 Years	% Change
Paleoindian	13,108–11,483	12,296	1,625	160	9.8	—
Early Archaic	11,483–10,204	10,844	1,279	154	12.0	22.4
Bifurcate	10,204–9019	9612	1,185	450	38.0	216.7
Middle Archaic	9019–6840	7930	2,179	306	14.0	–63.2
Late Archaic	6840–4858	5849	1,982	1,420	71.6	411.4
Transitional	4858–2903	3881	1,955	1,283	65.6	–8.4
Early Woodland	2903–1960	2432	943	175	18.6	–71.7
Middle Woodland	1960–1014	1487	946	227	24.0	29.0
Late Woodland	1014–400	707	614	1,421	231.4	864.2

Note: See Figure 3.6.

TABLE 3.5 Number of sites by time period in radiocarbon years BP

Time Period	Radiocarbon Dates BP	Midpoint BP	Duration in Years	Number of Sites	Sites per 100 Years	% Change
Paleoindian	11,200–10,000	10,600	1,200	160	13.3	—
Early Archaic	10,000–9000	9500	1,000	154	15.4	15.8
Bifurcate	9000–8100	8550	900	450	50.0	224.7
Middle Archaic	8100–6000	7050	2,100	306	14.6	–70.8
Late Archaic	6000–4300	5150	1,700	1,420	83.5	471.9
Transitional	4300–3200	3750	1,100	1,161	105.5	26.3
Early Woodland	3200–2000	2600	1,200	847	70.6	–33.1
Middle Woodland	2000–1100	1550	900	227	25.2	–64.3
Late Woodland	1100–350	725	750	1,421	189.5	652.0

Note: See Figure 3.7.

cover extremely long periods of time extending well into the Early Woodland period; moreover, the Late Woodland period is also overrepresented, if for no other reason than that Archaic triangular projectile points are mixed into the count. On the other hand, I would argue that, given the size of the PASS database, which comprises more than 8,400 dated prehistoric components, some of these problems are offset by the large numbers.

Evolution of the Adaptations

The following is a brief summary of the evolution of Transitional adaptations in the Susquehanna and Delaware drainage basins (Figure 3.8).

By the end of the Atlantic climatic episode, human population density had been steadily increasing for 5,000 years or more. In the Delaware and the Susquehanna drainage basins in the period from 4500 to 4200 BP, stemmed points such as Lamoka, Lackawaxen, or Kent's type E or D points are being made using local materials with an expedient tool kit. These points are associated with woodworking tools, netsinkers, grinding stones, and fire-cracked rock features. Because squash may have been a regular part of the diet, gardening was likely part of the subsistence pattern. As noted above, the climatic conditions of the Atlantic climatic episode probably represented an optimum period for a general foraging adaptation (Klein 1997; Wholey 2009:4). The technological innovations (woodworking tools, bannerstones, grinding stones, net weights) of the Archaic period represent incremental changes in response to an increasing population. They reflect the Late Archaic strategy to extract more calories

	4500 BP	4200 BP	3900 BP	3600 BP	3300 BP	3000 BP	2700 BP	2400 BP
	Late Archaic Period	**Transitional Period**					**Early Woodland Period**	
		Early Broadspear Phase		Late Broadspear Phase		Fishtail Phase		
Biface Type	Narrow-Stemmed	Koens-Crispin	Lehigh	Susquehanna and Perkiomen		Orient Dry Brook	Meadowood Hellgrammite	Lagoon Rossville
Bifacial Technology	Expedient Flake Cores	Bifacial Cores					Expedient Flake Cores	
Lithic Preference	Local	Local Preferences		Jasper, Metarhyolite, and Argillite			Onondaga and Local	Local
Fire-Cracked Features	Small	Larger	Large and Extensive			Very Large	Small	Disappear
Steatite Bowls				Large and Small Bowls				
Biface Caching	Scattered		Common				Common	Rare
Burial Ceremonialism			Savich Farm (New Jersey)			Orient Site (New York)		
Ceramics					Marcy Creek	Vinette I	Modified Vinette I	Grit-Tempered, Net-Impressed, and Cord-Marked
Subsistence			Hunting	Fishing		Gardening?		
		Squash Hickory Nuts White Acorns Walnuts	*Chenopodium* Little Barley Knotweed	Wild Rye Red Acorns Tubers	May Grass	*Chenopodium* Little Barley Knotweed		

FIGURE 3.8
Evolution of Transitional traits.

from the environment. Societies employing these technologies were successful, and their populations increased. Other than smaller seasonal rounds (reflected in lithic preferences) and larger sites, which suggest larger social groups than those in the Middle Archaic, there are no obvious changes in social organization. It is assumed that these groups were simple bilateral, egalitarian bands of foragers (Binford 1980). Although social organization was certainly a significant component in the adaptive strategy, it is not obviously reflected in the material culture of the Late Archaic period of this region.

At the onset of the Sub-Boreal episode, Snook Kill and Koens-Crispin broad-bladed bifaces are added to the Late Archaic assemblages. Late Archaic stemmed projectile point types decrease in frequency but seem to remain common. Changes in lithic preferences suggest changes in territorial boundaries (Robertson and Kingsley 1994) or the emergence of a trade and exchange system involving lithics (Stewart 1989). Broad-bladed bifaces are a technological response to increasing population density, aggravated by the change in climate and the resulting less predictable environment brought on by the Sub-Boreal. These bifaces are more flexible tool blanks that can be both easily modified to deal with an unpredictable environment and easily mass-produced for incorporation in a trade and exchange system. Although bifacial cores, a staged biface reduction system, and a curated tool technology are part of the same technological response, the consistent shapes or styles of broad-bladed bifaces suggest they have additional sociotechnic or ideotechnic meaning, representing broad regional groups who cooperate with one another in the exploitation of the environment.

Burial ceremonialism associated with broad-bladed bifaces is found in New York (Ritchie 1969) and New England (Snow 1980) and, in a different form, is certainly common in the Ohio and Mississippi Valleys. Although present in the Delaware Valley at the Savich Farm Site (Regensburg 1971) in New Jersey, it is generally rare in the drainage basins of both the Delaware and the Susquehanna, which suggests that a different form of social organization emerged in eastern Pennsylvania.

By 3700 BP, Lehigh broad-bladed bifaces are being produced primarily from jasper, metarhyolite, or argillite, but also from chert and quartzite. Initially, local lithics are common in the debitage, but, eventually, jasper, metarhyolite, or argillite dominates the debitage of Susquehanna and Perkiomen assemblages. Bifacial cores, a curated technology, and the trade and exchange for metarhyolite, argillite, or jasper increase. Fire-cracked rock features become extensive and large, suggesting a food resource that was available in large quantities and probably on a seasonal basis. These features may represent not only several different food-processing activities, such as drying, steaming, or stone boiling, but also large social events. Although fish may have been processed and consumed on a large scale, analysis of residues on tools and in steatite bowls also suggests the use of plant foods such as *Chenopodium* rather than fish; elements of the Eastern Agricultural Complex seem to be present in the region. Mainly associated with Susquehanna and Perkiomen bifaces, steatite bowls are added to the technological assemblage, reflecting a more effective method for processing food and an intensification of the adaptive strategy. As part of increasing social communication embodied in trade and shared designs, they were probably significant objects in regular social events. Beginning at roughly 3200 BP, fired clay in the form of steatite-tempered pottery (Marcy Creek) quickly begins to displace steatite bowls, which disappear over a 200-year period.

At 3000 BP, the Sub-Boreal ends and broad-bladed points and knives become narrow, taking the form of fishtail bifaces. A curated technology and lithic preferences continue and fire-cracked rock features become very large. Wetland tubers are added to the diet. Burial ceremonialism increases on Long Island in New York and may also be present within eastern Pennsylvania. The Transitional adaptive strategy clearly extends for a few more centuries into the more productive and predictable climate of the Sub-Atlantic episode. By about 2700 BP, fishtail bifaces disappear and Meadowood bifaces appear in the Upper Delaware and Susquehanna drainage basins. Although they probably do not represent the same type of sociocultural manifestation as broadspears or Lamoka projectile points, Meadowood bifaces are a useful chronological marker. Other biface forms or projectile points in perishable materials may be commonly associated with this phase or time period, but the picture is not clear. In the Lower Susquehanna and Middle Delaware Valleys, Hellgrammite projectile point types are more commonly found. Fire-cracked rock features decrease in size during the Hellgrammite phase, especially in assemblages associated with the Meadowood complex. Groups using a curated technology or processing food in ways that result in large amounts of fire-cracked rock no longer have a selective advantage. There continue to be lithic preferences and possibly a trade and exchange system, involving Onondaga chert for Meadowood bifaces, metarhyolite for Hellgrammite bifaces in the Lower Susquehanna Valley, and argillite for most Hellgrammite bifaces in the Middle Delaware Valley (Hummer 1991:309).

By 2400 BP, there is a return to using local lithics over much of eastern Pennsylvania. At least during the early Middle Woodland period in the Upper Delaware Valley, grinding and nutting stones increase in number (Kinsey 1972:368). Nondescript ceramics (Vinette I variations) become increasingly common; relatively nondistinctive bifaces, such as Rossville and Lagoon types, are being used. Social distinctions expressed in biface types over wide regions during the Transitional period become less important. Thus both the pottery and the projectile points are nondistinctive, making sites from the early Middle Woodland difficult to recognize. Middle Woodland components from this time period, though relatively common in the Upper Delaware Valley, are rare in the stratified contexts of the Susquehanna Valley, with notable exceptions at sites such as Harding Flats (East et al. 2001), Canfield Island (Bressler, Maietta, and Rockey 1983), and Three Mile Island (Smith 1979).

The above is presented as a broad working hypothesis. It is not unequivocally supported by the archaeological record; ambiguities in chronology, subsistence patterns, and the relationship and meaning of certain stylistic artifacts continue to be unresolved. Sites from this time period do not always contain broadspears or steatite, and radiometric dating is necessary for their identification. The diet of the Transitional period is very poorly understood, although more intensive excavation and analytical techniques are beginning to change this picture. The direct dating of residues and food remains should be a high priority. The relationship between the various Broadspear types is thought to be partly chronological, but more of these types need dating. Finally, sites must be excavated in a manner that allows changes in social groups to be identified. This requires highly controlled stratigraphic excavations (e.g., 5 cm levels), large horizontal exposures, and the detailed mapping (with point proveniences) of artifacts and features.

Conclusions

I have argued here that the artifacts, features, community patterns, and settlement systems of the Transitional period represent an evolving response to increasing population pressure, aggravated by the decrease in precipitation and the unpredictable climate of the Sub-Boreal. Late Archaic adaptive strategy first begins to change technologically with the use of standardized biface types, bifacial cores, a curated tool technology, and the intensive processing of food, resulting in fire-cracked rock features. The technology of the Early Broadspear phase represents a more flexible approach to an unpredictable environment. In addition, there are tantalizing data that may evidence the use of domesticated plants. The technological changes are associated with the use of nonlocal lithics, a change in lithic preferences from the Late Archaic period, or both, suggesting a change in concepts of territoriality. Social groups who selected these technological changes were more successful than groups who did not, and they increased in number through time.

During the Late Broadspear phase, the technological changes continue and include the use of more efficient steatite bowls. The social changes seem to become more pronounced during this time. There is an increase in social interaction in the form of shared distinctive broad-bladed bifaces and steatite bowls, trade and exchange of lithics, and rare instances of burial ceremonialism. It would seem that social groups who developed increased social communication and a more structured social organization were more successful than those who did not. This occurs on a regional level and suggests greater social communication within at least the Susquehanna and Delaware Valleys and probably a much larger area.

The changes seem to develop relatively quickly between 4300 and 3700 BP. The 600-year Early Broadspear phase is followed by the Late Broadspear phase, which comes to an end over a period of from 300 to 500 years. At approximately 3000 BP, artifacts of the Fishtail phase become very common, along with fire-cracked rock features and strong lithic preferences. By 2700 BP, however, the adaptive strategy has changed significantly, and most of the characteristics of the Transitional period have disappeared. The bifacial technology, an elaborate trade and exchange system, and the distinctive biface types were no longer necessary to exploit the Sub-Atlantic environment. Those social groups who adopted other lithic technologies, discontinued trade in lithics, and no longer produced socially distinctive bifaces or pottery types increased their numbers.

The Transitional adaptation is a response by human populations that had been increasing steadily over the 5,000 years of the Archaic period to a slight decrease in precipitation, brought on by the Sub-Boreal climatic episode. Having nearly maximized their Late Archaic adaptive strategy for exploiting their environment, these groups may have reached a "tipping point." In the fluctuating climate of the Sub-Boreal, broad-bladed bifaces, a curated tool technology, the mass processing of certain foods by roasting, stone boiling, or steaming, the use of domesticated plants, increased social communication, and the development of mutually beneficial relationships over broad regions were the core elements of the Transitional adaptation.

During the Transitional period, increased regional social communication is convincingly demonstrated by an increase in artifacts that reflect a more structured social organization, more frequent social interaction, and thus also increased cooperation within social groups. A more structured social organization represents an adjustment to increased population density, a mechanism by which to organize labor to more effectively collect, process, and consume calories from the environment. During the Transitional period, this more structured organization becomes clearly visible in the archaeological record of the Middle Atlantic region.

The Early Broadspear phase is characterized primarily by technological changes, whereas the Late Broadspear and Fishtail phases are characterized more by social changes. Trade and exchange in lithics focused on a limited variety of lithic types, Broadspear types become regionalized (Susquehanna and Perkiomen types), and steatite bowls with probable social roles became more common. By the time the environmental stresses end, social organization has changed forever, and Transitional groups begin focusing on a new food source, one that does not require or result in the accumulation of massive amounts of fire-cracked rock, possibly seed plants such as knotweed, little barley, or *Chenopodium*, rather than fish, root crops, or nuts.

The Transitional period represents a shift in adaptation in response to a change in the environment that resulted in reduced and less predictable food resources at a time when population density was approaching the carrying capacity for the Archaic adaptive strategy. Even when the Sub-Boreal ended and there was a return to the more favorable conditions of the Sub-Atlantic episode, which is to say, even when population pressure was reduced with the increase in precipitation and a more predictable environment, it was not possible to return to the Archaic adaptive strategy. The social organization and subsistence patterns had changed the cultural trajectory of Transitional peoples. They had shifted to exploiting a new type of food resource and to a new type of social organization. According to Sassaman (1999), the role of females in social and economic life may have increased in importance, although this is not easily testable. Transitional adaptation to the environment was distinct from Archaic or Woodland adaptation. A short-lived adjustment began a new and different cultural trajectory, which ended in the Late Woodland period, with its focus on domesticated plants and tribal social organization.

Archaeologists have typically divided the past into time periods that some considered distinct stages of cultural development (i.e., Paleoindian, Archaic, and Woodland). More recently, some archaeologists have suggested that these periods represent very broad adaptive strategies in response to cultural and environmental change. As defined above, the Transitional adaptation includes archaeological complexes that have traditionally been included in the Late Archaic and or the Early Woodland period. I would suggest that the terms "Transitional," "horizon," or "complex" are more appropriate than the term "Terminal Archaic." In the Susquehanna Valley, the exclusive use of Lackawaxen and Lamoka types represents the end of the Late Archaic adaptation and the Terminal Archaic period. The Transitional period marked a significant change from the foraging lifestyle of the Archaic period to a lifestyle in which social organization and the function and structure of human groups became more complex and made a greater contribution to adaptation. It also included the use of domesticated plants and possibly the changes in settlement systems required by gardening. It is neither an Archaic nor a Woodland adaptation. It represents a successful adaptation through interrelated technological and social changes that had not combined in the past. By the Middle Woodland period, the strategy had evolved into something different. The specifics are not clear in eastern Pennsylvania, but it seems to ultimately lead to horticulture and a tribal social organization in the Late Woodland period.

As we have always known, the chronological terms used by archaeologists are heuristic devices. Although Custer's (1996:21) proposed system based on cultural adaptations has not been widely adopted by the archaeological community, using such a system would avoid problems of relying on a limited number of "diagnostic artifacts" to define archaeological events. As cultural adaptations become understood in greater detail, chronologically based terms will have even less meaning and value. As a compromise, perhaps we should shift to the use of "phases."

Processual archaeology identifies and attempts to explain patterns in the prehistoric record, ultimately leading to a better understanding of the present and to possible applications for the future. In eastern Pennsylvania, we witness the evolution of a foraging adaptation in a temperate forest (Wholey 2009:15). One interpretation of that development is that, with increasing population density, simple technological innovations were no longer sufficient. At the beginning of the Transitional period, Native Americans changed their technology, but, what is more significant, they began to add a considerable social component to the adaptive strategy that more effectively organized the extraction of more calories from the environment to support a larger population. Many of the technological components and the archaeological manifestations of the social components disappear in the Early Woodland period after the Fishtail phase, and a new cultural trajectory emerges during the Middle Woodland that leads to the intensive use of domesticated plants. Is this a pattern that can be identified in other regions or on other continents? In contrast to eastern Pennsylvania, the social components at the beginning of the Early Woodland seem to intensify in the Ohio Valley, where Adena and Hopewell social organization become even more elaborate. Why are the two patterns different? Could it be that the Ohio and Mississippi Valleys had reached the Archaic carrying capacity at a much earlier date?

REFERENCES

Bergman, Christopher A., John F. Doershuk, Larry R. Kimball, and V. Riegel

1986 *Archaeological Data Recovery for Transcontinental Gas Pipe Line Corporation's 6.7 Mile Leidy Natural Gas Pipeline Expansion, Sands Eddy Site (36-Nm-12), Northampton County, Pennsylvania.* Report prepared for Transcontinental Gas Pipe Line Corporation, Houston, Texas. 3D/Environmental Services, Inc., Cincinnati, Ohio.

Bergman, Christopher A., Phillip LaPorta, John Doershuk, Heidi Fassler, David Rue, and Joseph Schuldenrein

1992 The Padula Site (36Nm15) and Chert Resource Exploitation in the Middle Delaware River Valley. *Archaeology of Eastern North America* 20: 39–66.

Binford, Lewis R.

1962 Archaeology as Anthropology. *American Antiquity* 28 (2): 217–25.

1965 Archaeological Systematics and the Study of Cultural Process. *American Antiquity* 31 (2; Part 1): 203–10.

1980 Willow Smoke and Dogs' Tails: Hunter-Gather Settlement Systems and Archaeological Site Formation. *American Antiquity* 45 (1): 4–20.

Blondino, Joseph R.

2008 How Can You Mend a Broken Hearth? Preliminary Results of Excavations at the Driftstone Site. *Journal of Middle Atlantic Archaeology* 24:167–75.

2009 An "Orient" Perspective on the Transitional Archaic in the Upper Delaware Valley. Paper presented at Annual Meeting of Pennsylvania Archaeological Council, Harrisburg.

Brennan, Louis A.

1967 The Taconic Tradition and the Coe Axiom. *Bulletin of the New York State Archaeological Association* 36:5–13.

Bressler, James P., Ricki Maietta, and Karen Rockey

1983 *Canfield Island Through the Ages: 36LY37.* North Central Chapter No. 8, Society for Pennsylvania Archaeology and Lycoming County Historical Society, Williamsport.

Burrow, Ian

1997 The Savich Farm Site: An Archaeological Survey of Phase 1 of the Long-Term Management Plan. *Bulletin of the Archaeological Society of New Jersey* 52:35–50.

Carbone, Victor A.

1976 *Environment and Prehistory in the Shenandoah Valley.* Ph.D. dissertation, Department of Anthropology, Catholic University of America, Washington, D.C. University Microfilms, Ann Arbor, Michigan.

Carr, Kurt W., Christopher A. Bergman, and Crista M. Haag

2010 Some Observations on Eastern Clovis Lithic Reduction Strategies and Percussion Blade Technology. *Lithic Technology* 35 (2): 91–125.

Cavallo, John A.

1996 *Area B Site (28Me1-B) Data Recovery.* Trenton Complex Archaeology: Report 8. Prepared for Federal Highway Administration and New Jersey Department of Transportation, Trenton. Cultural Resource Group, Louis Berger & Associates, Inc. East Orange, New Jersey.

Cavallo, John A., and Shari L. Kondrup

1986 Experimentally-Derived Interpretations of Prehistoric Stone Features in the Middle Delaware River Valley. Paper presented at Middle Atlantic Archaeological Conference, Rehoboth Beach, Delaware.

Cresson, Jack

1990 Broadspear Lithic Technology: Some Aspects of Biface Manufacture, Form, and Use History with Insights Towards Understanding Assemblage Diversity. In *Experiments and Observations on the Terminal Archaic of the Middle Atlantic Region*, edited by Roger W. Moeller, 105–30. Archaeological Services, Bethlehem, Connecticut.

Custer, Jay F.

1984 The Paleoecology of the Late Archaic: Exchange and Adaption. *Pennsylvania Archaeologist* 54 (3–4): 32–47.

1991 Notes on Broadspear Functions. *Archaeology of Eastern North America* 19:51–74

1996 *Prehistoric Cultures of Eastern Pennsylvania.* Anthropological Series 7. Pennsylvania Historical and Museum Commission, Harrisburg.

2001 *Classification Guide for Arrowheads and Spearpoints of Eastern Pennsylvania and the Central Middle Atlantic.* Pennsylvania Historical and Museum Commission, Harrisburg.

Custer, Jay F., and David C. Bachman

1985 Analysis of Projectile Point Morphology, Use Wear, and Activity Areas at the Hawthorn Site (7NC-E-46), New Castle County, Delaware. *Journal of Middle Atlantic Archaeology* 2:37–62.

Custer, Jay F., and Glenn S. Mellin

1986 Analysis of "Broadspears" from Delaware: Form, Function, and Distribution. *Bulletin of the Archaeological Society of Delaware* 22:1–29.

Deetz, James

1967 *Invitation to Archaeology.* American Museum of Natural History, New York.

East, Thomas C., Christopher T. Espenshade, Philip T. Fitzgibbons, and Frances B. King

2001 *Harding Flats Site 36Wo55 Phase II/III,* Volume 5: *Interpretations and Conclusions.* Report prepared for Pennsylvania Department of Transportation Engineering District 4-0. Skelly and Loy, Inc. Harrisburg and Monroeville, Pennsylvania.

Eren, Mitin I., Aaron Greenspan, and C. Garth Sampson

2008 Are Upper Paleolithic Blade Cores More Productive Than Middle Paleolithic Discoidal Cores? A Replication Experiment. *Journal of Human Evolution* 55:952–61.

Fehr, Elinor, Doris Freyermuth, Joseph Lopresti, Virginia Lopresti, Donald Kline, Barry C. Kent

1971 The Sandts Eddy Site. *Pennsylvania Archaeologist* 41:39–52.

Fiedel, Stuart J.

2001 What Happened in the Early Woodland? *Archaeology of Eastern North America* 29:101–42.

Fischler, Benjamin R., and James W. Mueller

1988 *Archaeological Discovery and Evaluation in Delaware Water Gap National Recreation Area, 1984–1987.* National Park Service, Denver Service Center Eastern Team, Rockville, Maryland.

Gardner, William M.

1987 Comparison of Ridge and Valley, Blue Ridge, Piedmont, and Coastal Plain Archaic Period Site Distribution: An Idealized Transect (Preliminary Model). *Journal of Middle Atlantic Archaeology* 3:49–80.

Hart, John P., and Nancy Asch Sidell

1997 Additional Evidence for Early Cucurbit Use in the Northern Eastern Woodlands East of the Allegheny Front. *American Antiquity* 62 (3): 523–37.

Hummer, Christopher C.

1991 *Biface and Ceramic Assemblage Variability in the Early Woodland: Continuity and Change at the Williamson Site, Hunterdon County, New Jersey.* Ph.D. dissertation, Department of Anthropology, Temple University, Philadelphia. University Microfilms, Ann Arbor, Michigan.

1994 Defining Early Woodland in the Delaware Valley: The View from the Williamson Site, Hunterdon County, New Jersey. In *Recent Research into the Prehistory of the Delaware Valley,* edited by C. A. Bergman and J. F. Doershuk, 141–52. Archaeological Services, Bethlehem, Connecticut.

Hunter, Charles E.

1970 *Broadspear and Fishtail Traditions in the Northeast.* Manuscript on file at the North Museum, Franklin and Marshall College, Lancaster, Pennsylvania.

Inashima, Paul Y.

2008 Establishing a Radiocarbon Date Based Framework for Northeastern Virginia Archaeology. *Archaeology Society of Virginia, Quarterly Bulletin* 63 (4): 1–99.

Jacoby, Robert, Robert Wall, Rhea Rogers, and John Killeen

1999 *Phase III Archaeological Investigations of Site 36Co17 and Sites 36Co18 for the Mifflinville Bridge Replacement, SR 2028, Mifflinville, Pennsylvania.* Report prepared for Pennsylvania Department of Transportation Engineering District 3-0, Montoursville, Pennsylvania. Cultural Resource Group, Louis Berger & Associates, Inc., East Orange, New Jersey.

Jehle, Patricia A., and Kurt W. Carr

1983 *The Southeast Pennsylvania Upland Archaeological Project: Intra-site Analysis of Plowzone Sites.* Report submitted to Pennsylvania Historical and Museum Commission. Pennsylvania Bureau of State Parks, Harrisburg.

Justice, Noel D.

1987 *Stone Age Spear and Arrow Points of the Midcontinental and Eastern United States: A Modern Survey and Reference.* Indiana University Press, Bloomington.

Kent, Barry C.

1996 Piney Island and the Archaic of Southeastern Pennsylvania. *Pennsylvania Archaeologist* 66:1–42.

1999 Notes on Susquehanna and Perkiomen Flakes and Points of Rhyolite. Manuscript in author's possession.

Kent, Barry C., Ira F. Smith, and Catherine McCann (editors)

1971 *Foundations of Pennsylvania Prehistory,* Anthropological Series 1, Pennsylvania Historical and Museum Commission, Harrisburg.

Kingsley, Robert G., James A. Robertson, and Daniel G. Roberts

1990 *The Archaeology of the Lower Schuylkill River Valley in Southeastern Pennsylvania.* Report prepared for Philadelphia Electric Company, Philadelphia. John Milner Associates, Inc., West Chester, Pennsylvania.

Kinsey, W. Fred, III (editor)

1972 *Archeology in the Upper Delaware Valley.* Anthropological Series 2. Pennsylvania Historical and Museum Commission, Harrisburg.

Kinsey, W. Fred, III, and Charles W. McNett

1972 Brodhead-Heller Site. In *Archaeology in the Upper Delaware Valley*, edited by W. Fred Kinsey III, 199–224. Anthropological Series 2. Pennsylvania Historical and Museum Commission, Harrisburg.

Klein, Michael J.

1997 The Transition from Soapstone Bowls to Marcey Creek Ceramics in the Middle Atlantic Region: Vessel Technology, Ethnographic Data, and Regional Exchange. *Archaeology of Eastern North America* 25:143–58.

Kraft, Herbert C.

1970 *The Miller Field Site, Warren County, New Jersey: A Study in Prehistoric Archaeology.* Part I: *Archaic and Transitional Stages.* Seton Hall University Press, South Orange, New Jersey.

1990 The Terminal Archaic in the Upper Delaware Valley: A Broad and Narrow Perspective. In *Experiments and Observations on the Terminal Archaic of the Middle Atlantic Region*, edited by Roger W. Moeller, 63–84. Archaeological Services, Bethlehem, Connecticut.

Maschner, Herbert D., and Steven Mithen

1996 Darwinian Archaeologies: An Introductory Essay. In *Darwinian Archaeologies*, edited by Herbert D. Maschner, 3–14. Plenum Press, New York.

McLearen, Douglas C.

1991 Late Archaic and Early Woodland Material Culture in Virginia. In *Late Archaic and Early Woodland Research in Virginia: A Synthesis*, edited by T. R. Reinhart and M. E. Hodges, 88–137. Special Publication 23. Archaeological Society of Virginia, Richmond.

Miller, Patricia E.

1995 *Archaeological Data Recovery: Sites 36Sn220 and 36Sn221 and Additional Phase II Survey: Site 36Sn21, Safer Highways for Economic Development Project, S.R. 0011, Section 003 (T.R. 11 and 15), Snyder County, Pennsylvania.* Report prepared for Pennsylvania Department of Transportation, Engineering District 3-0, Montoursville. Archaeological and Historical Consultants, Inc., Centre Hall, Pennsylvania.

1998 Lithic Projectile Point Technology and Raw Material Use in the Susquehanna Valley. In *The Archaic Period in Pennsylvania: Hunter-Gathers of the Early and Middle Holocene Period*, edited by Paul A. Raber, Patricia E. Miller, and Sarah M. Neusius, 91–119. Recent Research in Pennsylvania Archaeology 1. Pennsylvania Historical and Museum Commission, Harrisburg.

2009 The Transitional Archaic of the Susquehanna Valley, Part II. Paper presented at Annual Meeting of Pennsylvania Archaeological Council, Harrisburg, April 3.

Miller, Patricia E., Frank J. Vento, and James T. Marine

2007a *Archaeological Investigations: Susquehanna River Bridge, Dauphin and York Counties, Pennsylvania,* Volume 1: *Research Design and Prehistoric Context.* Report prepared for Pennsylvania Turnpike Commission. KCI Technologies, Inc., Mechanicsburg, Pennsylvania.

2007b *Archaeological Investigations: Susquehanna River Bridge, Dauphin and York Counties, Pennsylvania,* Volume 3a: *Phase II/III Archaeological Investigations at Site 36DA89 on Calver Island.* Report prepared for Pennsylvania Turnpike Commission. KCI Technologies, Inc., Mechanicsburg, Pennsylvania.

2009 *Archaeological Investigations, Route 11/15 Improvements (SR 0011, Section 008) Juniata and Perry Counties, Pennsylvania,* Volume 4: *Site 36Pe61.* Report prepared for Pennsylvania Department of Transportation, Engineering District 8-0, Harrisburg. KCI Technologies, Inc., Mechanicsburg, Pennsylvania. ER No. 1989-0381-042.

Moeller, Roger W. (editor)

1990 *Experiments and Observations on the Terminal Archaic of the Middle Atlantic Region.* Archaeological Services, Bethlehem, Connecticut.

Moeller, Roger W.

2009 Rethinking the Terminal Archaic in Pennsylvania: Hearths, Fish, and Pottery. Paper presented at Annual Middle Atlantic Archaeological Conference, Ocean City, Maryland.

Myers, J. Emlen, Aileen Dorney, and Janet Friedman

1995 *Archaeological Investigations at the City Island Site (36Da12), Harrisburg, Pennsylvania.* Report prepared for Pennsylvania Historical and Museum Commission, Harrisburg. Dames & Moore Cultural Resource Services, Bethesda, Maryland.

Parry, William J.

1994 Prismatic Blade Technologies in North America. In *The Organization of North American Prehistoric Chipped Stone Tool Technologies*, edited by Phillip J. Carr, 87–98. Archaeological Series 7. International Monographs in Prehistory, Ann Arbor, Michigan.

Raber, Paul A.

2008 The Early and Middle Woodland in the Upper Juniata River Drainage: Archaeological Visibility and Regional Population. *Pennsylvania Archaeologist* 78 (1): 16–40.

Reeve, Stuart A.

1992 Changes in Time: A Seriation Chronology for Southern Maryland Projectile Points. *Journal of Middle Atlantic Archaeology* 8:107–37.

Regensburg, Richard A.

1971 The Savich Farm Site: A Preliminary Report. *Bulletin of the Massachusetts Archaeological Society* 32 (1–2): 20–38.

Ritchie, William A.
1969 *Archaeology of New York State*. Revised edition. Natural History Press, Garden City, New York.

Robertson, James A., and Robert G. Kingsley
1994 The Lower Black's Eddy Site and Prehistoric Settlement Systems in the Middle Delaware Valley. *Journal of Middle Atlantic Archaeology* 10:85–104.

Sassaman, Kenneth E.
1993 *Early Pottery in the Southeast: Tradition and Innovation in Cooking Technology*. University of Alabama Press, Tuscaloosa.

1999 A Southeastern Perspective on Soapstone Vessel Technology in the Northeast. In *The Archaeological Northeast*, edited by Mary Ann Levine, Kenneth E. Sassaman, and Michael. S. Nassaney, 75–95. Bergin & Garvey, Westport, Connecticut.

2006 Dating and Explaining Soapstone Vessels: A Comment on Truncer. *American Antiquity* 71 (1): 141–56.

Schuldenrein, Joseph, Robert G. Kingsley, James A. Robertson, Linda Scott-Cummings, and Daniel R. Hayes
1991 Archaeology of the Lower Blacks Eddy Site, Bucks County, Pennsylvania: A Preliminary Report. *Pennsylvania Archaeologist* 61 (1): 19–75.

Shaffer, Gary D.
2008 Decorated Soapstone Vessels Discovered Along the Lower Susquehanna River. *Archaeology of Eastern North America* 36:1–24.

Shennan, Stephen
1996 Foreword. In *Darwinian Archaeologies*, edited by Herbert D. Maschner, ix–xiii. Plenum Press, New York

Siegel, Peter E., Robert G. Kingsley, and Tod L. Benedict
2001 Oberly Island: Trend and Tradition in the Lower Lehigh Valley. *Pennsylvania Archaeologist* 71 (2): 16–59.

Smith, Ira F.
1979 *Early and Middle Woodland Campsites on Three Mile Island, Dauphin County, Pennsylvania*. Pennsylvania Historical and Museum Commission, Harrisburg.

Snow, Dean R.
1980 *The Archaeology of New England*. Academic Press, New York.

Steponaitis, Laurie Cameron
1980 *A Survey of Artifact Collections from the Patuxent River Drainage, Maryland*. Maryland Historical Trust Manuscript Series 1. Maryland Historical Trust and the Coastal Resource Division, Tidewater Administration, Department of Natural Resources, Annapolis.

Stewart, R. Michael
1987 *Gropp's Lake Site (28Me100G), Data Recovery*. Trenton Complex Archaeology: Report 2. Prepared for Federal Highway Administration and New Jersey Department of Transportation, Trenton. Cultural Resource Group, Louis Berger & Associates, Inc., East Orange, New Jersey.

1989 Trade and Exchange in the Middle Atlantic Region. *Archaeology of Eastern North America* 17:14–78.

1998 Thoughts on the Origins of Ceramic Use and Variation. *Journal of Middle Atlantic Archaeology* 14:1–12.

2009 Problems, Problems, Problems: Working with the Archaeological Record of 3000 to 4000 BP. Paper presented at Annual Meeting of Pennsylvania Archaeological Council, Harrisburg.

2011 Stone Bowls and Early Pottery. *Journal of Middle Atlantic Archaeology* 27:147–64.

Truncer, James
1990 Perkiomen Points: A Study in Variability. In *Experiments and Observations on the Terminal Archaic of the Middle Atlantic Region*, edited by Roger W. Moeller, 1–62. Archaeological Services, Bethlehem, Connecticut.

2004 *Steatite Vessel Manufacture in Eastern North America*. BAR International Series 1326. Archaeopress, Oxford, England.

2006 Taking Variation Seriously: The Case of Steatite Vessel Manufacture. *American Antiquity* 71 (1): 157–63.

Turnbaugh, William A.
1975 *Man, Land, and Time: The Cultural Prehistory and Demographic Patterns of North-Central Pennsylvania*. Published for Lycoming County Historical Society, Williamsport, Pennsylvania. Unigraphic, Inc., Evansville, Indiana.

Vento, Frank J.
2009 Evidence for Climatic Variability During the Sub-Boreal/Transitional Period: Fact or Fiction. Paper presented at Annual Meeting of the Pennsylvania Archaeological Council, Harrisburg.

Vento, Frank. J., Harold B. Rollins, Anthony Vega, James M. Adovasio, Patricia Stahlman, David B. Madsen, and Jeffrey S. Illingworth
2008 Development of a Late Pleistocene–Holocene Genetic Stratigraphic Framework for the Mid-Atlantic Region: Implications in Archaeology. Paper presented at 73rd Annual Meeting of Society for American Archaeology, Vancouver, British Columbia, March 26–30.

Wall, Robert D.
2000 A Buried Lamoka Occupation in Stratified Contexts, West Branch Valley of the Susquehanna River, Pennsylvania. *Pennsylvania Archaeologist* 70 (1): 1–44.

Wall, Robert D., R. Michael Stewart, John Cavallo, Douglas McLearen, Robert Foss, Philip Perazio, and John Dumont
1996 *Prehistoric Archaeological Synthesis: Trenton Complex Archaeology*: Report 15. Report prepared

for Federal Highway Administration and New Jersey Department of Transportation, Bureau of Environmental Analysis, Trenton. Cultural Resource Group, Louis Berger & Associates, Inc., East Orange, New Jersey.

Walter, Robert C., and Dorothy J. Merritts
2008 Natural Streams and the Legacy of Water-Powered Mills. *Science* 319 (5861): 299–304.

Weed, Carol S., and William P. Wenstrom (editors)
1992 *Cultural Resources Investigations of 36LU90 (Jacobs Site) and 36LU105 (Gould Island Sites), Luzerne County, Pennsylvania.* Report prepared for Transcontinental Gas Pipe Line Corporation, Houston, Texas. Panamerican Consultants, Tuscaloosa, Alabama.

Wholey, Heather A.
2009 A Population Approach to the Middle Atlantic Archaic. *North American Archaeologist* 30 (1): 1–21.

Witthoft, John
1949 An Outline of Pennsylvania Indian History. *Quarterly Journal of the Pennsylvania Historical Association* 16 (3): 3–15.

1953 Broad Spear Points and the Transitional Period Cultures. *Pennsylvania Archaeologist* 24 (1): 4–31.

4.

The Transitional Archaic Period in the Susquehanna River Valley

Patricia E. Miller

ABSTRACT

Investigations at a number of stratified sites along the Susquehanna River have provided information on Transitional Archaic adaptation between 3800 and 3000 BP. The period was marked by the use of broadspears and the movement of rhyolite and steatite up the Susquehanna River. This chapter synthesizes data from radiocarbon-dated components to provide an overview of the period, including the rise and fall of a trade network. The information from the Susquehanna River valley is compared to archaeological data from the Late Archaic and Early Woodland periods.

Investigations at stratified sites in the Susquehanna River valley conducted over the last two decades have provided information documenting cultural changes that took place between 3800 and 3000 BP (Figure 4.1). The cultural changes associated with this 800-year period are often referred to as the "Broadspear tradition" or "Broadspear horizon" and consist primarily of the intensive use and trade in rhyolite, the use of steatite, and the use of broadspear points. In Pennsylvania, the tradition is confined almost entirely to the Susquehanna River drainage basin. A search of Pennsylvania's Cultural Resources Geographical Information System (CRGIS) revealed 194 sites having Susquehanna broadspears associated with either rhyolite or steatite or both in the Susquehanna River basin, as opposed to only nineteen in the Delaware River basin and only eleven in the Ohio River basin.

John Witthoft (1953) defined the Transitional period as a change in adaptive strategy involving a more intensive use of rivers both for associated food resources and for transportation. A number of researchers have argued that climate change was the primary driving force behind the adaptation, but the data on the climate are not definitive, and some researchers do not agree with this interpretation (Joyce 1988; Miller 1993). Insights into the period can be derived by examining data from Transitional Archaic components at stratified sites along the Susquehanna River and by comparing these components both with Late Archaic and, to the degree possible, with Early Woodland components at these sites. This approach, detailed here, indicates that the major change of the Transitional Archaic period in the Susquehanna Valley was the operation of a trade network that led to a focus of settlement along the

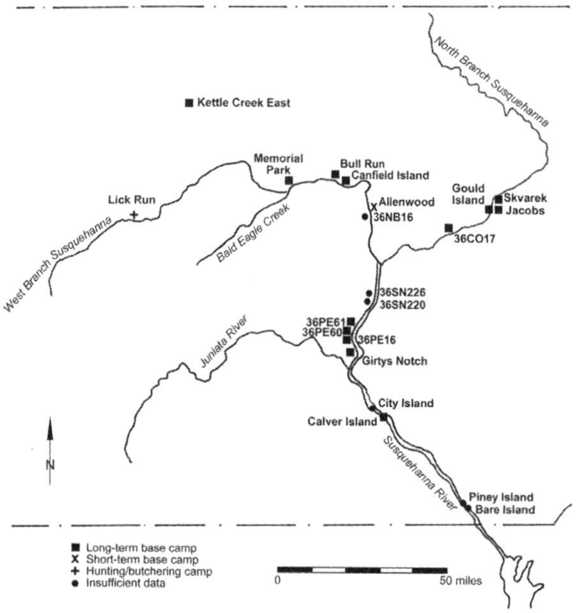

FIGURE 4.1
Transitional Archaic sites excavated in Susquehanna River Valley.

river. The network was overlaid on a hunter-gatherer adaptation that was evolving, driven primarily by an increase in population density rather than by climate change.

Geomorphological Context

At many stratified sites along the Susquehanna, evidence of Transitional Archaic occupations is found within and immediately below the plow zone. For example, at Site 36PE60 (Miller et al. 2009), located near Liverpool, Pennsylvania, features dating between 3600 and 3000 BP were found at the base of the plow zone. The underlying sandy soil stratum was 22 centimeters thick and represents an accumulation of sediments extending over 280 years. At sites such as Calver Island (36DA89), however, the Transitional Archaic components occurred 20 centimeters or more below the base of the plow zone (Miller, Marine, and Vento 2007).

The soil matrix of Transitional Archaic components is often, though not always, sandy, which differs from the underlying Late Archaic deposits and suggests high-energy flooding. However, the stratigraphy at Site 36PE60 and two other sites investigated in the Liverpool area indicates that the effects of these high-energy floods were somewhat localized and that such floods occurred into the Early Woodland period. The soil profile at the Wallis Site (36PE16) shows the effect of distance from the active river channel (Figure 4.2), with Transitional Archaic cultural material found in sandy C-horizon deposits (CB, C1/BC) closest to the river and in silty B-horizon soils (Bw1, Bw2, Bw3) in more distant locations (Miller et al. 2009).

Early Woodland artifact assemblages at stratified sites along the Susquehanna River are often entirely within the plow zone and cannot be isolated from those of later Woodland components. However, at the Calver Island, Gould Island (36LU105), Jacobs (36LU90), and Woodworkers (36SN220) Sites, the Transitional Archaic components were found 20 centimeters or more below the plow zone and Early Woodland components were preserved in the upper portion of the subsoil (Miller 1995; Miller, Marine, and Vento 2007; Weed and Wenstrom 1992). Thus there is good information on the Early Woodland from some sites, but not from others.

Late Archaic components generally occur in silty or silty-clay soils, which suggests low-energy flooding.

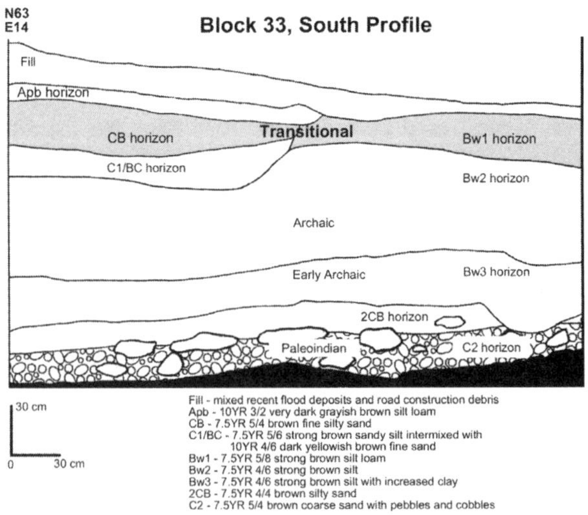

FIGURE 4.2
Soil profile, Wallis Site (36PE16).

But because rates of deposition were generally somewhat greater in the Late Archaic, components from this period appear to have fewer superimposed occupations than components from later periods. The differences in floodplain deposition clearly indicate that something different was happening in the Transitional Archaic environment, although there is still disagreement on what the difference was and how it affected human adaptation (Miller 1993; Vento et al. 1992; Vento, Chapter 1, this volume).

The Broadspear Tradition

Rhyolite

The likely source of rhyolite in the Susquehanna River valley is the Blue Ridge province of southern Pennsylvania. Studies of the distributions of diagnostic rhyolite points indicate that the material was used throughout prehistory, especially beginning in the Early Archaic period (Stewart 1984). The proportions of rhyolite in debitage assemblages, however, reveal a dramatic focus on the material between 3800 and 3000 BP not seen during any other period (Figure 4.3). The proportion of rhyolite in the debitage of Broadspear tradition components ranges as high as 88%. At Sites 36PE60 and 36PE61 and the Jacobs Site, well-defined rhyolite chipping clusters were preserved (Miller et al. 2009). On Calver Island, the southernmost of the sites, the intensive use of rhyolite began somewhat later. Debitage in components dating between 3800 and 3400 BP was predominantly a local argillite, but the assemblage also contained a high proportion of rhyolite tools. Debitage in components dating between 3300 and 3000 BP was more than 80% rhyolite.

The tools from these components were also predominantly rhyolite (Figure 4.4), although the proportions of rhyolite were not as high as those in the debitage. Rhyolite was used primarily to manufacture Susquehanna broadspears and other points, as well as hafted drills and scrapers. Some knives and scrapers were fashioned through bifacial retouching of large flakes. Expedient cores of rhyolite are virtually absent from Transitional Archaic components.

In the upper reaches of the Susquehanna Basin, the use of rhyolite was somewhat less intensive. Little

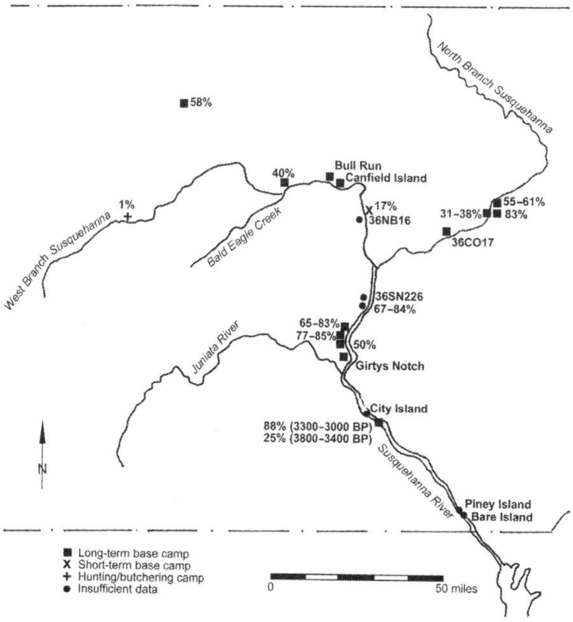

FIGURE 4.3
Proportion of rhyolite in debitage of Transitional Archaic components.

FIGURE 4.4
Rhyolite tools from Wallis Site (36PE16).

rhyolite debitage and no rhyolite tools were found at the Lick Run Site (36CD102), located on the West Branch of the river in Clearfield County (Miller et al. 2006). Instead, gray chert and Onondaga chert predominated. Of the Transitional Archaic artifacts at the Kettle Creek East Site (36CN199), 58% are made of rhyolite, with chert a strong second in importance (Petraglia, Knepper, and Rissetto 1998). Jasper is an important part of the lithic assemblages at several sites on the North Branch of the Susquehanna, indicating that trade in this area extended eastward into the Delaware River basin. At excavated sites well off the Susquehanna River, such as the Jacks Mill Site (36CE230) in Centre County (Hay and Graetzer 1985) and the Sugartown Site (36BL36) in Blair County (Dinsmore et al. 1995), Susquehanna and other broadspears of rhyolite were found, but very little rhyolite debitage was recovered, supporting a pattern in which rhyolite was traded up the river, fashioned into bifaces at sites along the riverbanks, and traded to the interior regions.

R. Michael Stewart (1989:54) has noted examples of what he terms "hoarding" in the Lake Ontario region, where large numbers of rhyolite points or blades indicate that rhyolite trade involving finished or near-finished rhyolite tools extended north of the Susquehanna Valley. Unfortunately, the data within the valley itself are not sufficient to identify the presence of hoarding or to reconstruct specific patterns of falloff in rhyolite tools or debitage. In light of many lines of evidence indicating increased sedentism during the Transitional Archaic, however, it is unlikely that task groups residing in areas as distant as the North and West Branches of the Susquehanna River would travel on procurement forays as far as 200 kilometers or more, given that suitable, even higher-quality, materials were present much closer.

The rhyolite trade network can be characterized as involving trade in quarry blanks or preforms from the quarry region upstream to sites along the Susquehanna River and its major branches. At these sites, the blanks were reduced to bifaces or tools, some for use and some for trade into the interior regions, as well as northward and eastward beyond the Susquehanna River drainage basin.

Steatite

Steatite, used primarily for the production of cooking vessels, was widely traded in the Midwest and Southeast. Indeed, thousands of steatite vessels were traded through the Poverty Point network alone. Kenneth Sassaman (1993, 1997) has argued that, in some areas of the Southeast, the network of trade in steatite was so important that it delayed the adoption of ceramics. In Pennsylvania, steatite moved primarily in the Susquehanna River basin. The number of sites in the CRGIS reporting steatite in the Delaware (N = 14) and Ohio (N = 8) River basins is small compared to that in the Susquehanna River basin (N = 124). There are seven known steatite quarry sites in the Lower Susquehanna River valley (Wholey 2011). Steatite occurs in nearly all of the major Transitional Archaic components along the Susquehanna River. Although fragments of thick-walled square vessels are found, there is a tremendous variety of vessel forms and decorations, including incised, gouged, and scalloped-rim decorations (Figure 4.5). Relatively few vessels are found at each site, however, and drill holes from repairs are common, suggesting that

FIGURE 4.5
Steatite bowl fragments from Site 36PE61.

FIGURE 4.6
Steatite beads (*left*) and pendant (*right*) from Sites 36AL480 and 36DA89, respectively.

steatite was a relatively scarce commodity. Although unmodified steatite fragments occur on sites along the Susquehanna River, the sample size is small, and it is unclear whether the steatite trade involved raw material, finished objects, or both.

Steatite was also used to manufacture beads and pendants, including a pendant from Calver Island (36DA89) and two disk-shaped beads from the Leetsdale Site (36AL480), located along the Ohio River (Figure 4.6; Miller and Marine 2005). Chemical sourcing of the steatite found at Leetsdale revealed that it most likely came from the southeastern Pennsylvania quarries, representing another example of the extension of the trade network to regions outside the Susquehanna Valley (Vento and Stahlman 2005).

Broadspears

Broad-bladed point forms such as those found at the Wallis Site (Figure 4.7) are common throughout the eastern United States during the Transitional Archaic period: Savannah River forms along the eastern coast and Piedmont; Genesee, Snook Kill, Perkiomen, and Susquehanna forms in New York, Pennsylvania, and into the Midwest; and the Mansion Inn/Wayland series in southern New England. Jay Custer (1996:172) notes that broadspears have been subjected to a variety of interpretations, including "specialized adaptations, migrations, and simple additions to the local tool kit."

FIGURE 4.7
Rhyolite points from Wallis Site (36PE16).

It has been argued that their large size makes broadspears unsuited for use as spear points (Moeller 1990). Jay Custer and Glenn Mellin (1986) examined broad-bladed points and found that they had lower penetrating capacity than narrow bifaces did. Wear and breakage patterns indicated that most of the broadspears in their sample of 599 were used as knives rather than as projectiles. In contrast, microwear analysis of points from Calver Island and three stratified sites excavated for the Route 11/15 project revealed no apparent differences in the use of broadspears versus stemmed and notched point types. All major point types were used as spear points or as knives; in many cases, spear points with impact fractures were subsequently used as knives. Of the sixty-nine broadspears analyzed by Larry Kimball (2004a, 2004b, 2006), which included Susquehanna as well as Perkiomen and Koens-Crispin broadspears,

70% showed macro- or microimpact fractures, and half had both impact fractures and evidence of use for butchering.

Data from these sites do support Custer's (1996) position that broadspears were not the only point type in use during this period. Stemmed points predominated over broadspears in the Transitional Archaic assemblages at Calver Island. Stemmed, notched, and triangular points were all present in assemblages from the Route 11/15 sites.

Custer's (1996) proposition that Snook Kill, Savannah River, and Lehigh/Koens-Crispen points are earlier than Susquehanna and Perkiomen points finds some support at Calver Island, where Savannah River, Koens-Crispin, and Perkiomen points predate 3300 BP, and Susquehanna broadspears are later. Susquehanna broadspears do occur, however, in contexts prior to 3300 BP farther upstream at Sites 36PE60 and 36PE61 and the Skvarek Site (36LU132) on the North Branch of the Susquehanna (Miller 1994). Along with the lack of rhyolite debitage, the absence of Susquehanna broadspears in the Piedmont and Lower Susquehanna River valley during the earlier half of the period may indicate that the trade network initially bypassed this region.

Those who have argued that broadspears were an adaptation to a warmer and drier climate have not specified exactly how this point type was beneficial under those conditions (Carr and Bergman 2001). Rather, evidence suggests that, as an addition to the tool kit, broadspears apparently represented a technological innovation that did not withstand the test of time. Although Susquehanna broadspears differ from Perkiomen and other types in being narrower and larger than earlier or later forms, the transition from Susquehanna broadspear to Orient fishtail does not appear to involve much more than a reduction in overall size. Along with microwear results, the formal characteristics of Susquehanna broadspears seem to argue against their being a specialized adaptation, although they may have been a distinctive marker of the rhyolite trade network.

The Late Archaic to Early Woodland Transition

In this section, the data from stratified sites are examined for differences among Late Archaic through Early Woodland components, with a focus on tools and tool use, tool-manufacturing technology, features, and subsistence, in an effort to identify and interpret adaptive changes might be taking place.

Tools and Tool Use

The stratified sites along the Susquehanna River show no evidence of significant changes in tool types or the increased use of any particular tool type from the Late Archaic through the Early Woodland period. Netsinkers, which have been cited as evidence for an increase in net fishing in the Transitional Archaic period and as part of the posited riverine focus, are found in Late Archaic occupations at the Canfield Island, Allenwood (36UN82), and Skvarek Sites on the North and West Branches of the Susquehanna (Bressler, Maietta, and Rockey 1983; Miller 1994; Wall 2000), at Sites 36PE60 and 36PE61 on the Central Susquehanna, and at the Calver Island Site in the Lower Susquehanna. There is no evidence at these sites that the use of net fishing increased from the Late Archaic to the Transitional Archaic. Heavy woodworking tools such as axes, adzes, and celts, which would have been used for building dugout canoes, were also used during both periods and are found in Late Archaic contexts at Calver Island, Memorial Park (36CN164), and 36PE61 (Hart et al. 1995; Miller, Marine, and Vento 2007; Miller et al. 2009). These data argue against a change in fishing techniques or an increase in heavy-duty woodworking as adaptive changes associated with the Transitional Archaic.

As noted above, broadspears, which have been cited as an adaptation to environmental change, were an additional point type rather than a replacement. Stemmed, notched, and triangular points continued in use during the Transitional Archaic period, with stemmed points most common in the

Lower Susquehanna Valley and notched points more common in the Upper. Susquehanna broadspears morphed into fishtails during the Orient phase, but stemmed and notched points continued in use into the Early Woodland period.

Extensive microwear analysis of points and tools from three Perry County sites was conducted as part of the Route 11/15 project (Kimball 2004a, 2004b, 2006). Unfortunately, because Early Woodland components at the three sites were intermixed in the plow zone with Middle and Late Woodland components, there are no definitive data from that period. Table 4.1 summarizes microwear data from the three sites for broadspears only. The interpretation of points as projectiles was based primarily on the presence of impact fractures. The analysis reveals that broadspears were used primarily as projectiles, with butchering usually a secondary use after the point was broken. No other uses for broadspears were identified.

Table 4.2 provides a summary of stemmed, notched, and other point types from Transitional Archaic contexts at the three sites. The distribution shows that these nonbroadspear point types, though used primarily as projectiles and for butchering, were also used for wedging, sawing, and boring materials such as antler, wood, and bone, among other activities. Points from Late Archaic contexts revealed a similar pattern, but with slightly heavier use for butchering after impact fractures and limited use for other activities (Table 4.3).

The microwear analysis indicates a greater variety of activities at Transitional Archaic sites. Transitional Archaic points other than broadspears were used more frequently than Late Archaic points for tasks other than butchering, a difference that holds even when broadspears and nonbroadspears are combined (Table 4.4). The wider variety of activities represented at the Transitional Archaic sites likely reflects site function and length of occupation at these sites rather than changes in point function or adaptive change. It does seem clear, however, that broadspears were apparently suited primarily for hunting and for butchering and not for working bone, wood, antler, and other materials. But nothing in the microwear analysis suggests that broadspears were an adaptation involving new and different tasks required by different environmental conditions.

TABLE 4.1 Microwear evidence: Broadspears from three sites

	Projectile Only	Butchery Only	Projectile and Butchery	Other Tasks
Susquehanna (N = 39)	15	6	18	0
Snook Kill (N = 4)	2	0	2	0
Perkiomen (N = 6)	3	0	3	0
Other (N = 10)	3	3	4	0
Total (N = 59)	23	9	27	0
Proportion	39%	15%	46%	0

TABLE 4.2 Microwear evidence: Transitional Archaic nonbroadspears from three sites

	Projectile Only	Butchery Only	Projectile and Butchery	Other Tasks
Notched (N = 22)	3	1	11	7
Stemmed (N = 13)	3	3	4	3
Other (N = 12)	5	1	5	1
Total (N = 47)	11	5	20	11
Proportion	23%	11%	43%	23%

TABLE 4.3 Microwear evidence: Late Archaic points from three sites

	Projectile Only	Butchery Only	Projectile and Butchery	Other Tasks
Notched (N = 20)	3	1	14	2
Stemmed (N = 6)	1	2	3	0
Other (N = 17)	8	1	8	0
Total (N = 43)	12	4	25	2
Proportion	28%	9%	58%	5%

TABLE 4.4 Microwear evidence from Late Archaic and Transitional Archaic periods

	Projectile Only	Butchery Only	Projectile and Butchery	Other Tasks
Late Archaic	28%	9%	58%	5%
Transitional Archaic	29%	12%	40%	19%

Tool-Manufacturing Technology

It has been argued that a change to a bifacial tool technology took place during the Transitional Archaic period and was related to climate change. Although rhyolite cores other than bifacial cores are virtually absent from Transitional Archaic components, and only 10 of 171 expedient cores reported from stratified contexts (fewer than 6%) are of rhyolite, core-and-flake tool technology is well represented in other lithic materials. The relative proportion of bifaces to cores increased during the Transitional Archaic at Calver Island, but was unchanged at three sites in Perry County (Table 4.5; differences in overall values between site locations are the result of differences in counting methods). The bifacial technology is overwhelmingly represented by rhyolite, which was used for points and hafted drills (Table 4.6).

William Andrefsky (1994) and Douglas Bamforth (1986) argue that raw material shortages can result in curated technologies and that such shortages can occur as a result of behavior as well as geography. Thus a material such as rhyolite that was acquired primarily through trade would likely be used for formal, or curated, technologies. Thus the apparent increase in bifacial technology is likely related to the trade network rather than to environmental adaptation.

TABLE 4.5 Biface:core ratios

	Calver Island		
	Bifaces	Cores	Ratio
Late Archaic	109	106	1:1
Transitional Archaic	30	19	1.6:1
Early Woodland	4	4	1:1
	Sites 36PE16, 36PE60, 36PE61		
	Bifaces	Cores	Ratio
Late Archaic	27	92	0.3:1
Transitional Archaic	39	113	0.3:1

TABLE 4.6 Calver Island biface:core ratios by lithic material

Rhyolite	Argillite	Chert	Slate
14.7:1	0.9:1	0.5:1	4.5:1

Features

The Susquehanna River data document the regional change in feature types from the Late Archaic to the Transitional Archaic. Nearly all of the sites excavated along the main stem of the Susquehanna River contain evidence of intensive Transitional Archaic occupations, as represented by the reuse of hearths and roasting pits and by relatively high artifact densities, particularly fire-cracked rock. In contrast, Late Archaic occupations at many of these sites appear to be much less intensive. These conclusions need to be considered within a geomorphological context: because sedimentation rates were higher during the Late Archaic, evidence of successive occupations in this period is vertically separated in the soil profile, whereas evidence of successive occupations during the Transitional Archaic may be more closely superimposed, thus making these later occupations appear to be more intensive. But differences in feature types are notable.

Late Archaic features are generally hearths with little evidence of reuse. On Calver Island, for example, features from the 5200–5000 BP occupations were generally small hearths, although one smudge pit or earth oven was found. Features of similar types were associated with occupations dating to 4400–4300 BP, but also include a single circular roasting pit with oxidized soil, a layer of charcoal lining the base, and a dense layer of fire-cracked rock (Figure 4.8), an early example of a type of feature that is relatively common in Transitional Archaic and later occupations.

Evidence was found of an increase in the intensity of occupation on Calver Island at around 3900 BP. It must be noted that the occupation zone is on an incipient A horizon, indicating a more stable surface and the likelihood of multiple superimposed occupations. But in addition to the higher artifact density, there is a distinct change in the type of features in this component. Although few of the Late Archaic hearths had fire-cracked rock, virtually all of the features from ca. 3900 BP contained fire-cracked rock, which was densely scattered outside them. The component also

FIGURE 4.8
Transitional Archaic roasting pit: Feature 47, Site 36DA89 (scale bar: 100 cm).

included a deep pit, possibly used for storage, and two earth oven–type features with bark layers.

After 3800 BP, roasting features become common and show clear evidence of reuse. Living floors are scattered with fire-cracked rock, some of which is likely from the cleaning and reuse of hearths, and some of which is in tight clusters suggesting dumps from stone boiling. The density of fire-cracked rock in dumps and scatters outside of features increased during the Transitional Archaic and occurred at about three times the density of Late Archaic occupations. This increase in fire-cracked rock has been recognized throughout the Middle Atlantic region. Along with steatite bowls for stone boiling and bark-lined earth ovens, the roasting pits indicate a change in cooking techniques likely involving food preparation for larger groups.

Features dated to the Early Woodland period include hearths, hearth refuse pits, and roasting pits and suggest a continuation of Transitional Archaic trends. Overall, the feature data suggest continuity with the Transitional Archaic.

Subsistence

Flotation analysis of Late Archaic, Transitional Archaic, and Early Woodland feature fill has consistently produced fragments of hickory nuts, walnuts, acorns, hazel nuts, and beechnuts, along with occasional seeds of fruits or berries. Although the botanical and faunal evidence clearly indicates a hunter-gatherer adaptation, changes in the specific focus of food procurement that might result from environmental change would be difficult to detect in the archaeological record. Residue analysis of steatite bowl fragments from Calver Island and two of the Route 11/15 sites indicates that native seeds, including possibly little barley and *Chenopodium*, were cooked in the vessels, likely using stone-boiling techniques. Since most of the evidence for the use of native seeds is from residues of steatite vessels, however, seeds could have been used in the Late Archaic period or earlier. Charred *Chenopodium* seeds from a dated feature suggest that native seeds were in use on Calver Island by 3900 BP (Miller, Marine, and Vento 2007). Squash rind has been found and dated to ca. 5405 BP at Memorial Park (Hart et al. 1995; Hart and Sidell 1997) and to ca. 3780 BP at Site 36SN21 (Miller 1995). Overall, the subsistence data suggest a gradually expanding use of food resources, which could be a response to either climate change or increased population density.

Conclusions

Based on the data discussed above, a number of conclusions were reached regarding the Transitional Archaic period in the Susquehanna River valley.

1. Data from stratified sites along the Susquehanna River show no changes in the types of tools that were used or in the ways they were used, from the Late Archaic through the Early Woodland period.
2. Broadspears were an addition to the tool kit and were used for hunting and butchering. Their size and shape likely made them unsuitable for other tasks such as working bone, wood, or antler. But there is no evidence that they represent an adaptive response to changed environmental conditions.

3. The apparent increase in bifacial technology is related to trade in rhyolite. The high proportions of debitage at sites along the river suggest that rhyolite raw material was being reduced to bifaces for trade up the Susquehanna River and its tributaries. Expedient tools of materials other than rhyolite were used from the Late Archaic through the Early Woodland.
4. The length of occupation and possibly group size appear to have increased during the Transitional Archaic at sites along the river. Changes in cooking methods, including the use of roasting pits and earth ovens, suggest food preparation for larger groups. The wider variety of tasks indicated by tools from Transitional Archaic components implies longer occupations, as do the use of steatite vessels and the reuse of hearths.
5. Evidence suggests that the diet was broadening to include native seed plants and squash, as occurred in the Midwest at about this time. But nuts and berries still dominate the botanical data, and there is no evidence of any significant changes in the basic hunter-gatherer procurement strategy.

Transitional Archaic occupations along the Susquehanna River were intensive, a definition based on the presence of elaborate cooking features such as roasting pits and earth ovens, hearth refuse pits indicating considerable reuse of hearths, and abundant fire-cracked rock. The use of steatite vessels suggests increased sedentism. Short-term camps such as those found during the Late Archaic period are not apparent along the Susquehanna River during the Transitional Archaic period. The Transitional Archaic settlement strategy entailed reduced mobility and occupations longer than those during the Late Archaic. Although excavated Early Woodland components are relatively rare, the settlement strategy during this period appears to revert to one more like that of the Late Archaic, with both long- and short-term base camps, as the importance of the rhyolite trade decreased. Although social relationships cannot be determined from archaeological data, it is possible that the Late Archaic/Early Woodland pattern represents a seasonal fissioning process generally referred to as a "macroband/microband" type of social organization. And although smaller, possibly microband camps dating to the Transitional Archaic are identifiable in tributary valleys of the Susquehanna River, periodic fissioning appears to have been abandoned along the main stem of the river during the Transitional Archaic, and the intensive occupations were focused along major tributaries to take advantage of the benefits of the trade network.

Whereas the upriver portion of the trade network that was in place during the period from 3800 to 3000 BP is clearly represented in the archaeological record by the distributions of rhyolite and steatite, nothing is preserved of whatever materials were moving in the downstream portion of the network. These may have included basketry or items fashioned of bone or wood that were not preserved.

The use of and trade in rhyolite decline after about 3000 BP. Debitage proportions on Calver Island dropped from 81% to 50% by 2600 BP, and steatite largely disappeared. Rhyolite proportions dropped from 83% to 51% in the Orient component at the Jacobs Site; rhyolite is present in only a very small proportion of later Woodland assemblages.

The reasons for the development and disappearance of the trade network are unclear, despite the addition of so many Transitional Archaic components to the archaeological database. Trade networks begin to appear throughout the eastern United States in the Late and Transitional Archaic periods, during which population density and competition for resources were increasing. Although both occurred in the Transitional Archaic period between hunter-gathering and horticulture phases, the trade network of the Susquehanna River and that of Poverty Point in the southeastern United States differed radically in scale and underlying social organization. What is more, Poverty Point was a regional distribution center, whereas no such center was present in the Susquehanna River valley.

In summary, the Broadspear tradition of the Transitional Archaic period was a time of increasing population density and experimentation with new food sources. Steatite bowls represent an innovation in methods of cooking. The site data suggest a relatively high degree of sedentism, with large group sizes. Sites located along the major tributaries of the Susquehanna were likely situated there to facilitate participation in a basin-wide trade network. In turn, the trade network mitigated risk associated with high population density and the need to intensify food production and bring new food sources into the diet. It is possible that population density actually did decrease during the Early Woodland period, as people moved out of the Susquehanna Valley to participate in developments associated with the Adena and Meadowood cultures. With a smaller population and less competition, the advantages of the Susquehanna River trade network diminished and settlement returned to the Late Archaic pattern.

Acknowledgments

Most of the sites discussed in this chapter were investigated in projects funded by the Pennsylvania Department of Transportation, the Pennsylvania Turnpike Commission, the U.S. Army Corps of Engineers, and other state and federal agencies. Numerous individuals and organizations completed field investigations and data analysis for these sites. Most of the data and photographs used in this chapter are from projects conducted by KCI Technologies. Larry Kimball of Appalachian State University conducted microwear analysis. Justine Woodward McKnight conducted the botanical analysis.

REFERENCES

Andrefsky, William, Jr.
1994 Raw-Material Availability and the Organization of Technology. *American Antiquity* 59 (1): 21–34.

Bamforth, Douglas B.
1986 Technological Efficiency and Tool Curation. *American Antiquity* 51 (1): 38–50.

Bressler, James P., Ricki Maietta, and Karen Rockey
1983 *Canfield Island Through the Ages: 36LY37*. North Central Chapter 8, Society for Pennsylvania Archaeology and Lycoming County Historical Society, Williamsport.

Carr, Kurt W., and Christopher Bergman
2001 Late Pleistocene Blade Core, Paleoindian Bifacial Core, Broadspear Biface Technology, and Cultural Ecology in the Middle Atlantic Region. Paper presented at 66th Annual Meeting of the Society for American Archaeology, New Orleans.

Custer, Jay F.
1996 *Prehistoric Cultures of Eastern Pennsylvania*. Anthropological Series 7. Pennsylvania Historical and Museum Commission, Harrisburg.

Custer, Jay F., and Glenn S. Mellin
1986 Analysis of "Broadspears" from Delaware: Form, Function, and Distribution. *Bulletin of the Archaeological Society of Delaware* 22:1–29.

Dinsmore, Douglas, Gary F. Coppock, Patricia E. Miller, and Conran A. Hay
1995 *Data Recovery at Sugartown, Site 36B136, L.R. 1061, Sections 001 and 002, Blair County, Pennsylvania.* Report prepared for Pennsylvania Department of Transportation, Engineering District 9-0, Hollidaysburg. Archaeological and Historical Consultants, Inc., Centre Hall, Pennsylvania.

Hart, John P., and Nancy Asch Sidell
1997 Additional Evidence for Early Cucurbit Use in the North Eastern Woodlands East of the Allegheny Front. *American Antiquity* 62 (3): 523–37.

Hart, John P., Jeffrey R. Graybill, David L. Cremeens, Michael G. Spitzer, John P. Nass, Nancy Asch Sidell, et al.
1995 *Archaeological Investigations at the Memorial Park Site (36Cn164), Clinton County, Pennsylvania*. Report prepared for U.S. Army Corps of Engineers, Baltimore District. GAI Consultants, Inc., Monroeville, Pennsylvania.

Hay, Conran A., and Mary A. Graetzer
1985 *Archaeological Investigations at the Jacks Mill Site (36Ce230): Final Mitigation Research*. Report prepared for Boalsburg Limited Partnership, Boalsburg, Pennsylvania. Archaeological and Historical Consultants, Inc., Centre Hall, Pennsylvania.

Joyce, Arthur A.

1988 Early/Middle Holocene Environments in the Middle Atlantic Region: A Revised Reconstruction. In *Holocene Human Ecology in Northeastern North America*, edited by George P. Nicholas, 185–214. Plenum Press, New York.

Kimball, Larry R.

2004a *Microwear Analysis of Archaic Tools from 36Pe60, Pennsylvania.* In Patricia E. Miller, Frank J. Vento, James T. Marine, Sharon White, and Eloisa A. Pollack, *Phase III Archaeological Data Recovery, Route 11/15 Improvements (SR 0011, Section 008), Juniata and Perry Counties, Pennsylvania*, Volume 3, Section 9.9.1, III-833–III-965. Report prepared for Pennsylvania Department of Transportation, Engineering District 8-0, Harrisburg. KCI Technologies, Inc., Mechanicsburg, Pennsylvania, 2009.

2004b *Microwear Analysis of Lithic Tools from 36Pe61, Pennsylvania.* In Patricia E. Miller, Frank J. Vento, James T. Marine, Sharon White, and Eloisa A. Pollack, *Phase III Archaeological Data Recovery, Route 11/15 Improvements (SR 0011, Section 008), Juniata and Perry Counties, Pennsylvania*, Volume 4, Section 9.9.1, IV-550–IV-635. Report prepared for Pennsylvania Department of Transportation, Engineering District 8-0, Harrisburg. KCI Technologies, Inc., Mechanicsburg, Pennsylvania, 2009.

2006 *Microwear Analysis of Paleo-Indian and Archaic Tools from 36Pe16, Pennsylvania.* In Patricia E. Miller, Frank J. Vento, James T. Marine, Sharon White, and Eloisa A. Pollack, *Phase III Archaeological Data Recovery, Route 11/15 Improvements (SR 0011, Section 008), Juniata and Perry Counties, Pennsylvania*, Volume 2, Section 9.6, II-852–II-909. Report prepared for Pennsylvania Department of Transportation, Engineering District 8-0, Harrisburg. KCI Technologies, Inc., Mechanicsburg, Pennsylvania, 2009.

Miller, Patricia E.

1993 *Prehistoric Settlement Patterns in the Bald Eagle Creek Drainage of Central Pennsylvania.* Ph.D. dissertation, Department of Anthropology, Pennsylvania State University, University Park. University Microfilms, Ann Arbor, Michigan.

1994 *Archaeological Data Recovery, The Skvarek Site (Site 36LU132), Proposed Shickshinny/Mocanaqua Bridge Replacement (S.R. 0239), Salem and Conyngham Townships, Luzerne County, Pennsylvania.* Report prepared for Luzerne County Commissioners and Pennsylvania Department of Transportation, Engineering District 4-0, Wilkes-Barre. Archaeological and Historical Consultants, Inc., Centre Hall, Pennsylvania.

1995 *Archaeological Data Recovery: Sites 36Sn220 and 36Sn221 and Additional Phase II Survey: Site 36Sn21, Safer Highways for Economic Development Project, S.R. 0011, Section 003 (T.R. 11 and 15), Snyder County, Pennsylvania.* Report prepared for Pennsylvania Department of Transportation, Engineering District 3-0, Montoursville. Archaeological and Historical Consultants, Inc., Centre Hall, Pennsylvania.

Miller, Patricia E., and James T. Marine

2005 *Investigations in Area 2, Prehistoric Component (Chapter 7), Data Recovery at Site 36AL480, Leetsdale Industrial Park, Leetsdale, Pennsylvania, Monongahela Locks and Dams Numbers 2, 3, and 4 Modernization Project.* Report prepared for U.S. Army Corps of Engineers, Pittsburgh District. KCI Technologies, Inc., Mechanicsburg, Pennsylvania.

Miller, Patricia E., James T. Marine, N. Sheehan, and Frank J. Vento

2006 *Phase III Archaeological Data Recovery, The Irwin Site (36CD102), SR 0879, Section A01, Lick Run Bridge Replacement Project, Clearfield County, Pennsylvania.* Report prepared for Pennsylvania Department of Transportation, Engineering District 2-0, Clearfield. KCI Technologies, Inc., Mechanicsburg, Pennsylvania.

Miller, Patricia E., James T. Marine, and Frank J. Vento

2007 *Phase II/III Archaeological Survey at Site 36Da89 on Calver Island, Susquehanna River Bridge Replacement Project, Dauphin and York Counties, Pennsylvania.* Report prepared for Pennsylvania Turnpike Commission, Harrisburg. KCI Technologies, Inc., Mechanicsburg, Pennsylvania.

Miller, Patricia E., Frank J. Vento, James T. Marine, Sharon White, and Eloisa A. Pollack

2009 *Phase III Archaeological Data Recovery, Route 11/15 Improvements (SR 0011, Section 008), Juniata and Perry Counties, Pennsylvania*, Volumes 1–6. Report prepared for Pennsylvania Department of Transportation, Engineering District 8-0, Harrisburg. KCI Technologies, Inc., Mechanicsburg, Pennsylvania.

Moeller, Roger W.

1990 *Experiments and Observations on the Terminal Archaic of the Middle Atlantic Region.* Archaeological Services, Bethlehem, Connecticut.

Petraglia, Michael, Dennis Knepper, and John Rissetto

1998 The Nature of Prehistoric Activities on Kettle Creek, An Upland Tributary of the West Branch of the Susquehanna. *Journal of Middle Atlantic Archaeology* 14:13–38.

Sassaman, Kenneth E.

1993 *Early Pottery in the Southeast: Tradition and Innovation in Cooking Technology.* University of Alabama Press, Tuscaloosa.

1997 Refining Soapstone Vessel Chronology in the Southeast. *Early Georgia* 25 (1): 1–20.

Stewart, R. Michael

1984 South Mountain (Meta) Rhyolite: A Perspective on Prehistoric Trade and Exchange in the Middle Atlantic Region. In *Prehistoric Lithic Exchange Systems in the Middle Atlantic Region*, edited by Jay F. Custer, 14–44.

Monograph 3. Center for Archaeological Research, University of Delaware, Newark.

1989 Trade and Exchange in Middle Atlantic Region Prehistory. *Archaeology of Eastern North America* 17:14–78.

Vento, Frank J., Harold B. Rollins, R. Michael Stewart, Paul A. Raber, and William Johnson

1992 *Genetic Stratigraphy, Climate Change, and Deep Burial of Archaeological Sites in Alluvial Contexts within the Susquehanna, Ohio, and Delaware River Drainages.* Report prepared for Bureau for Historic Preservation, Pennsylvania Historical and Museum Commission. Harrisburg. Clarion University of Pennsylvania, Clarion.

Vento, Frank J., and Patty Stahlman

2005 *NAA of Selected Steatite Samples from the Leetsdale Site (36A1480), Allegheny County, Pennsylvania.* Report prepared U.S. Army Corps of Engineers, Pittsburgh District. Clarion University of Pennsylvania, Clarion.

Wall, Robert D.

2000 *Phase III Archaeological Investigations, 36Un82, Allenwood Federal Correctional Complex, Sanitary Water Treatment Facility, Union County, Pennsylvania.* Report prepared for U.S. Department of Justice, Federal Bureau of Prisons, Washington, D.C. Cultural Resource Group, Louis Berger & Associates, Inc., Washington, D.C.

Weed, Carol S., and William P. Wenstrom (editors)

1992 *Cultural Resources Investigations of 36LU90 (Jacobs Site) and 36LU105 (Gould Island Sites), Luzerne County, Pennsylvania.* Report prepared for Transcontinental Gas Pipe Line Corporation, Houston, Texas. New World Research, Inc., New Orleans.

Wholey, Heather A.

2011 Steatite: A Landscape Perspective. *Journal of Middle Atlantic Archaeology* 27:113–20.

Witthoft, John

1953 Broad Spear Points and the Transitional Period Cultures. *Pennsylvania Archaeologist* 23 (1): 4–31.

5.

Rethinking the Transitional Archaic Period in the Upper Delaware Valley

A VIEW FROM THE "ORIENT"

Joseph R. Blondino

ABSTRACT

The term "Transitional" can be somewhat problematic when applied to archaeological or cultural periods. Although it can indeed be argued that all cultures are in a constant state of flux, and therefore always "transitional," it can also be demonstrated that certain time periods have been marked by cultural change at an accelerated rate; an example from the relatively recent past would be the Industrial Revolution of the eighteenth–nineteenth centuries. I have chosen the term "Transitional Archaic" to refer to a roughly 1,000 year period bridging what has otherwise been considered the late Late Archaic and the early Early Woodland, an implicit acknowledgment that a sufficiently accelerated rate of cultural change during this period is evident in the archaeological record to warrant use of the term "Transitional." This chapter will discuss some of my own views on the Transitional Archaic period from the perspective of research in the Upper Delaware Valley. Although first focusing on the Orient phase, this research has led to a necessary expansion to the whole of the Transitional Archaic period in the Upper Delaware, which I define as encompassing the Broadspear through Fishtail (Orient) phases. I hope that what follows, though admittedly based on a combination of empirical data and informed speculation regarding the Transitional Archaic populations of the Upper Delaware, will nonetheless provide some useful insights into the way we think about this period of regional prehistory.

The Orient Phase

Following the Broadspear phase of the Transitional Archaic period, the prehistory of the Upper Delaware Valley enters what is referred to in the regional literature as the "Orient phase," defined largely by the introduction of a new narrow-bladed biface variant, the fishtail point (Custer 1996:178; Kinsey 1972:355). Although the lifeways of Orient peoples seem largely a continuation of those of the earlier broadspear-using populations, some important technological developments occur during Orient times; perhaps most significant among these is the continued development of durable (i.e., nonperishable) container technology. And although use of carved soapstone bowls continues from Broadspear times, early pottery is also a hallmark of the Orient phase, a development that has caused some researchers to designate the Orient phase as marking the beginning of the Woodland period (e.g., Kraft 2001). I would argue, however, that the relatively small amount of early pottery found at Orient sites, though certainly an important technological innovation, represents no real cultural watershed and does not justify setting the Orient phase apart from the preceding phases of the Transitional Archaic; indeed, the early pottery vessels from Orient sites appear to have been used in a similar fashion to their carved stone antecedents. Of course, among the most archaeologically salient aspects of the Transitional Archaic are the ever-present fire-cracked rock (FCR) features, and the Orient phase marks the peak of their use in the Middle Atlantic region, in terms of both size and number (Cavallo 1987:279). Viewed in the light of the apparent focus of Transitional Archaic settlement on high-order streams like the Delaware River, FCR features have typically been interpreted as relating to the processing of riverine resources (e.g., Kraft 1970). The remainder of this chapter will briefly review some aspects of the Orient phase as it is manifested in the Upper Delaware Valley; it will offer a closer consideration of the locations of Orient and earlier Transitional Archaic sites on the landscape with an eye toward the possible functions of fire-cracked rock features and the nature of the resources they may have been used to process.

The Transitional Archaic period is dated to roughly 3750–2750 BP (1800–800 BC) in the Upper Delaware Valley, with the Orient phase occupying approximately the last 400 years of that range (Table 5.1). It should be noted, however, that not only are there

TABLE 5.1 Radiocarbon chronology for Transitional Archaic sites in Upper Delaware Valley

Site	Association	Date in Years BP	Laboratory Number	Calibrated Dates	Reference
Driftstone	Broadspear (Lehigh/Snook Kill)	3740 ± 70	Beta-131311	4159–3982 BP or 2348–1943 BC	Blondino 2008
Peters-Albrecht	Broadspear (Lehigh)	3670 ± 100	Y-1826	4293–3704 BP or 2344–1755 BC	Kinsey 1972
Miller Field	Broadspear (Perkiomen)	3670 ± 120	Y-2587	4300–3695 BP or 2351–1746 BC	Kraft 1970
Zimmerman	Broadspear (Susquehanna)	3600 ± 80	Y-2344	4098–3693 BP or 2149–1744 BC	Kinsey 1972
Miller Field	Broadspear (Perkiomen)	3590 ± 100	Y-2588	4156–3632 BP or 2207–1683 BC	Kraft 1970
Brodhead-Heller	Broadspear (Perkiomen)	3570 ± 100	Y-2340	4101–3612 BP or 2152–1663 BC	Kinsey 1972
Faucett	Broadspear (Perkiomen)	3450 ± 120	Y-2478	3992–3445 BP or 2043–1496 BC	Kinsey 1972
Driftstone	Unknown	3270 ± 30	UGAMS-02949	3571–3445 BP or 1622–1496 BC	Blondino 2008
Zimmerman	Fishtail (Dry Brook)	3230 ± 120	Y-2343	3726–3158 BP or 1777–1209 BC	Kinsey 1972
Miller Field	Fishtail (Orient)	3170 ± 120	Y-2589	3646–3065 BP or 1697–1116 BC	Kraft 1970
Brodhead-Heller	Fishtail (Orient)	3120 ± 120	Y-2339	3594–2993 BP or 1645–1044 BC	Kinsey 1972
Driftstone	Fishtail (Orient)	3070 ± 80	Beta-43899	3452–3057 BP or 1503–1108 BC	Blondino 2008
Driftstone	Fishtail (Orient)	2920 ± 30	UGAMS-02948	3160–2969 BP or 1211–1020 BC	Blondino 2008
Faucett	Fishtail (Orient)	2760 ± 100	Y-2477	3159–2729 BP or 1210–780 BC	Kinsey 1972
Smithfield Beach	Steatite Vessel Fragment (Orient?)	2710 ± 150	Beta-15568	3180–2420 BP or 1231–471 BC	Fischler and Mueller 1988

Note: Although other dates falling within the Transitional Archaic range exist for Upper Delaware Valley sites, only those having definite association with Transitional archaeological deposits and diagnostic artifacts are presented. UGAMS-02949 was not associated with diagnostic artifacts, but was stratigraphically between Fishtail and Broadspear components. All dates calibrated using Calib 7.0.

relatively few dates for this phase, but also that, with the exception of those from the recent excavations at the Driftstone Site, where samples were assayed using accelerator mass spectrometry (AMS), all dates were made using the traditional radiometric technique and have rather large standard deviations. As a result, it is somewhat difficult to establish firm bracketing dates for either the Broadspear or the Orient phase. Additionally, it is uncertain whether apparent overlaps with the bracketing dates for earlier and later cultural manifestations, and possibly also overlaps between dates for Fishtail and Broadspear components, have any basis in prehistoric reality. It is therefore difficult to establish the Broadspear and Orient phases as cultural rather than temporal units. More data from well-stratified sites are needed to refine the chronology and address some of these basic issues.

One of our best opportunities to study the Orient phase in the Upper Delaware Valley comes from the Driftstone Site (36NM244), located along the Delaware River just south of Portland, Pennsylvania. Having been made aware of the site a few years ago by its discoverer, local avocational archaeologist Donald Kline, I made arrangements to renew excavations there. In the summer of 2007, Temple University conducted a field school in prehistoric archaeology at the Driftstone Site. Between Kline's excavations and Temple's, approximately 285 square meters (3,050 ft^2) of the site have been excavated (Blondino 2008). Investigations at the site have produced numerous Orient bifaces, a portion of a carved steatite bowl, and a small amount of steatite-tempered pottery. Because the Orient component at the site is stratigraphically separated from other components present by thick packages of sterile sediment both above and below the Orient level, mixing of components is not an issue here. Additionally, the identification of "dead zones" across the site, where few or no artifacts were recovered, suggests that only a single occupation is present since a revisited site would appear as a relatively continuous artifact deposit.

Of course, as at any proper Orient site in the Upper Delaware, large fire-cracked rock features were also identified. Portions of four of these have been excavated, two by Kline and two by the Temple field school, and at least one other large stone feature has been revealed by probing. Two distinct types of FCR features were identified at Driftstone. A feature of the first type, a dense concentration of fire-cracked rock lying within a shallow, basin-shaped pit, is extremely rich in organic material, but with very little ash or charcoal. A similar feature ("Hearth #8") is described for the Transitional Archaic component at the Miller Field Site (Kraft 1970:43). A feature of the second type, a "classic" Transitional Archaic FCR feature, consists of a large scatter of highly fractured rock having little depth and apparently sitting directly on the ancient ground surface and measures more than 140 by 185 centimeters (4.6 by 6.1 ft.), as revealed by excavation and probing. Features of the second type are found on all of the major Orient sites in the Upper Delaware and are commonly quite large, easily in excess of 140 centimeters along their greatest dimension, with some being much larger than that (Kinsey 1972:163, 1975:86, 309; Kraft 1970:40). Like those encountered at Driftstone, these features generally contain relatively little ash or charcoal, and what is present seems to be scattered within and around the features rather than concentrated within them. Although some charcoal was noted among and beneath the rocks in some of the FCR features at the Miller Field and Brodhead-Heller Sites, it does not appear to be present in great quantities, and although these features are referred to as "hearths," it is unclear whether fires were actually burned directly on their stones.

Fire-Cracked Rock Features

Elucidating the function of FCR features is clearly of critical importance to our understanding of the lifeways of Orient and other Transitional Archaic peoples. Several hypotheses for the functions of such features have been proposed. The larger fire-cracked rock features of the type most common on Upper

Delaware Valley Orient sites have traditionally been interpreted as large hearths used for the smoking or drying of fish or other meats (e.g., Kraft 2001). But the fact that the features tend to contain relatively little ash or charcoal and the sediments beneath them show no visible evidence of thermal alteration seems quite problematic for the traditional interpretation: fires maintained long enough to create such copious quantities of fire-cracked rock would be expected to leave behind far more evidence of burning. On the other hand, experimental work by William Schindler (2006) has demonstrated that large, hot fires are not necessary for smoking meats, and that low, smoky fires are sufficient. And observation of Schindler's experimental smoking platform revealed that much of the charcoal overlying the rock pavement was washed away with spring flooding (R. Michael Stewart, personal communication, July 25, 2011). Given the amount of time that fires would have likely been maintained on these stone platforms, however, some ash and charcoal among the FCR in quantities suggestive of in situ burning and some evidence of thermally altered sediments would still be expected.

Although we could certainly spend plenty of time trying to defend the "platform hearth" hypothesis despite its problems, the simplest explanation is most likely the correct one: if there is no strong evidence of fires being burned directly on these platforms, then the simplest explanation for the FCR features is, of course, that they were dumps for shattered stones transported from other areas where fires were actually burned. Based on work at sites in the Middle Delaware Valley, John Cavallo (1987) has suggested that some of the features are pot boiler dumps related to stone-boiling activities; evidence that may support this has been recovered from the Abbott Farm Area B Site. Alternatively, FCR dumps could represent residue from cooking in earth ovens. This may be the case at the Driftstone Site, where two distinct feature types are present (Blondino 2008). It is possible that one feature type relates to the use of hot rock, whereas the other relates to the discard of such rock; the proximity of the two types at one locus at Driftstone could represent an earth oven and associated dump for stones too fractured to be of any further use. Finally, we cannot discount the possibility that multiple activities involving the use of hot rock are taking place during the Transitional Archaic period and that aspects of all of the above hypotheses are correct.

No matter the specific activity or activities that created these features, it seems safe to assume that they were related to the processing of some sort of food resource. The sheer amount of fire-cracked rock found in them suggests intensive resource extraction and processing, most likely organized at a community level (Kinsey 1972), and a concomitant shift in hunter-gatherer economy from a simpler foraging strategy to one focused on the collection of particular types of food resources. Augusto Oyuela-Caycedo and Renee Bonzani (2005:41, 48) have pointed out that redundant features (multiple features of the same type in a given location) are suggestive of intensive processing of resources. This certainly seems to be the case at Upper Delaware Valley Transitional Archaic sites, where FCR features are so common as to be a hallmark of the time period.

Environment, Resource Use, and Subsistence

The question then becomes one of identifying the resources that are being so intensively exploited at sites with FCR features. It has often been assumed (e.g., Kraft 2001) that the obvious answer is fish since the sites containing these features are typically located on the floodplains of high-order streams such as the Delaware River. But if these features are related to fish processing, then we must wonder why we do not see such extensive FCR platforms at sites from later time periods, when we know or can assume that large-scale fish harvesting was occurring. Let us therefore consider the possibility that the resources processed using all of this hot rock during the Transitional Archaic period might have been processed less intensively, or at least differently, before and after that time.

Transitional Archaic subsistence practices are usually interpreted as being linked to resources available in the two major features dominating the landscape of the Upper Delaware Valley: the river itself, which would have provided fish, and the adjacent uplands, which would have provided mast-producing trees and abundant game. But there is a third landscape feature adjacent to the Upper Delaware sites that warrants serious consideration: the small streams linking the river to the uplands. While working at the Driftstone Site, I was struck by the location of what seemed to be a major site along a tiny, first-order stream that, during the summer months, was barely more than a swampy rut with a trickle of water going through it. In looking at the locations of other large Orient sites in the Upper Delaware, I noticed that they were often in similar settings. In an attempt to determine whether the pattern I seemed to perceive had any validity, I turned to the Pennsylvania Archaeological Site Survey (PASS) files to assess the locations of Orient sites throughout the Upper Delaware.

For the purposes of this study, the Upper Delaware Valley was defined as the section of the valley between the confluence of the Delaware and Lehigh Rivers at Easton and the large bend in the river at Matamoras, where the river exits the rather narrow and steep-sided gorge through which its upper reaches flow. Within this section, the boundaries of the area under consideration extended 2,000 meters from the river in order to encompass the river's floodplain, ancient terraces, and immediately adjacent uplands. Using Pennsylvania's Cultural Resources Geographical Information System (CRGIS), I reviewed the site survey files for all archaeological sites that fell within this zone. I considered only those sites for which diagnostic point data were available. Each site that had yielded Orient or Dry Brook fishtail points, or both, was examined, plotted on a topographic map, and the order of the nearest stream other than the Delaware River was recorded, as was the distance of the site from that stream. Stream order was defined following the Strahler scheme as described by Luna Leopold (1994:225), in which a first-order stream is defined as one having no tributaries feeding into it, a second-order stream as formed by the junction of two streams of the first order, and so on.

In all, twenty-five sites containing fishtail points were found to be located within the study area (Table 5.2). Of these, sixteen (64%) were situated in locations where the nearest stream other than the Delaware River was a first-order stream. If we include the two sites that are adjacent to second-order streams, the percentage increases to 72%. Based on this admittedly rather simple exercise, there would appear to be a correlation between the location of Orient sites and low-order streams. As this apparent pattern emerged, however, I began to question whether it reflected an actual preference by Orient peoples for such settings, or whether what I was seeing was merely a function of the physiography of the Upper Delaware Valley. After all, in most locations in the Upper Delaware, the closest stream other than the river is a first- or second-order stream. But it is the proximity of the sites to these low-order streams that is telling. Of the eighteen sites situated on a first- or second-order stream, twelve (or 67%) are within 200 meters of that stream. Additionally, only two of the confluences of *major* streams (third-order or higher) with the Delaware have mapped Orient sites associated with them: the Egypt Mills Site on Tom's Creek and the Peters-Albrecht Site (36PI22) on Bushkill Creek. Although, for purposes of this exercise, I quantified only data relating to Orient sites, a review of mapped locations of sites dating to other time periods appears to show a random distribution with regard to proximity to first- and second-order streams, with many of these sites located at considerably greater distances from these low-order streams and associated with the more major confluences. Interestingly, 80% of the Orient sites in the study area also contain Broadspear components, suggesting that this apparent preference for locations near low-order streams may hold true not simply for the Orient phase but for the whole of the Transitional Archaic period.

TABLE 5.2 Orient Fishtail site data from Upper Delaware Valley study area in Pennsylvania

Site	Order of Nearest Stream	Distance from Nearest Stream in Meters	Broadspear Component?
36NM4	1	600	X
36NM12	3	200	X
36NM15	1	100	X
36NM45	6	60	X
36NM244	1	150	X
36NM254	1	25	—
36MR5	1 (extinct)	5	X
36MR12	1	260	—
36MR43	6	110	—
36MR179	6	15	X
36PI2	1	100	X
36PI7	1	220	X
36PI12	3	530	—
35PI13a	2	540	X
36PI14	1	40	X
36PI21	3	120	—
36PI30	2	10	X
36PI33	1	40	X
36PI35	1	80	X
36PI46	1	960	X
36PI131	1	540	X
36PI132	Delaware River	10	X
36PI158	1	150	—
36PI160	1	200	X
36PI238	1	550	X

What might be the appeal of these low-order stream settings? Why settle next to a trickle of water when there are otherwise identical landforms situated on the larger tributaries of the Delaware River? It may have more to do with the ecosystems surrounding those low-order streams than with the streams themselves. There are mapped wetlands associated with most of these smaller tributaries and the sites that are located adjacent to them. As mentioned previously, the stream entering the Delaware River just above the Driftstone Site is little more than a sluggish trickle through low swampy ground during the summer months. The Brodhead-Heller Site (36PI7) is located next to a similar stream and associated wetland, as is Site 36PI35 nearby. Because national wetlands inventory maps (U.S. Fish and Wildlife Service 2011) show the wetlands at Brodhead-Heller as having been partially drained or ditched to facilitate drainage, it is likely that they were considerably more extensive in prehistoric times. Although the Peters-Albrecht Site lies along a third-order stream, the Bushkill Creek, it is located near extensive wetlands that border the creek as it traverses the floodplain near its confluence with the Delaware River. Because New Jersey does not yet have a system like Pennsylvania's CRGIS, I have thus far not been able to obtain corresponding data from the New Jersey side of the river; however, similar associations are apparent at the two major Orient sites on the New Jersey side. The Harrys Farm Site (Kraft 1975) is located roughly equidistant between two first-order streams draining the adjacent uplands and is only a short distance downstream from a fairly large wetland area near Dimicks Ferry. Just upstream, the Miller Field Site is surrounded by extensive mapped wetlands along Vancampens Brook; Herbert Kraft (1970:6) notes that this is an area preferentially dammed by beaver, which may well have been the case in prehistoric times as well. Interestingly, these two sites are located adjacent to the only large wetland areas mapped for this stretch of the Delaware Valley between the Delaware Water Gap and Wallpack Bend on the New Jersey side of the river.

Although the archaeological significance of wetlands in the Middle Atlantic region and the Northeast has certainly been discussed elsewhere (e.g., Funk 1992; Hasenstab 1991; Nicholas 1991:31–32, 1998a), researchers interested in the prehistoric importance of such environments have focused primarily on large marshes, swamps, tidal zones, and other rather extensive wetland areas. They have largely ignored smaller wetlands, such as those bordering low-order streams, despite their rich, if areally limited, biological resources. For purposes of the present discussion, I define wetlands following George Nicholas (1998b:721) as "land that is (a) seasonally or periodically water-covered or saturated, (b) supports hydrophytic vegetation, and/or (c) has hydric soils." Event-controlled saturated areas such as flood chutes and floodplain backswamps would therefore qualify as wetlands under this definition. Even though many of these locations may not be mapped as wetlands because of their relatively small size or because of sampling error in regional wetland identification surveys, they are nonetheless important landscape features that must be considered along with other geomorphic, hydrologic, and environmental controls on prehistoric site selection.

To meet the above criteria as a wetland, an area need not be large; it need only have saturated soils or a shallow water cover, and the landscape of the Upper Delaware Valley contains many such areas. Low-order streams draining the eastern front of the Appalachian Plateau in Pennsylvania reach the low relief of the Delaware River's floodplains and carve out shallow channels as they cross broad expanses of alluvial bottomland and low terraces. As they traverse the floodplain, the channels of these streams often contain only moist soils with no significant water flow or a sluggish flow only a few centimeters deep. Stream flow in some cases, such as at the Driftstone Site, is so low that significant slackwater areas exist at the confluence with the Delaware River, even at times of normal flow for the larger stream. Low-lying areas within the floodplain of the Upper Delaware hold great potential for having been important event-controlled wetlands, possibly even more so in Transitional Archaic times, for which there is abundant evidence of overbanking events. The soils of an inundated flood chute may remain wet for quite some time following the recession of floodwaters, and seasonally persistent backwater swamps may form where recently flooded bottomland meets an influx of surface runoff at the slope break to the uplands.

All of the above types of wetland environments, although perhaps somewhat limited in extent, could have produced numerous resources important to prehistoric populations. Referring primarily to larger wetland areas, Nicholas (1991) has pointed out that "temperate zone swamps and marshes are among the most biologically productive ecological zones known anywhere." We must not, however, discount the equally productive, if smaller, wetland environs bordering low-order, low-gradient (floodplain) streams. Though I do not propose to provide an exhaustive list of economically useful plants available in such environments, I will point out that wetlands are host to numerous plant species that may have provided Transitional Archaic peoples with important resources. Just a few of the wetland species with food value include *Sagittaria* (duck potato), *Typha* (cattail), *Pontederia cordata* (pickerelweed), and *Peltandra* (arrow arum), all of which are known to have been used by native peoples (Densmore 1974; Messner 2008; Rountree, Clark, and Mountford 2007:51). In addition to food resources, wetland environments also produce a number of other economically useful plants, such as *Asclepias incarnata* (swamp milkweed) and *Apocynum cannabinum* (Indian hemp), which may produce raw materials for textiles, cordage, basketry, and other goods.

Just as wetland ecosystems directly provide habitat for numerous economically useful plants, so they are also home to several animal species useful for food, fur, and hides (Nicholas 1998b), and their presence as part of a landscape can serve as an attractor for many others. Frogs, turtles, and crayfish are common in low-order streams, and muskrats may be found in the wetlands that border them. The areas of slackwater present at the confluence of these streams with the Delaware River provide habitat for both fish and amphibians; indeed, such areas are referred to as "frogwater" in the local vernacular. Moreover, the ecotones at the wetland-field/forest transition are frequented by fringe environment–seeking species such as deer and may also attract bear and other game. This is particularly true in the Upper Delaware Valley, where these environments occur at the convergence of the floodplain and adjacent high-elevation uplands.

Wetland areas were clearly rich in resources that would have attracted native populations, and people were undoubtedly exploiting them for this reason throughout prehistory. But it is not until the Transitional Archaic period that wetlands seem to have become a major criterion for site selection in the Upper Delaware Valley; paleoenvironmental data for the Transitional Archaic offer some insight into why. Environmental reconstructions of this period place it within the Sub-Boreal climatic episode, during which generally warm and dry conditions prevailed, which may represent a xerothermic maximum for the Holocene based on palynological, sedimentological, and stratigraphic data (Carbone 1976; Dent 1979; Stewart 1991; Vento et al. 2008). Alluvial sequences are particularly useful for reconstructing major climatic episodes because of their sensitivity to climatic change and their ability to demonstrate both change and stability through time as well as across space (Carbone 1982; Curry and Custer 1982; Custer 1988; Knox 1983, 1993). Additionally, alluvial sequences tend to show more immediate response to climate change than does the palynological record, which may be skewed by "lags" between climate change and resulting shifts in plant communities (Joyce 1988:193).

The phase of the Transitional Archaic period roughly corresponding to the Broadspear tradition marks a major spike in vertical floodplain accretion in the Upper Delaware Valley (Stewart 1991:102–6). At the Driftstone Site, more than a meter of sediment separates the Fishtail component from the underlying Broadspear deposits. Radiocarbon dates on the archaeological deposits bracketing this sedimentary package (see Table 5.1) suggest that all of these sediments were deposited over the course of roughly 800 years (Blondino 2008). Increased overbank deposition during this period is also apparent at other sites in the upper portions of the Delaware Valley, such as the Faucett Site (36PI13a) in the Upper Delaware, and the Byram Site on the New Jersey side of the river in the Middle Delaware Valley (Kinsey 1975:63, 66–67; Ritter, Kinsey, and Kauffman 1973:374; Stewart 1991:90–91). Increased vertical accretion of floodplains for the time period encompassing the Transitional Archaic has been noted in the Upper Susquehanna Valley as well (Scully and Arnold 1981:341), and Victor Carbone (1976:123) has attributed increased sedimentation in the Shenandoah Valley during this time period to moisture stress on vegetation and "extreme climatic conditions."

High rates of overbank deposition are consistent with the warm and dry conditions of the Sub-Boreal climatic episode: reduced vegetal cover on the landscape made sediments more easily entrained by floodwaters, and resulted in increased upland erosion, which would also lead to greater sediment load in streams (Knox 1983:28; Scully and Arnold 1981:341). Thus, increased sedimentation might actually have been facilitated by a reduction in annual precipitation, or at least a shift in the time of year that most of the precipitation fell. Moreover, James Knox (1993:432) has pointed out that relatively small changes in annual temperature and precipitation can have major effects on the frequency and magnitude of flooding events. On the other hand, evidence for increased deposition during the Transitional Archaic period is not present in every stratigraphic sequence, alluvial deposition being affected by many site-specific variables. For example, Joseph Schuldenrein (2003) sees an overall *decrease* in sedimentation rates for the Transitional Archaic, which he attributes to a "dry cycle" for the Delaware Valley, culminating at approximately 3500 BP. A rough terminal date for the xerothermic conditions of the Broadspear phase, 3000 BP, is provided by the presence of subsequent Fishtail and Early Woodland components within cambic horizons (Blondino 2008:168–69; Hummer 1991:27; Stewart 1991:93), which indicate stabilizing landscapes and ameliorating climatic conditions around that time. Carbone (1976:123) also recognizes paleosol formation for the Broadspear phase in the Shenandoah Valley and attributes it to stabilizing climatic conditions.

Although evidence for climate changes during the Late/Transitional Archaic period is abundant, not all models for this Middle Holocene climatic shift agree on the precise timing and nature of these changes (see discussions in Custer 1988 and Cavallo 1987). Several researchers have suggested that the period of maximum warmth and dryness for the Holocene predated the Transitional Archaic (e.g., Cavallo 1987; Joyce 1988). Disagreements over the changes are largely a function of different approaches to climatic reconstruction (palynological versus sedimentological) and scales of study (physiographic versus regional). But even though some of the data conflict with regard to the *timing* of the period of maximum warmth for the Middle Holocene, data for the Delaware Valley region tend to agree that a generally *warm and dry* period coincides with Transitional Archaic cultural manifestations. Recent evidence from lake sediment cores in northern New Jersey implies dry conditions for this period: palynological data from a well-dated core from Lake Grinnell show a marked decline in hemlock, whose intolerance of dry conditions make it a good indicator of reduced precipitation, between 5300 and 3000 BP (Zhao, Yu, and Zhao 2010). Richard Scully and Richard Arnold (1981:341) report that decline of hemlock as a major tree species in the forest communities of eastern North America roughly coincides with an increase in vertical floodplain accretion in the Upper Susquehanna Valley around 4700 BP (mid-third millennium BC); they attribute this to a possible reduction in annual precipitation. In addition to the decrease in hemlock pollen, the Lake Grinnell core data show a coincident stable oxygen isotope shift that is also interpreted as an indicator of dry conditions (Zhao, Yu, and Zhao 2010).

Although there is certainly nothing new or revolutionary about demonstrating environmental shifts during the Transitional Archaic period, the sudden spike in vertical floodplain accretion and associated stratigraphic discontinuity seen at the Upper Delaware Valley sites suggest that this change may have occurred fairly rapidly, as do data from other sources (e.g., Zhao, Yu, and Zhao 2010). If this is the case, then local populations would have had to rather quickly adjust their subsistence practices to cope with the shift in both the nature and the locational availability of various resources brought on by this change, all the more stressful for Upper Delaware Valley populations in light of the preceding Atlantic climatic episode, which Richard Dent (1979:217, 265) has characterized as supporting a "lush understory" with a greatly increased biotic carrying capacity. The relatively rapid onset of xerothermic conditions would have particularly affected groups who had become increasingly reliant on plant resources during the preceding phase of the Late Archaic. Floodplain locations undoubtedly would have become more attractive to local populations as resources in other areas began to dry up, and people were forced to look to areas where resources would be the most concentrated. Frank Vento and colleagues (2008) have suggested that the shift to settlement near larger streams may be linked to the more stable discharges of these higher-order fluvial systems during dry conditions. But it might not be only the major streams that are attracting people to the landscapes being heavily utilized during the Transitional Archaic, but also the wetlands associated with the low-order streams that traverse the floodplains at these site locations. Although the trend toward floodplain habitation sites represents a continuation of a pattern seen earlier in the Late Archaic, local populations during the Transitional Archaic were becoming more selective regarding the *types* of floodplain locations they chose. Even when limited in size, wetland ecosystems contain the highest levels of biodiversity to be found at these locations; being able to exploit both riverine and wetland resources at the junctions of river and wetland environments would have been particularly attractive in a time when resource-rich zones were relatively patchy in their distribution across the landscape.

Carbone (1976:200) postulates that the period of maximum warmth and dryness corresponding to the Transitional Archaic period would have been a time of environmental stress for native populations and that significant cultural and technological change can be precipitated by this stress. But such change need not be a drastic reordering of lifestyle and subsistence practice; rather, it may simply represent attempts by populations to maintain a state of equilibrium with their world and the ways they make a living in it (Carbone 1982:50). Nonetheless, focusing on the interrelatedness of environment and the technologies used to extract a living from it can sharpen our view of the archaeological record of times during which both environmental and cultural transitions are taking place. Not all of the innovations of the Transitional Archaic can be neatly attributed to mechanisms of coping with environmental stress of course, but it may be useful to consider some of the archaeological hallmarks of the period in light of such stress.

Technological Adaptations

Broadspears have been interpreted as generalized processing tools designed to serve a variety of different functions (Cresson 1990; Custer 1996:172; Truncer 1990). Could groups whose subsistence base had become unreliable and unpredictable prefer multifunction tools capable of processing a variety of resource types to more specialized tools? A multifunction tool, especially one capable of serving as a core from which expedient flake tools might be struck, would have been more useful than a specialized tool on longer forays from primary habitation sites to locate and procure resources. The proliferation of Broadspear sites in interior and upland settings could reflect the necessity for more frequent foraging excursions into these areas. Most campers would agree that, if you find yourself in the wilderness with only one tool, it should be one capable of handling a variety of tasks, and the broadspear may, in effect, be the "survival knife" of the Transitional Archaic period. Additionally, the width of broadspear forms allows for extensive resharpening, which may have been an important factor for groups processing ever greater quantities of tough, fibrous plant materials.

Another important innovation of the Transitional Archaic is, of course, durable container technology in the form of carved soapstone bowls, followed by flat-bottomed pottery vessels. The correlation between the adoption of a new cooking technology and a shift in subsistence practices is clear and need not be elaborated in any great detail. Increasing reliance on new food resources often requires new cooking techniques and utensils. This may be particularly true if additions to the diet include items such as seeds that are best processed using wet-cooking techniques to render them edible and appetizing. Although I have also argued that the relatively small quantities of early durable containers at Transitional Archaic sites argue against their use as an "everyday" cooking technology, their very use at this time is nonetheless suggestive of additions to the subsistence base that required new methods of processing and cooking foods. It may also be telling that not until climatic conditions stabilize during the Early to Middle Woodland period do we see evidence for the widespread adoption of pottery in quantities that indicate it has become a primary mode of cooking and thus also that the types of resources being processed with pottery were becoming more predictably available and therefore more important as dietary staples.

Of course, one of the most significant characteristics of Upper Delaware Valley Transitional Archaic sites is the presence of large fire-cracked rock features. Although FCR features in themselves are certainly nothing new, the size and configuration of such features at sites of this time period suggests that they are serving a different function from those in earlier periods, or serving the same function much more intensively. Again, it is safe to assume that they are being used for relatively large-scale resource processing, and the question remains as to the nature of the resources being processed using all of this hot rock. It is interesting that the number and extent of large FCR features decrease through the Woodland period as pottery continues its development and becomes an everyday cooking technology, possibly pointing to both pottery and hot rock being used to process similar resources and to one technology eventually supplanting the other. Perhaps we have simply been looking in the wrong place to find those resources.

As Nicholas (1991) has pointed out, archaeological site surveys have largely focused on areas that make sense as habitation sites to the investigators. To this I would add that not only do we focus on places that make sense to *us* in our search for habitation sites, but we also interpret the functions of sites in particular locations based on how *we* would prioritize the importance of particular landscape features. Plant foods available in the wetlands adjacent to the sites may very well be a larger part of Transitional Archaic subsistence than previously thought. As noted above, wetlands are a rich source of edible plants, including many varieties of edible tubers, shoots, and seeds. Many of these potential foods require some degree of processing prior to consumption, such as the arrow arum, or tuckahoe, used extensively by native peoples inhabiting the tidal zones of the Middle Atlantic region during the Late Woodland and Contact periods (Messner and Schindler 2010; Rountree, Clark, and Mountford 2007). Cooking with hot rocks can provide a simple way to process large amounts of such foods very efficiently, particularly if used in a roasting pit or earth oven (what I have called the "crock pot" of prehistory), which requires no tending once the cooking process is initiated. In light of this, we should perhaps shift our focus from the more obvious riverine food resources to investigate what plants may have been available in the wetlands adjacent to the low-order streams that are such a prominent hydrologic feature on the landscape of the Upper Delaware Valley. Furthermore, analytical techniques now available to paleobotanists offer us an additional means to answer some of the pressing questions about subsistence during the Transitional Archaic period. Plant microfossils such as starch grains and phytoliths recovered from sediments within and beneath fire-cracked rock features and from tools found nearby have the potential to change the way we think about what may have been going on at these sites. Recent work in the Delaware Valley has already shown that identifiable starch grains can be recovered from surprising places if only we think to look for them there (Messner 2008, Messner and Dickau 2005).

Conclusions

The preceding thoughts and observations are preliminary, and much more work is clearly required to properly address the issues they raise. The site location exercise described above was undertaken simply as a "thought experiment," although the results, however preliminary, are nonetheless compelling. The extent to which sampling error is reflected in the limited information of the digitized site files is unknown and must be considered. A similar site location exercise has to be undertaken for the New Jersey side of the river to see whether the apparent association between Transitional Archaic sites and low-order streams holds up there as well, and data on the relationships between stream order and sites dating to other time periods must be quantified to put Transitional Archaic site location in perspective and to empirically determine whether this apparent pattern is real. Moreover, many of the data on the nature of these low-order streams and associated wetlands have thus far come only from looking at mapped site locations. Some field visits, including limited testing and geomorphological assessment, may be required to determine to what extent activity during the historic period has altered the nature of stream hydrology and the adjacent landscapes.

Further consideration of these types of small wetland environments and the nature and quantity of the resources they could have provided to prehistoric populations is certainly warranted. Interpretations of prehistoric site selection have often focused on the more prominent landscape features and on our modern conceptions of what constitutes an economically productive landscape or environment. The size of a particular ecosystem may not be as limiting a factor in terms of its productivity as we might at first assume. Even the fairly small wetland areas discussed above may have produced sufficient resources for a limited-duration encampment of a relatively small group of people, particularly a group of people who were attuned to the seasonal productivity of such areas. And even though we cannot always rely on existing wetland maps and inventories, which may not be scaled at a level of resolution sufficient to capture all of the potentially important resource extraction zones for prehistoric populations, this does not mean that such areas should not figure prominently into predictive models for site location (Hasenstab 1991:59–60). Indeed, if we are to more fully understand why particular locations were chosen for settlement and how they were used, a view of archaeological landscapes that considers the *total* range of ecological diversity present within them is called for.

REFERENCES

Blondino, Joseph R.

2008 How Can You Mend a Broken Hearth? Preliminary Results of Excavations at the Driftstone Site. *Journal of Middle Atlantic Archaeology* 24:167–75.

Carbone, Victor A.

1976 *Environment and Prehistory in the Shenandoah Valley.* Ph.D. dissertation, Department of Anthropology, Catholic University of America, Washington, D.C. University Microfilms, Ann Arbor, Michigan.

1982 Environment and Society in Archaic and Woodland Times. In *Practicing Environmental Archaeology: Methods and Interpretations*, edited by Roger W. Moeller, 39–52. Occasional Papers 3. American Indian Archaeological Institute, Washington, Connecticut.

Cavallo, John

1987 *Area B Site (28Me1-B), Data Recovery.* Trenton Complex Archaeology: Report 8. Prepared for Federal Highway Administration and New Jersey Department of Transportation, Bureau of Environmental Analysis, Trenton. Cultural Resource Group, Louis Berger & Associates, Inc., East Orange, New Jersey.

Cresson, Jack

1990 Broadspear Lithic Technology: Some Aspects of Biface Manufacture, Form, and Use with Insights Towards Understanding Assemblage Diversity. In *Experiments and Observations on the Terminal Archaic of the Middle Atlantic Region*, edited by Roger W. Moeller, 105–30. Archaeological Services. Bethlehem, Connecticut.

Curry, Dennis C., and Jay F. Custer

1982 Holocene Climatic Change in the Middle Atlantic Area: Preliminary Observations from Archaeological Sites. *North American Archaeologist* 3:275–85.

Custer, Jay F.

1988 Late Archaic Cultural Dynamics in the Central Middle Atlantic Region. *Journal of Middle Atlantic Archaeology* 4:39–59.

1996 *Prehistoric Cultures of Eastern Pennsylvania.* Anthropological Series 7. Pennsylvania Historical and Museum Commission, Harrisburg.

Densmore, Frances

1974 *How Indians Use Wild Plants for Food, Medicine, and Crafts.* Dover Publications, New York. Reprint of *Uses of Plants by the Chippewa Indians*, 44th Annual Report of the Bureau of American Ethnology, 1928.

Dent, Richard J.

1979 *Ecological and Sociocultural Reconstruction in the Upper Delaware Valley.* Ph.D. dissertation, American University, Washington, D.C. University Microfilms, Ann Arbor, Michigan.

Funk, Robert E.

1992 Some Major Wetlands in New York State: A Preliminary Assessment of Their Biological and Cultural Potential. *Man in the Northeast* 43:25–41.

Hasenstab, Robert

1991 Wetlands as a Critical Variable in Predictive Modeling of Prehistoric Site Locations: A Case Study from the Passaic River Basin. *Man in the Northeast* 42:39–61.

Hummer, Chris C.

1991 *Biface and Ceramic Assemblage Variability in the Early Woodland: Continuity and Change at the Williamson Site, Hunterdon County, New Jersey.* Ph.D. dissertation, Department of Anthropology, Temple University, Philadelphia. University Microfilms, Ann Arbor, Michigan.

Joyce, Arthur A.

1988 Early/Middle Holocene Environments in the Middle Atlantic Region: A Revised Reconstruction. In *Holocene Human Ecology in Northeastern North America*, edited by George P. Nicholas, 185–214. Plenum Press, New York.

Kinsey, W. Fred, III (editor)

1972 *Archeology in the Upper Delaware Valley.* Anthropological Series 2. Pennsylvania Historical and Museum Commission, Harrisburg.

Kinsey, W. Fred, III

1975 Faucett and Byram Sites: Chronology and Settlement in the Delaware Valley. *Pennsylvania Archaeologist* 45 (1–2): 1–103.

Knox, James C.

1983 Responses of River Systems to Holocene Climates. In *Late-Quaternary Environments of the United States*, Volume 2: *The Holocene*, edited by H. E. Wright Jr., 26–41. University of Minnesota Press, Minneapolis.

1993 Large increases in flood magnitude in response to modest changes in climate. *Nature* 361 (6411): 430–32.

Kraft, Herbert C.

1970 *The Miller Field Site, Warren County, New Jersey*, Part 1: *Archaic and Transitional Stages*. Archaeological Research Center, Seton Hall University, South Orange, New Jersey.

1975 *The Archaeology of the Tocks Island Area*. Archaeological Research Center, Seton Hall University Museum, South Orange, New Jersey.

2001 *The Lenape-Delaware Indian Heritage: 10,000 B.C. to A.D. 2000*. Lenape Books, Stanhope, New Jersey.

Leopold, Luna B.

1994 *A View of the River*. Harvard University Press, Cambridge, Massachusetts.

Messner, Timothy C.

2008 *Woodland Period People and Plant Interactions: New Insights from Starch Grain Analysis*. Ph.D. dissertation, Department of Anthropology, Temple University, Philadelphia. University Microfilms, Ann Arbor, Michigan.

Messner, Timothy C., and Ruth Dickau

2005 New Directions, New Interpretations: Paleoethnobotany in the Upper Delaware Valley and the Utility of Starch Grain Research in the Middle Atlantic. *Journal of Middle Atlantic Archaeology* 21:71–82.

Messner, Timothy C., and William Schindler

2010 Plant Processing Strategies and Their Effect on Starch Grain Survival When Rendering *Peltandra virginica* (L.) Kunth, Araceae Edible. *Journal of Archaeological Science* 37 (2): 328–36.

Nicholas, George P.

1991 Putting Wetlands into Perspective. *Man in the Northeast* 42:29–38.

1998a Assessing Climatic Influences on Human Affairs: Wetlands and the Maximum Holocene Warming in the Northeast. *Journal of Middle Atlantic Archaeology* 14:147–60.

1998b Wetlands and Hunter-Gatherers: A Global Perspective. *Current Anthropology* 39 (5): 720–31.

Oyuela-Caycedo, Augusto, and Renee M. Bonzani

2005 *San Jacinto 1: A Historical Ecological Approach to an Archaic Site in Colombia*. University of Alabama Press, Tuscaloosa.

Ritter, Dale F., W. Fred Kinsey III, and Marvin E. Kauffman

1973 Overbank Sedimentation in the Delaware River Valley During the Last 6,000 Years. *Science* 179 (4071): 374–75.

Rountree, Helen C., Wayne E. Clark, and Kent Mountford

2007 *John Smith's Chesapeake Voyages: 1607–1609*. University of Virginia Press, Charlottesville.

Schindler, William

2006 *Middle Woodland Exploitation of Migratory Fish in the Delaware Valley*, Ph.D. dissertation, Department of Anthropology, Temple University, Philadelphia. University Microfilms, Ann Arbor, Michigan.

Schuldenrein, Joseph

2003 Landscape Change, Human Occupation, and Archaeological Site Preservation at the Glacial Margin: Geoarchaeological Perspectives from the Sandts Eddy Site (36NM12), Middle Delaware Valley, Pennsylvania. In *Geoarchaeology of Landscapes in the Glaciated Northeast*, edited by D. L. Cremeens and J. P. Hart, 181–210. New York State Museum and Science Service Bulletin 497. University of the State of New York, State Education Department, Albany.

Scully, Richard W., and Richard W. Arnold

1981 Holocene Alluvial Stratigraphy in the Upper Susquehanna River Basin, New York. *Quaternary Research* 15:327–44.

Stewart, R. Michael

1991 Archaeology and Environment in the Upper Delaware Valley. In *The People of Minisink: Papers from the 1989 Delaware Water Gap Symposium*, edited by David G. Orr and Douglas V. Campana, 79–115. National Park Service, Philadelphia.

Truncer, James J.

1990 Perkiomen Points: A Study in Variability. In *Experiments and Observations on the Terminal Archaic of the Middle Atlantic Region*, edited by Roger W. Moeller, 1–62. Archaeological Services, Bethlehem, Connecticut.

U.S. Fish and Wildlife Service

2011 Wetlands Mapper, National Wetlands Inventory. Available online at http://www.fws.gov/wetlands/data/Mapper.html. Accessed July–August 2011.

Vento, Frank J., Harold B. Rollins, Anthony Vega, James M. Adovasio, Patricia Stahlman, David B. Madsen, and Jeffrey S. Illingworth

2008 Development of a Late Pleistocene–Holocene Genetic Stratigraphic Framework for the Mid-Atlantic Region: Implications in Archaeology. Paper presented at73rd Annual Meeting of the Society for American Archaeology, Vancouver, British Columbia, March.

Zhao, Yan, Zicheng Yu, and Cheng Zhao

2010 Hemlock (*Tsuga canadensis*) Declines at 9800 and 5300 cal. yr. BP Caused by Holocene Climatic Shifts in Northeastern North America. *Holocene* 20 (6): 877–86.

6.

Transitional Archaic Settlement Density in Eastern Pennsylvania

Heather A. Wholey

ABSTRACT

Population density is the ratio of the raw or estimated number of people occupying a specified territorial unit to the area of that unit. Relative density estimates for hunter-gatherer populations may correlate to the intensity or strategy of mobility and subsistence, social organization, or kinship structures. Whereas generalized prehistoric population models suggest that population density increases continuously through time, regional models illustrate that density is locally specific and related to land use, settlement makeup, and localized environmental carrying capacity. More than population growth alone, population density may be a factor in cultural and technological innovation, as groups seek to modify their local carrying capacity or respond to social or environmental stress. This chapter explores the role of population density as an indicator of social organization in the Transitional Archaic period in the Susquehanna and Delaware Basins.

In *Trend and Tradition in the Prehistory of the Eastern United States*, Joseph Caldwell (1958) defined the Eastern Woodlands Archaic as a period of gradual economic intensification and sociocultural elaboration. The term "Transitional," first applied by John Witthoft (1953), is often used to describe a unique period from about 4300 to 2700 BP (see Carr, Chapter 3, for radiometric dates) that is associated with "transitions" toward residential stability, technological efficiency, heightened sociocultural complexity, and greater sociocultural diversity. Caldwell's model of innovation and intensification is exemplified during the Transitional Archaic period by the manufacture of steatite vessels, the cultivation of edible plants, such as cucurbits and *Chenopodium*, an increase in interregional trade and mortuary ceremonialism, and the establishment of large settlements, often with sizable features. Explanatory frameworks for these developments are often constructed around the theme of change in climate (Vento, Chapter 1) or in population (Carr, Chapter 3). In further exploring the role of population during the Transitional Archaic period in the Delaware and Susquehanna River basins of Pennsylvania, this chapter identifies localized population clusters or areas of high-intensity use and considers the role of population density as an indicator of social organization in these locations.

Population Density

Population density is calculated by dividing the raw or estimated number of people occupying a specified territorial unit by the area of that unit. Rather than the necessary outcome of population growth, population pressure is instead the result of an imbalance in the population to resources ratio. A group of people may not experience or perceive stress through population growth so long as territorial expansion (Graber 1990) or economic intensification (Graber 1997) is possible. Thus the people of a "densely" occupied area may not be stressed so long as their group's size can be supported by the local carrying capacity. Overall low population density is thought to characterize most hunting and gathering groups because of their low fertility and high mobility. In fact, global hunter-gather density projections rarely exceed two individuals per square mile (two per 2.5 km^2; Deevey 1960; Hassan 1978), with the ratio of one person per square mile or two and a half square kilometers being offered as ideal (Hassan 1975, 1978; Lee and DeVore 1968). The so-called magic numbers of hunter-gatherer demography proposed during the 1968 "Man the Hunter" symposium are twenty-five individuals for the local group, or microband, and 500 for the aggregate group, or macroband (Lee and DeVore 1968).

Within the Eastern Woodlands, local groups are estimated at up to ten exogamous families, and aggregate groups, up to 100 families with affinal ties to one another (Kent 1993). Given these figures, a single microband would minimally require at least 65 square kilometers (25 mi^2), but ideally more like 130 square kilometers (50 mi^2). The macroband would require at least 1,300 square kilometers (500 mi^2), but ideally up to 6,500 square kilometers (2,500 mi^2). In addition to social organization or kinship structures, hunter-gatherer population density may also correlate to intensity or strategy of mobility and subsistence. For example, lower population density not only enables, but may also require, significant mobility over large areas (Madden 1983). For hunter-gatherers, an increase in density may first be accompanied by a decrease in mobility, with a shift from a residentially mobile to a logistically oriented extractive strategy and to increased reliance on resource management within a restricted spatial range (Binford 1980). Continuous density increase may first trigger expansion into previously "marginal" areas and may eventually lead to resource overuse or social conflict, which may manifest as ecological damage or firmer territorial boundaries.

Study Delineation

The study reported in this chapter synthesizes data from the Pennsylvania Archaeological Site Survey (PASS) to generate population densities for each watershed within the Delaware and Susquehanna Basins and several subbasins of the Susquehanna Basin (Figure 6.1). Watersheds are catchment areas that often crosscut physiographic zones, incorporate various geological and biotic landscapes, and accommodate a range of human settlement behaviors (McDougal and Funk 2006); for these reasons, they are often employed as a spatial analytic unit in analyzing archaeological settlement patterns. Although watershed boundaries do not define the operating space of any given population, for this study, they are considered spatial-territorial units and, along with the number of Broadspear and Orient components recorded in the PASS system, are used to calculate localized population densities.

Population ecology regularly employs proxies to record the size of populations and to examine fluctuations in that size. For example, animal biologists use indirect indicators such as numbers of nests and burrows or signs such as the presence of animal tracks and droppings to estimate the relative population of a given species. Archaeologists also widely apply diagnostic indicators within site file data sets as proxies to construct historical frameworks and interpretive models. Although these proxy data cannot be used to precisely model population, they can yield accurate estimations so long as variability in occupational duration, intensity of land use, and frequency of site

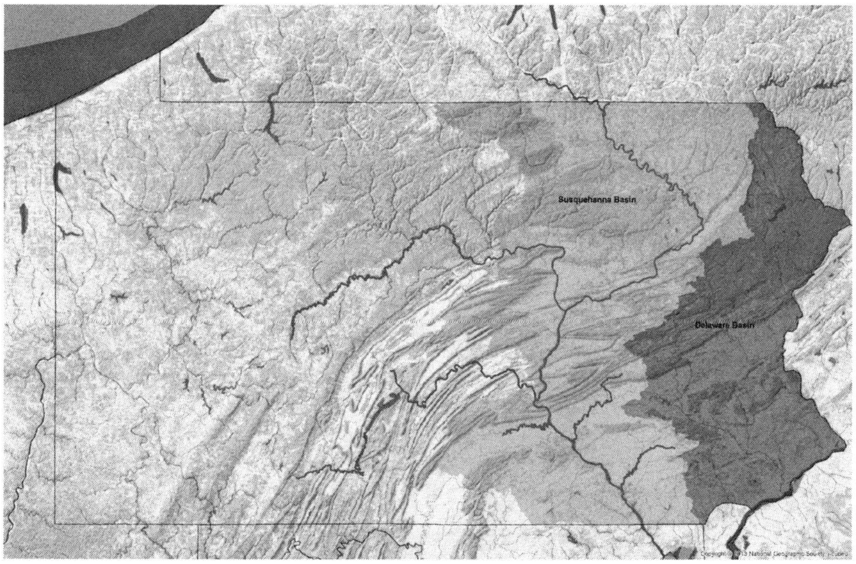

FIGURE 6.1 Susquehanna and Delaware Basins.

TABLE 6.1 Transitional Archaic diagnostic components

Early Transitional Archaic	Broadspear Phase	ca. 4350–3150 BP
	Lehigh/Snook Kill	
	Perkiomen	
	Susquehanna	
	Savannah River	
Late Transitional Archaic	Fishtail Phase	ca. 3150–2650 BP
	Fishtail	

Note: See Carr (Chapter 3) for available radiometric dates.

relocation is taken into consideration (Dewar 1991; Hassan 1978; Varien and Potter 1997). To account for variability in occupational duration and potential site reoccupation and to apply a standard spatial-temporal measurement, population units are calculated from the presence of a particular diagnostic component, not the actual number of artifacts belonging to it, at a given site. Each diagnostic listed in Table 6.1 is counted as a single component. Thus a single site with one or more Orient points is considered a single Orient component, whereas a single site with one or more Perkiomen *and* one or more Susquehanna points is counted as two Broadspear components.

Transitional Archaic Settlement Density

Settlement systems for the Transitional Archaic period throughout much of eastern Pennsylvania have been described as micro-/macroband systems, whose base camps are associated with the terraces of major river valleys, and whose smaller foraging camps are associated with upland settings in smaller stream valleys (Custer 1996; Siegel, Benedict, and Kingsley 1999; Siegel, Kellogg, and Kingsley 2001). Riverine environments were stable, productive zones, permitting in situ population growth (Custer 1996). Transitional Archaic sites within the watersheds of the Delaware and Susquehanna Basins are found in a range of settings, with the majority on floodplains, terraces, or stream benches. Most Transitional Archaic sites in the Susquehanna Basin are located on floodplains, whereas sites in the Delaware Basin are almost evenly distributed among those three settings (Figure 6.2).

There are nearly twice as many Transitional Archaic components in the Susquehanna Basin as in the Delaware Basin due to the higher number of Broadspear components (Figure 6.3). More Broadspear components and more floodplain sites in the Susquehanna Basin indicate a core settlement/use area during the Broadspear phase. The following finer-grained analysis at the watershed scale isolates areas within the two river basins with the most intensive use or highest population density.

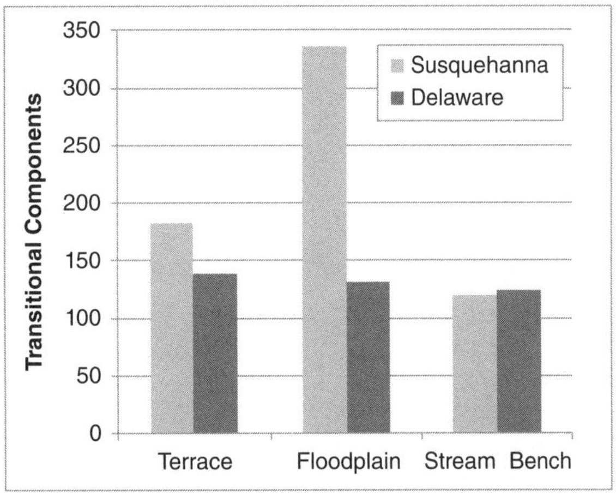

FIGURE 6.2
Comparison of Transitional Archaic components in three most common ecological settings.

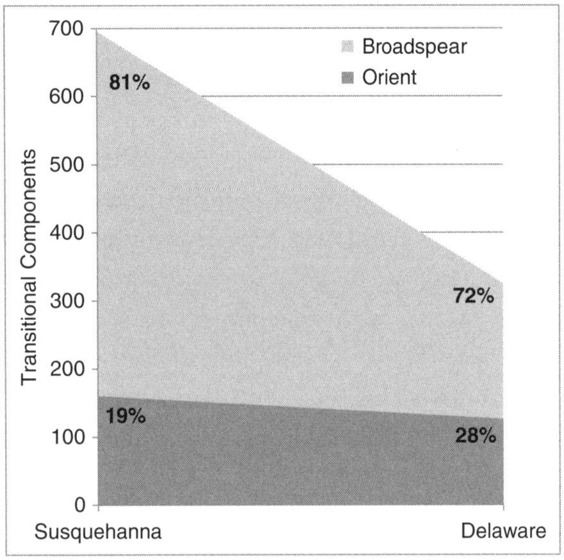

FIGURE 6.3
Transitional Archaic components in Susquehanna and Delaware Basins.

Delaware Basin

Comprising 21,813 square kilometers (8,422 mi²) and the twenty-two watersheds that drain the Upper, Central, and Lower Delaware Subbasins, the physiographically diverse Delaware Basin in Pennsylvania encompasses portions of the Coastal Plain, Piedmont Uplands, Reading Prong, Great Valley, Blue Mountain, Anthracite Upland, and Glaciated Low Plateau sections of eastern Pennsylvania (Delaware Water Plan 2014). There are nearly twice as many Broadspear components as Orient components in the Delaware Basin, with Broadspear component density averaging 1.8 per square kilometer and Orient component density averaging 1.1 per square kilometer.

Upper Delaware Subbasin

Comprising the 4,703 square kilometers (1,816 mi²) that drain into the Delaware River above the Lehigh River, the Upper Delaware Subbasin includes the watersheds of the Shehawken-Rattlesnake Creeks, Lackawaxen River, and Wallenpaupack, Bushkill, and Brodhead Creeks (Delaware Water Plan 2014). All Transitional Archaic sites in the subbasin are located within 200 meters of the nearest surface water, most in a floodplain or terrace setting, with a few also on the stream bench. The highest component density for both Broadspear and Orient traditions is in watersheds of the Bushkill and Shehawken-Rattlesnake Creeks (Table 6.2).

Central Delaware Subbasin

Primarily situated in the Piedmont Lowlands, although also traversing portions of the Reading Prong and Great Valley, the Central Delaware Subbasin comprises 5,030 square kilometers (1,942 mi²) and

TABLE 6.2 Transitional Archaic component densities in Upper Delaware Subbasin

		Components Present	
Watershed	**Area**	**Broadspear**	**Orient**
Shehawken-Rattlesnake Creeks	756 km² (292 mi²)	2.4/km² (n = 18)	1.7/km² (n = 13)
Lackawaxen River	956 km² (369 mi²)	0.3/km² (n = 3)	0.1/km² (n = 1)
Wallenpaupack Creek	593 km² (229 mi²)	0.2/km² (n = 1)	0.2/km² (n = 1)
Shohola-Bushkill Creeks	1,121 km² (433 mi²)	2.8/km² (n = 31)	1.5/km² (n = 17)
Brodhead Creek	800 km² (309 mi²)	0.3/km² (n = 2)	0.3/km² (n = 2)
Jacoby-Bushkill Creeks	477 km² (184 mi²)	2.1/km² (n = 10)	0.8/km² (n = 4)

Note: n = number of components present, not number of component artifacts or number of sites.

TABLE 6.3 Transitional Archaic component densities in Central Delaware Subbasin

Watershed	Area	Components Present	
		Broadspear	Orient
Upper Lehigh River	1,088 km² (420 mi²)	0.2/km² (n = 2)	0.1/km² (n = 1)
Middle Lehigh River	1,197 km² (462 mi²)	0.3/km² (n = 4)	0.1/km² (n = 1)
Lower Lehigh River	1,240 km² (479 mi²)	5/km² (n = 62)	1.5/km² (n = 19)
Cooks-Tohickon Creeks	546 km² (211 mi²)	2.4/km² (n = 13)	1.1/km² (n = 6)
Pidcock-Mill Creeks	347 km² (134 mi²)	0.6/km² (n = 2)	0 (n = 0)
Neshaminy Creek	611 km² (236 mi²)	2.1/km² (n = 13)	1/km² (n = 6)

Note: n = number of components present, not number of component artifacts or number of sites.

includes the watersheds of the Lehigh River and Cooks-Tohickon, Pidcock-Mill, and Neshaminy Creeks (Delaware Water Plan 2014). All Transitional Archaic sites are located within 300 meters of the nearest surface water, most in floodplain or stream bench settings, with fewer on terraces or in upland or interior settings. The highest component density for both Broadspear and Orient traditions is in the watersheds of the Lower Lehigh River, Cooks-Tohickon Creeks, and Neshaminy Creek (Table 6.3).

Lower Delaware Subbasin

Primarily situated in the Atlantic Coastal Plain province, the Lower Delaware Subbasin has a total drainage area of 7,014 square kilometers (2,708 mi²) and includes the watersheds of the Schuylkill River and Maiden, Tulpehocken, Manatawny-French, Perkiomen, Darby-Crum, Brandywine, White Clay, and Pennypack Creeks (Delaware Water Plan 2014). All Transitional Archaic sites are located within 300 meters of the nearest surface water, with most on terraces, although many are also on the floodplain or on stream benches. The highest component density for both Broadspear and Orient traditions is in the watersheds of the Manatawny-French, Perkiomen, and Brandywine Creeks (Table 6.4).

TABLE 6.4 Transitional Archaic component densities in Lower Delaware Subbasin

Watershed	Area	Components Present	
		Broadspear	Orient
Upper Schuylkill River	883 km² (341 mi²)	0.2/km² (n = 2)	0 (n = 0)
Lower Schuylkill River	585 km² (226 mi²)	1.4/km² (n = 8)	0.3/km² (n = 2)
Maiden Creek	777 km² (300 mi²)	2.3/km² (n = 18)	0.6/km² (n = 5)
Tulpehocken Creek	927 km² (358 mi²)	1.9/km² (n = 18)	0.4/km² (n = 4)
Manatawny-French Creeks	855 km² (330 mi²)	5.5/km² (n = 47)	1.9/km² (n = 16)
Perkiomen Creek	938 km² (362 mi²)	4.7/km² (n = 44)	1.9/km² (n = 18)
Darby-Crum Creeks	632 km² (244 mi²)	0.2/km² (n = 1)	0.3/km² (n = 2)
Brandywine Creek	780 km² (301 mi²)	3.2/km² (n = 25)	0.9/km² (n = 7)
White Clay Creek	254 km² (98 mi²)	1.2/km² (n = 3)	0.4/km² (n = 1)
Pennypack Creek	386 km² (149 mi²)	0 (n = 0)	0 (n = 0)

Note: n = number of components present, not number of component artifacts or number of sites.

Susquehanna Basin

Comprising 54,488 square kilometers (21,038 mi²) and the watersheds that drain the Upper, Upper Central, Lower Central, and Lower Susquehanna, as well as its Upper West, Central West, and Lower West Branches, and the Upper and Lower Juniata Subbasins, the physiographically diverse Susquehanna Basin encompasses portions of the Piedmont, Blue Ridge, Ridge and Valley, and Appalachian Plateau provinces of Pennsylvania (Susquehanna Water Plan 2014a, 2014b). There are more than four times as many Broadspear as Orient components in the portion of the Susquehanna Basin outlined for this study. Broadspear component density averages 2.1 per square kilometer, and Orient component density averages 0.5 per square kilometer.

Lower Susquehanna Subbasin

Located in the Piedmont Lowlands and Uplands, the Lower Susquehanna Subbasin comprises 10,769 square kilometers (4,158 mi²) in the lowermost reaches of the

Susquehanna River in Pennsylvania and includes the watersheds of Sherman, Conondoguit, Clark-Paxton, Swatara, Yellow Breeches, Conewago, Chickies, Codorus, and Kreutz-Muddy Creeks, the Conestoga River and Pequea-Octorara Creeks (Table 6.4). Most Transitional Archaic sites are located on floodplains or terraces, and all are within 250 meters of the nearest surface water. The highest component density for the Broadspear tradition is in the watersheds of Swatara Creek, Conestoga River, Clark-Paxton Creeks, and Conewago Creek (Table 6.5). All but the Conestoga River watershed also have the highest density for the Orient tradition. The very low density of the Orient tradition in the Conestoga River watershed could indicate a shift in settlement structures, resource exploitation, or population relocation. These will be explored further in a subsequent section of this chapter.

Lower Central Susquehanna Subbasin

Located in the Ridge and Valley physiographic province, the Lower Central Susquehanna Subbasin encompasses 3,753 square kilometers (1,449 mi²) and includes the watersheds of the Penns-Middle, Mahoney-Shamokin, and Mahantango Creeks (Table 6.6). Most Transitional Archaic sites are located on floodplains or terraces, and all are within 120 meters of the nearest surface water. There is relatively low component density for both Broadspear and Orient traditions in all three watersheds.

TABLE 6.5 Transitional Archaic component densities in Lower Susquehanna Subbasin

		Components Present	
Watershed	Area	Broadspear	Orient
Sherman Creek	795 km² (307 mi²)	0.9/km² (n = 7)	0.3/km² (n = 2)
Conondoguit Creek	1,357 km² (524 mi²)	0.8/km² (n = 11)	0.3/km² (n = 4)
Clark-Paxton Creeks	458 km² (177 mi²)	5.5/km² (n = 25)	2/km² (n = 9)
Swatara Creek	1,476 km² (570 mi²)	12/km² (n = 178)	1.5/km² (n = 22)
Yellow Breeches Creek	614 km² (237 mi²)	2.3/km² (n = 14)	0.5/km² (n = 3)
Conewago Creek	1,321 km² (510 mi²)	4.1/km² (n = 54)	1.4/km² (n = 18)
Chickies Creek	655 km² (253 mi²)	3.5/km² (n = 23)	0.5/km² (n = 3)
Codorus Creek	759 km² (293 mi²)	0.8/km² (n = 6)	0.7/km² (n = 5)
Muddy Creek	780 km² (301 mi²)	0.3/km² (n = 2)	0.3/km² (n = 2)
Conestoga River	1,272 km² (491 mi²)	7.9/km² (n = 100)	0.7/km² (n = 9)
Pequea-Octorara Creek	1,282 km² (495 mi²)	1.3/km² (n = 17)	0.1/km² (n = 1)

Note: n = number of components present, not number of component artifacts or number of sites.

TABLE 6.6 Transitional Archaic component densities in Lower Central Susquehanna Subbasin

		Components Present	
Watershed	Area	Broadspear	Orient
Penns-Middle Creeks	1,510 km² (583 mi²)	1.2/km² (n = 18)	0.1/km² (n = 2)
Mahoney-Shamokin Creeks	883 km² (341 mi²)	0.2/km² (n = 2)	0.1/km² (n = 1)
Mahantango Creek	1,360 km² (525 mi²)	0.9/km² (n = 12)	0.4/km² (n = 5)

Note: n = number of components present, not number of component artifacts or number of sites.

Central Susquehanna Subbasin

Located mainly in the Appalachian Plateau and Ridge and Valley provinces, the Central Susquehanna Subbasin encompasses 4,561 square kilometers (1,761 mi²) and includes the watersheds of the Lackawanna River and Toby-Wapwallopen, Fishing, Nescopeck, and Catawissa-Roaring Creeks (Table 6.7). Most Transitional Archaic sites are located on terraces or stream benches, and all are within 520 meters of the nearest surface water. The highest component density for the Broadspear tradition is in the Toby-Wapwallopen Creeks watershed. There is a relatively low component density for the Orient tradition in all five watersheds.

Upper Susquehanna Subbasin

Located mainly in the Allegheny Mountain and Appalachian Plateau provinces, the Upper Susquehanna Subbasin comprises 8,511 square kilometers (3,286 mi²) and includes the watersheds of the Tioga-Cowanesque Rivers, Wappesining Creek–Chemung River, and Sugar-Towanda, Wysox-Wyalusing, Tunkhannock, and Mehoopany-Bowman Creeks, as

TABLE 6.7 Transitional Archaic component densities in Central Susquehanna Subbasin

		Components Present	
Watershed	Area	Broadspear	Orient
Lackawanna River	901 km² (348 mi²)	0.4/km² (n = 4)	0.2/km² (n = 2)
Toby-Wapwallopen Creeks	1,044 km² (403 mi²)	2.6/km² (n = 27)	0.7/km² (n = 7)
Fishing Creek	1,000 km² (386 mi²)	0.1/km² (n = 1)	0.1/km² (n = 1)
Nescopeck Creek	676 km² (261 mi²)	1.8/km² (n = 12)	0.4/km² (n = 3)
Catawissa-Roaring Creeks	940 km² (363 mi²)	0.3/km² (n = 3)	0.0/km² (n = 0)

Note: n = number of components present, not number of component artifacts or number of sites.

TABLE 6.8 Transitional Archaic component densities in Upper Susquehanna Subbasin

		Components Present	
Watershed	Area	Broadspear	Orient
Tioga-Cowanesque Rivers	1,751 km² (676 mi²)	0.5/km² (n = 8)	0.3/km² (n = 5)
Wappesining Creek–Chemung River	901 km² (348 mi²)	0.9/km² (n = 8)	0/km² (n = 0)
Sugar-Towanda Creeks	1,210 km² (467 mile²)	1/km² (n = 12)	0.3/km² (n = 4)
Wysox-Wyalusing Creeks	1,432 km² (553 mi²)	0.6/km² (n = 9)	0.2/km² (n = 3)
Great Bend	800 km² (309 mile²)	2/km² (n = 16)	0.8/km² (n = 6)
Tunkhannock Creek	1,070 km² (413 mi²)	0.4/km² (n = 4)	0.1/km² (n = 1)
Mehoopany-Bowman Creeks	1,347 km² (520 mi²)	1.3/km² (n = 17)	0.4/km² (n = 6)

Note: n = number of components present, not number of component artifacts or number of sites.

well as the Great Bend watershed (Table 6.8). Most Transitional Archaic sites are located on terraces, and all are within 250 meters of the nearest surface water. The highest component density for the Broadspear tradition is in the Great Bend watershed. There is relatively low component density for the Orient tradition in all seven watersheds.

Lower West Branch Susquehanna Subbasin

Located mainly in the Ridge and Valley province, the Lower West Branch Susquehanna Subbasin is 4,685 square kilometers (1,809 mi²) in extent and includes

TABLE 6.9 Transitional Archaic component densities in Lower West Branch Susquehanna Subbasin

		Components Present	
Watershed	Area	Broadspear	Orient
Antes-Lycoming Creeks	1,290 km² (498 mi²)	0.8/km² (n = 10)	0.2/km² (n = 2)
Loyalsock Creek	1,331 km² (514 mi²)	0.8/km² (n = 10)	0.4/km² (n = 5)
White Deer–Buffalo Creeks	886 km² (342 mi²)	2/km² (n = 18)	0.9/km² (n = 8)
Muncy-Chillisquaque Creeks	1,178 km² (455 mi²)	5.2/km² (n = 61)	1.8/km² (n = 21)

Note: n = number of components present, not number of component artifacts or number of sites.

the watersheds of Antes-Lycoming, Loyalsock, White Deer–Buffalo, and Muncy-Chillisquaque Creeks (Table 6.9). Most Transitional Archaic sites are located on terraces, and all are within 220 meters of the nearest surface water. The highest component density for both Broadspear and Orient traditions is in the Muncy-Chillisquaque Creeks watershed.

Transitional Archaic "Core" Areas

The data contained in Tables 6.2 through 6.8 illustrate patterning and variability in Transitional Archaic settlement density. Three things are clear from the tabular analysis: (1) there is a higher density of Broadspear than Orient components across the study area; (2) river settings tend to be more intensively utilized or densely populated, and interior locations tend to be more extensively utilized or less densely populated throughout the Transitional Archaic period; and (3) there tends to be continuity in the more intensively utilized or densely populated areas from the earlier to later Transitional Archaic phases (e.g., Broadspear to Orient). Figures 6.4 and 6.5 interpolate these trends. The two maps illustrate component density for the earlier (Broadspear) and later (Orient) phases of the Transitional Archaic period with shading correlating with component density (darker with higher density; lighter with lower density; Table 6.10).

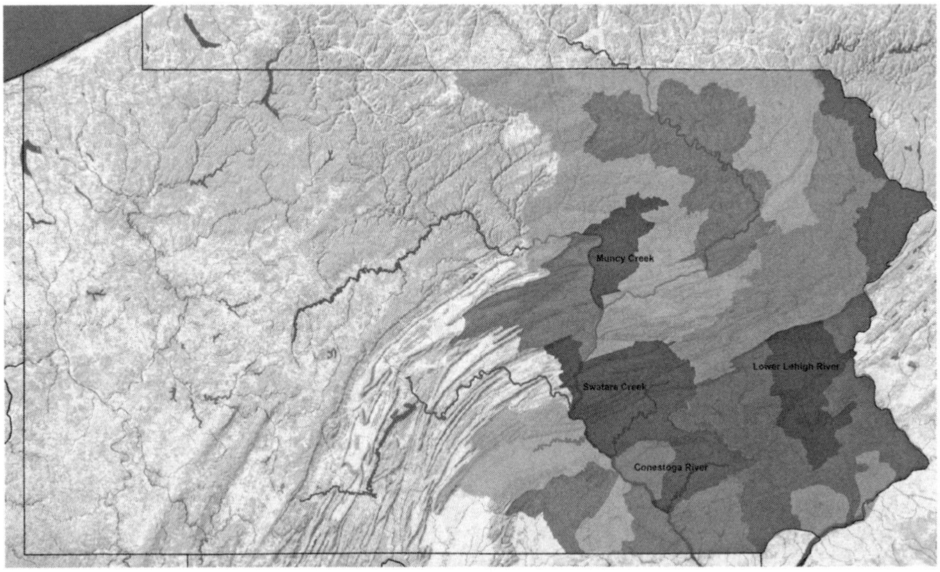

FIGURE 6.4
Density of Broadspear components (darker = higher density; lighter = lower density).

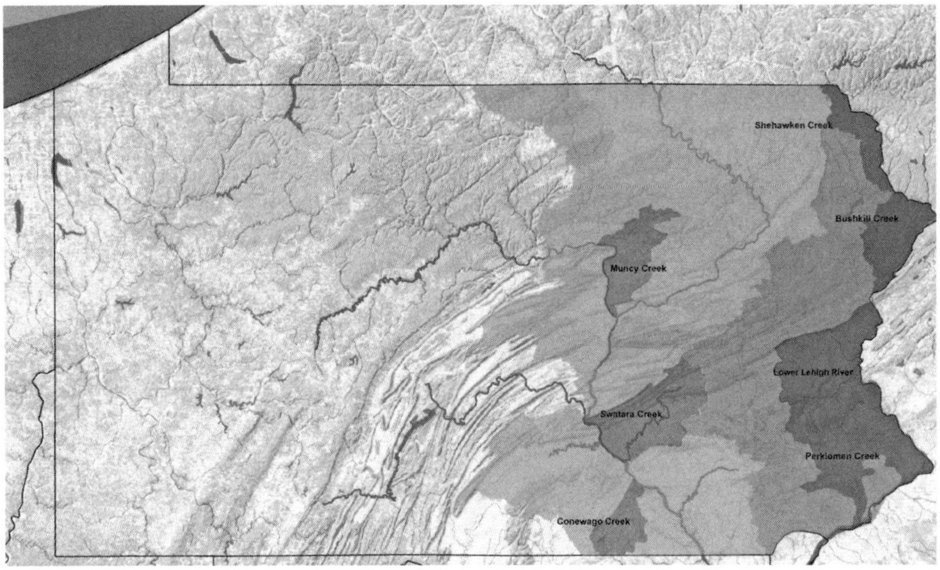

FIGURE 6.5
Density of Orient components (darker = higher density; lighter = lower density).

As illustrated in Figure 6.4, the highest Broadspear component density is in the Swatara Creek and Conestoga River watersheds, with secondary concentrations in the Muncy Creek and Lower Lehigh River watersheds. These are all locations with five or more components per square kilometer. The carrying capacity of these "core" settlement areas during the Broadspear phase may have been able to sustain more intensive utilization or higher population densities than "core" areas during the Orient phase because of a diverse resource base and stable riverine settings.

As illustrated in Figure 6.5, the highest Orient component density is in the watersheds of Swatara, Conewago, Muncy, Perkiomen, Bushkill, and Shehawken Creeks and the Lower Lehigh River. These are all locations with one to five components per square kilometer. The figure's distribution map shows more tightly focused riverine settlement in the Orient than in the Broadspear phase, although none of these settlement areas are more intensively utilized, or more densely populated than those in the Broadspear phase. The Conestoga River watershed displays the greatest difference from the earlier to later phases, with density

TABLE 6.10 Key to Figures 6.4 and 6.5

Grade 1 (lightest shade)	< 1 component/km^2
Grade 2	1–5 components/km^2
Grade 3	5–10 components/km^2
Grade 4 (darkest shade)	> 10 components/km^2

dropping from more than ten to fewer than one component per square kilometer.

Population Density and Social Organization in the Transitional Archaic Period

Results of the study reported in this chapter essentially support earlier statements by Witthoft (1953) that Transitional settlement is largely river oriented, but also point to particular "core" use or settlement areas. These "core" areas remain consistent from the earlier Transitional Archaic Broadspear tradition to the later Orient tradition, with the main difference being a higher overall density of Broadspear components in those locations. This may reflect the methodology employed in this study, which counts each Broadspear type as a discrete component. Although, due to variability in use and discard rates, there is no direct correlation between density of materials and the number of people, the study proposes that the trends presented here are accurate and significant for understanding social organization and cultural developments during the Transitional Archaic Period. And although the decline of archaeological components from the Broadspear to the Orient phase may merely signify the beginning of what Andrew Wyatt (2003) and Paul Raber (2008) suggest is the invisibility of the Early and Middle Woodland Periods in Pennsylvania due to biased site recordation and the poorly defined material culture of these periods, it may instead reflect significant shifts in social organization. Binford (1980) suggests that increased population density may require greater resource management within a restricted spatial range, and during the Broadspear phase this may have entailed a focus on macroband organization. Macrobands would have been composed of smaller groups with affinal ties to one another that may have resulted in cohesive territorial units, such as within the watersheds of Muncy, Swatara, and Conestoga Creeks and the Lower Lehigh River. These riverine locations also correspond to high concentrations of steatite vessels, procured in some cases from more than 200 kilometers away (Wholey and Shaffer 2014); the locations would have been desirable not only for facilitating the transport of steatite vessels from relatively great distances, but also for coping with the dry climate conditions of the time. Drought-resistant, seed-producing herbaceous plants such as *Chenopodium* and little barley would have thrived in these settings; the dry conditions would have slowed sea level rise and allowed for seasonal migratory fish runs and shellfish communities. Acquiring nonlocal steatite, harvesting seasonal fish runs, and managing stands of herbaceous food plants are all activities that would have required a level of cooperative behavior likely possible only through a macroband organizational focus.

During the Orient phase, the "core" areas within the watersheds of Muncy, Swatara, Perkiomen, Bushkill, Shehawken Creeks and the Lower Lehigh River appear to have been less intensively utilized. Although, as noted above, this may be due to the "invisibility" of the Early Woodland period, it may instead reflect an economic "scaling back" after the relative intensity of the Broadspear phase. Or it may represent a "budding off" into smaller, more residentially mobile microbands with less emphasis on the cooperative activity and territorial cohesion of the macroband organizational unit.

Early stages of population pressure would include both population expansion into underutilized or "marginal" areas and technological innovation, particularly related to resource acquisition or production. Sustained population pressure would be expressed through social conflict, ecological damage, and even territorial abandonment. Although higher population density in the "core" locations during the Broadspear phase may represent productive ecologies capable of supporting intensive utilization, higher population densities, and larger social groups, overuse or short-term population pressure may have triggered organizational shifts during the Orient phase.

REFERENCES

Binford, Lewis R.

1980 Willow Smoke and Dogs' Tails: Hunter-Gatherer Settlement Systems and Archaeological Site Formation. *American Antiquity* 45 (1): 4–20.

Caldwell, Joseph

1958 *Trend and Tradition in the Prehistory of the Eastern United States*. American Anthropological Association Memoir 88. Menasha, Wisconsin.

Custer, Jay F.

1996 *Prehistoric Cultures of Eastern Pennsylvania*. Anthropological Series 7. Pennsylvania Historical and Museum Commission, Harrisburg.

Deevey, Edward S.

1960 The Human Population. *Scientific American* 203 (1): 194–204.

Delaware Water Plan

2014 *Pennsylvania's Watershed Regions: Delaware*. Available online at http://www.pawaterplan.dep.state.pa.us/docs/Publications/09-delaware_region.pdf. Accessed October 2014.

Dewar, Robert E.

1991 Incorporating Variation in Occupation Span into Settlement-Pattern Analysis, *American Antiquity* 56 (4): 604–20.

Graber, Robert Bates

1990 Areal Decrease, Density Increase, and Circumscription: A Mathematical Model. *American Antiquity* 55 (3): 546–49.

1997 A Rigorous Approach to Population Pressure's Contribution to Cultural Evolution. In *Integrating Archaeological Demography: Multidisciplinary Approaches to Prehistoric Population*, edited by Richard R. Paine, 263–84. Occasional Papers 24. Southern Illinois University Center for Archaeological Investigations, Carbondale.

Hassan, Fekri

1975 Determination of the Size, Density, and Growth Rate of Hunting-Gathering Populations. In *Population, Ecology, and Social Evolution*, edited by S. Polgar, 27–52. Mouton, Hague.

1978 Demographic Archaeology. In *Advances in Archaeological Method and Theory*, Volume 1, edited by Michael Schiffer, 49–104. Academic Press, New York.

Kent, Barry C.

1993 Archaic Society. *Journal of Middle Atlantic Archaeology* 19:155–62.

Lee, Richard B., and Irven DeVore

1968 Problems in the Study of Hunter-Gatherers. In *Man the Hunter*, edited by Richard B. Lee and Irven DeVore, 3–12. Aldine, Chicago.

Madden, Marcie

1983 Social Network Systems Amongst Hunter-Gatherers Considered Within Southern Norway. In *Hunter-Gatherer Economy in Prehistory: A European Perspective*; edited by Geoff Bailey, 191–201. Cambridge University Press, Cambridge.

McDougal, Steven, and Chan Funk

2006 The Watershed Model, Local Contexts, and Settlement Pattern Studies. Paper presented at 77th Annual Meeting of Society for Pennsylvania Archaeology, Washington, Pennsylvania.

Raber, Paul A.

2008 The Early and Middle Woodland in the Upper Juniata River Drainage: Archaeological Visibility and Regional Population. *Pennsylvania Archaeologist* 78 (1): 16–40.

Siegel, Peter E., Tod L. Benedict, and Robert G. Kingsley

1999 *Archaeological Data Recoveries at the Fahs II and Oberly Island Sites: Structure, Function, and Context in the Lower Lehigh Valley*. Report prepared for URS Greiner, King of Prussia, Pennsylvania. John Milner Associates, Inc., West Chester, Pennsylvania.

Siegel, Peter E., Doulas C. Kellogg, and Robert G. Kingsley

2001 *Prehistoric Settlement Patterns in Upland Settings: An Analysis of Site Data in a Sample of Exempted Watersheds: Brandywine Creek Watershed (Watershed H) Chester, Lancaster, and Delaware Counties, Pennsylvania*. Report prepared for Pennsylvania Historical and Museum Commission, Harrisburg. John Milner Associates, Inc., West Chester, Pennsylvania.

Susquehanna Water Plan

2014a *Pennsylvania's Watershed Regions: Lower Susquehanna*. Available online at http://www.pawaterplan.dep.state.pa.us/docs/Publications/07-lower_susquehanna_region.pdf. Accessed October 2014.

2014b *Pennsylvania's Watershed Regions: Upper/Middle Susquehanna*. Available online at http://www.pawaterplan.dep.state.pa.us/docs/Publications/06-upper_middle_susquehanna_region.pdf. Accessed October 2014.

Varien, Mark D., and James M. Potter

1997 Unpacking the Discard Equation: Simulating the Accumulation of Artifacts in the Archaeological Record. *American Antiquity* 62 (2): 194–213.

Witthoft, John

1953 Broad Spear Points and the Transitional Period Cultures. *Pennsylvania Archaeologist* 23 (1): 4–31.

Wyatt, Andrew

2003 Early and Middle Woodland Settlement Data for the Susquehanna Basin. In *Foragers and Farmers of the Early and Middle Woodland Periods in Pennsylvania*, edited by Paul Raber and Verna Cowin, 35–47. Recent Research in Pennsylvania Archaeology 3. Pennsylvania Historical and Museum Commission, Harrisburg.

7.

The Transitional Dilemma in Pennsylvania

HEARTHS, FISH, AND POTTERY

Roger Moeller

ABSTRACT

Across the United States, the Archaic period is noted for having many local, specialized adaptations, each with its own distinctive tool kits: Maritime, Piedmont, and Desert, to name three. Some researchers in the Northeast see the Transitional period as marking a specialized adaptation, with its Broadspear cultures bridging the gap between the Late Archaic and Early Woodland periods. Although many topics will be discussed in this chapter, the primary focus will be a characteristic feature of the Transitional: large—sometimes huge—hearths filled with fire-cracked rock and located on the floodplains of major rivers and their tributaries. If these hearths were indeed a necessary part of that period's specialized adaptation related to the intensive processing of anadromous fish, how were these fish processed differently before and after then in the absence of large hearths? Answers to the Transitional dilemma will be sought.

Background

The major problem with studies on broadspears is that those who have excavated these components attempt to fit their observations into published interpretations without first completely analyzing their own sites. Whenever I hear "Terminal Archaic," "Transitional," "broadspear," or "broad blade," I think of the very large hearths and jasper bifaces I encountered on the banks of the Upper Delaware River. In this context, the broadspears include not only Lehigh, Susquehanna, and Perkiomen broadspears, but also Orient and Dry Brook fishtails. Although they do not have broad blades, the Orient and Dry Brook fishtails are included because I see a continuity of form from the Susquehanna broadspears and their association with large hearths.

The first site that I worked on more than forty years ago was the Peters-Albrecht Site (lower terrace) in Bushkill, Pennsylvania, which had a Transitional component with a huge hearth (Kinsey 1972:301–11). I next worked on the upper terrace of Peters-Albrecht, where I saw a lone Lehigh point with pot-lid fractures in a charcoal-filled pit (Kinsey 1972:318). Two years later, I excavated Orient fishtail points from a hearth 6 meters in diameter and 50 centimeters deep, filled with fire-cracked rock and bits of poorly fired Vinette I pottery at the Faucett Site (Kinsey 1972:188–90).

My subsequent excavations and analyses of surface collections from New York, Connecticut, New Jersey, and other parts of Pennsylvania yielded broadspears (including Orient and Dry Brook fishtails). Even if the sites were not known to have large hearths, I still thought these were a necessary part of the culture. After years of reflection, I have changed my mind. Broadspears and fishtails are found at sites lacking large hearths. They are found in nonriverine, nonfloodplain settings. The large hearths were not a necessary part of the culture in all econiches. Heather Wholey (2009; Chapter 6, this volume) makes this same point using data gleaned from a far more systematic search of the Pennsylvania Archaeological Site Survey (PASS) files and crosscutting a variety of river subbasins. On the other hand, I have seen very few sites in the Northeast and Middle Atlantic regions that had large hearths and lacked a Transitional component. Why were large hearths on the floodplain during the Transitional period? Why are large accumulations of fire-cracked rock so uncommon in Paleoindian, Early, Middle, and Late Archaic, and Early, Middle, and Late Woodland components—with the significant exception of Middle Woodland components at Abbott Farm (Cavallo 1984, 1987)? To answer these questions, I considered artifacts, ecofacts, and features from a variety of Transitional and pre- and post-Transitional components in widely different areas.

Overview of Regional Components

The following brief snapshots of Broadspear components (including Orient and Dry Brook fishtails) in different parts of the Northeast and Middle Atlantic regions highlight the artifacts, features, and ecofacts from selected sites to illustrate the range of what has been found. These data may or may not be typical of finds at all sites in each region. Putting broadspears into a regional context enhances our understanding of comparable Pennsylvania contexts. I also considered non-Transitional components having extensive or numerous hearths. The detailed archaeological data and interpretations can be found in the original references. If a similar package of traits for the Transitional period is not found across the Northeast and Middle Atlantic regions, then this cannot be a specialized adaptation.

New York State

The first two excavated Orient phase sites, Orient Number 1 and Number 2, on eastern Long Island were cemeteries dating to 2894 ± 250 BP (M-494; 3611–2420 BP or 1662–471 BC calibrated; Ritchie 1965:Figure 1). Habitation sites (e.g., Baxter, Stony Brook, and Muskeeta Cove) later found on Long Island showed a dietary focus on saltwater shellfish (quahog, scallop, clam, whelk, and oyster), large and small mammals and small reptiles (deer, raccoon, woodchuck, and turtle), medium-sized birds (turkey and duck), and hickory nuts. The notable features were middens, pits, earth ovens, burials, and fired earth, with small amounts of fire-broken cobbles. Although Orient fishtail bifaces (points, drills, knives) were common, soapstone bowl fragments, anvil stones, Vinette I pottery, slate gorgets, shell beads, paint stones, celts, adzes, gouges, bannerstones, and debitage were only recovered from some sites (Ritchie 1965:164–77).

New Jersey Ridge and Valley Province

Bradford Botwick and Robert Wall (1994:63–73) found Orient fishtail points at an upland site (28SX324) on the New Jersey side of the Delaware River with Late Archaic Bare Island, Brewerton, Egypt Mills, Lackawaxen, Lamoka, Poplar Island, and Eshback points; Transitional Perkiomen and Susquehanna points, Early Woodland Rossville points, and Late Woodland Levanna and Madison points. Site 28SX324 had a small cluster of fire-cracked rocks lacking cultural affiliation. Although Perkiomen and Susquehanna bifaces were found with a variety of Late Archaic ones, there is no indication they were associated with the same occupation. The site was obviously occupied repeatedly by people using a variety of bifaces, but there was no evidence for which ones were contemporaneous, and every recognizable type could have been brought by people from different bands at different times. The important point for this discussion is that Transitional bifaces were found at an upland camp in the absence of a large accumulation of fire-cracked rock.

West Branch Susquehanna Valley

The Terminal Archaic component at the Allenwood Site (Wall 2000) on the West Branch of the Susquehanna River included a mix of Perkiomen, Snook Kill, and Susquehanna broadspears, with fishtail points found stratigraphically above and below the broadspears. Twelve hearths ranging from small to large and a burned area were identified, with several discrete concentrations of features and artifact clusters. The presence of netsinkers, manos, choppers, abraders, and drills suggested a variety of base camp activities.

Main Stem Susquehanna Valley

Three stratified sites, 36PE60, 36PE16 (Wallis), and 36PE61, have been excavated by Patricia Miller (Miller et al. 2003; Miller, Marine, and Vento 2004, 2007) on a six-kilometer stretch of the Susquehanna River near Liverpool, Pennsylvania. Broadspear components there displayed a predominance of rhyolite debitage in chipping clusters. Features included basin-shaped pits, roasting pits, hearths, refuse pits, and fire-cracked rock dumps, which might be from stone boiling or intensively used hearths. Walnut and hickory nut fragments were common in the hearths, but there was very little bone. Use-wear analysis of tools indicated a variety of activities, including butchering, bone/antler working, dry hide working, soft stone working, and woodworking.

The Calver Island Site (36DA89) was very deeply stratified and included as many as eight discrete Transitional/early Early Woodland occupations dating from 3800 to 2600 BP and, on the basis of artifact density and variety of tasks represented, both short- and long-term in nature. A few of these occupations will be discussed to illustrate their similarities and differences (Miller et al. 2010:92–94). Two and possibly three Early Woodland occupations dated from 3000 BP to sometime after 2600 BP. These were most likely short-term base camps with stemmed bifaces, fishtail points, a Susquehanna broadspear, Otter Creek point, and Brewerton eared-notched point; small piles of fire-cracked rock near an earth oven suggest stone boiling. Activities represented in the microwear analysis included cutting and scraping wood or antler, hide working, butchering, cutting plants and soft material, and working soft stone.

At least two Late Transitional occupations on the island dated to between 3300 and 3000 BP. The artifact assemblages included steatite vessel fragments and a steatite pendant. Rhyolite predominated in the artifact assemblage, which included stemmed points, Susquehanna broadspears, drills, a knife, end scraper, axe, pestle, abrader, and flake tool. Three features (two hearths and a roasting pit) had charred hickory and acorn nutshells. There was microwear evidence of butchering, hide working, and working with wood, bone, or antler. Based on the relatively high densities of artifacts and fire-cracked rock, the occupations were interpreted as a long-term base camp.

An occupation likely occurring ca. 3200 BP had a hearth containing hickory nutshells and grass associated with two steatite bowl fragments. Rhyolite debitage predominated, but argillite and other lithics (e.g., steatite) were present. No specific activities were apparent. The occupation was interpreted as a base camp.

An occupation dating to ca. 3430 BP included six features: two hearths, a pit hearth, storage pit, hearth refuse pit, and fire-cracked rock dump. A Susquehanna broadspear, Orient fishtail, side scraper, and drill were found in the same level as the features. The presence of a fishtail point in this context seems early given dates from other sites. Microwear revealed evidence of cutting soft materials.

The earliest occupation at the Calver Island Site, likely dating to ca. 3800 BP, had a fire-cracked rock cluster and a roasting pit in an area of relatively high artifact density. Point types included Pequea, Steubenville stemmed, Genesee, Rossville, Bare Island, and Savannah River. Tools other than points consisted of three pestles, a chopper, cobble tool, and netsinker.

These components represent quite a diversity of tools, features, functions, floral remains, and lengths of occupations. Wood, bone, antler, and hide working, food preparation, tool manufacture or retouching, and butchering are evidenced. Susquehanna broadspears, Orient fishtails, and Snook Kill, Koens Crispin, Poplar Island, Savannah River, Steubenville stemmed, Genesee, Rossville, Pequea, and Bare Island points were identified. Other artifacts included a bead, bowls, and fragments of steatite as well as drills and pestles, a knife, scraper, axe, abrader, netsinker, chopper, and debitage of rhyolite and argillite. Features included a possible storage pit, chipping cluster, roasting pit, pit hearth, and surface hearth, as well as hearth refuse and FCR dumps. Food remains were hickory nut, black walnut, and acorn shells and *Chenopodium*, little barley, rye grass, or wheatgrass seeds.

Upper Delaware Valley

In his comparison of Broadspear (i.e., Perkiomen) and Orient traits at the Miller Field (New Jersey), Brodhead-Heller (Pennsylvania), and Faucett (Pennsylvania) Sites, W. Fred Kinsey (1972:Table 10) shows the same components or levels had large hearths and shared many implements (e.g., bifacial scrapers, knives, drills, strike-a-lights, netsinkers, choppers, grinding stones, hammerstones, axes, celts, spearthrower weights, steatite bowls, and mullers) not used in fish processing. The primary items not found in the Orient components at these occupations were early cord-marked and steatite-tempered pottery and other items made from steatite (spoons, ladles, cups, pendants, and beads). The only ecofact found was a small amount of charcoal. Although this was expected from the Brodhead-Heller and Miller Field Sites, where large-scale flotation was not employed, I conducted flotation on all the soil from an entire Orient hearth that was more than 6 meters in diameter at the Faucett Site in 1972 and recovered only a scant amount of charcoal (Moeller 2009).

In comparing the Upper Delaware Valley Orient components to the Long Island ones, Kinsey (1972:Table 10) notes the absence of large hearths, choppers, steatite-tempered pottery, and steatite items other than bowls, all present on Long Island. The major features found on Long Island but not in the Upper Delaware Valley are cremation burials.

Herbert Kraft excavated a huge hearth at the Harrys Farm Site on the New Jersey side of the Delaware River, opposite and slightly downstream from the Faucett Site. Based on a radiocarbon date of 1660 BP ± 95 (I-4748; 1743–1362 BP or AD 207–588 calibrated) from Feature G-F58 located within the hearth (Kraft 1975:51, Figure 29), he assigned it to the Middle Woodland period. Some years later, however, Kraft (2001:155, Figure 5.7) apparently changed his mind, describing this same hearth as a "cobble-filled drying platform associated with the Orient culture on the Harry's Farm site [that] measured 47 feet by 26 feet [14.5 by 8 m]." Although he does not explain why he changed his mind, given similar features on the Pennsylvania side of the river, I am suggesting that the hearth was indeed constructed and utilized during Orient times, but that features were later dug into it, giving a misleading radiocarbon date.

Lower Delaware Valley

In their excavations in the Piedmont Uplands of Chester County, Pennsylvania, at the Woodward Site (36CH374), David Rue and Christopher Bergman (1991:127) found "a variety of projectile point forms, including Brewerton, Lackawaxen small stemmed, Rossville contracting stemmed, and Broadspears . . . utilized during the same occupational episode." These bifaces were found close to a pit hearth radiocarbon dated to 3950 ± 60 BP (Beta 26700; 4537–4229 BP or 2588–2280 BC calibrated; Rue and Bergman 1991:133–34). Rue and Bergman's findings support the invalidity of certain point typologies as chronological markers. Tasks at the site were dominated by woodworking rather than butchering (Rue and Bergman 1991:127).

Piscataway, Maryland

South of Washington, D.C., where Piscataway Creek joins the Potomac River, the water is brackish. Intermittent freshwater streams flowing across the broad expanse of low-relief floodplain become brackish at their mouths and support marshes. William Gardner (1987:74–75) discusses the variety of econiches present:

> This zone contains the maximum number of all the available habitats in the area including a major river (the Potomac); a major embayed high order stream (Piscataway Bay); smaller embayed areas and associated swamps (mouths of the intermittent creeks); numerous intermittent creeks; a broad floodplain and the immediately contiguous uplands. . . . The second order stream valleys (Gardner 1976) have their headwaters in the uplands and pass through several micro-zones. These include the embayed areas at the mouths; a zone of low terraces; a zone of deep, slightly U-shaped valleys; and a zone of narrow, shallow valleys. The mouths of the streams on which we have worked have low flood free areas on at least one side and project peninsula-like out into a tidal swamp. During high tide, the stream backs up to the edge of the low flood free areas, and in low tide it reverts to the normal channel. . . . [We] uncovered an extensive archaeological site spanning the period from the Late Archaic through the terminal Middle Woodland (Mockley). The site was literally continuously covered with hearths and contained quantities of projectile points/knives and debitage. With the exception of a few fragments of soapstone, all of the lithic material was derived from cobbles available nearby. This situation was replicated by work we did in other areas along the Piscataway.

South Fork of the Shenandoah River

Numerous Late Archaic (and, by inference, Transitional) sites on low-order streams intersecting the Shenandoah were most likely there for fishing purposes. These sites have numerous hearths, but none are very large. On the other hand, by the Late Archaic period, sites on the floodplain of the South Fork do have large hearths, suggesting the radiation of riverine resources such as fish, which can be heavily exploited seasonally (Gardner 1987:65). Although large anadromous fish runs did not occur in the South Fork, schools of anadromous species of the sucker family (Catostomidae) were common there (Gardner 1987:57).

Interpretations of Regional Components

Overviews

Based solely on these quick snapshots from Transitional sites across the Middle Atlantic region, one would conclude that broadspears were not functioning within a specialized economy. The wide diversity of site functions, of associated artifacts, ecofacts, and econiches suggests that the broadspear was a highly generalized implement modified for the circumstances at hand. Were there small, highly mobile bands exploiting a diversity of econiches throughout their seasonal round? Were frequent contacts among mobile bands spreading the basic technology, which was locally modified? Large-scale or numerous hearths or fire-cracked rock dumps are not unique to the Transitional period. When not found in that period, the association is with intensive fishing, the implication being that the Transitional hearths were also used in fish processing. Various researchers examined the components in their region and drew various conclusions.

Long Island Sound Area

Based on his research and that of colleagues across Long Island Sound in Connecticut, Rhode Island, Massachusetts, and elsewhere in New York State, William Ritchie (1965:173) concluded that "the Orient phase conveys the distinct impression of having achieved its climax on Long Island. Except for the mortuary aspects, it would seem to have been quite prosaic and utilitarian, the product of a small population of semisedentary food gatherers firmly rooted in regional Archaic traditions."

Upper Delaware Valley

Kinsey's *Archeology in the Upper Delaware Valley* (1972:354) is probably the most frequently cited source for associating broadspears with very large hearths for processing great quantities of anadromous fish taken from the Upper Delaware Valley. Looking at just the summary chapter, one might assume he is making an argument for a specialized fishing economy. Individual site reports elsewhere in the volume, however, list artifacts *not* directly associated with fishing. Thus fishing might have been the reason people came to the floodplain, but it was not their only activity after they arrived.

Middle Delaware Valley

Joseph Blondino's (2008) work at the Driftstone Site (36NM244) uncovered Orient, Perkiomen, and Lehigh/Snook Kill components with extensive hearths. His discussion on whether the fire-cracked rocks broke from being used as stone boilers or from being repeatedly heated in platform hearths (Blondino 2008:172–73) does not resolve the question, however. The necessary associated features and artifacts are absent, either because they were never there or because they completely disappeared.

New Jersey

Herbert Kraft's (1972) research at the Miller Field Site revealed the typical association of Perkiomen broadpoints with hearths on a floodplain site. Broadening his perspective to other sections of New Jersey, Kraft (1990:69–70) commented:

> Perkiomen broadpoints and artifacts associated with this culture are found not only near major streams; they occur near swamps, at the headwaters of streams, on high terraces, on glacial kames overlooking swamps, and in the interior uplands near springs (Staats 1986:39; LaPorta, personal communication, January 31 and March 10, 1989). They have also been reported from the Abbott Farm site (Cavallo 1987), and in backwater floodplains and upland settings in other parts of the Middle Delaware River Valley, and from the interior of the New Jersey Coastal Plain in the vicinity of large expanses of cedar swamps (Ibid.:VIII/28–29), and on the "cuesta" interface between the inner and outer coastal plains (Cresson, personal communication March 1, 1989). These riverine and interior occurrences and the relative scarcity of broadpoints on coastal sites call into question the presumption that broadpoints are a reflection of a maritime economy (Cook 1976; Turnbaugh 1975).

Jack Cresson (1990:125) summarized his analysis of more than 1,200 broadspears from many inland locations in New Jersey:

> Most researchers agree that broadspear bifaces can be multi-functional tools exhibiting a range of mixed uses that seem to be aligned to size, configuration, fracture history, and environmental setting. What they disagree on is the extent of primary and secondary functional uses within the variation of broadspear subforms. What most failed to do, with the exception of Custer and Mellin (although fault

cannot be placed because of the limited scopes of research) is to look at the larger realm of the broadspear phenomenon as part of a more complex system of biface tools developed to provide a continuum of both specialized and generalized, curated and expedient tool forms for multi-functional uses.

Pennsylvania, New Jersey, Maryland, and Virginia

James Truncer (1990:33–34) conducted a use-wear analysis on nearly 500 Perkiomen points from sites in these four states:

> One of the more important findings is that Perkiomen points show evidence of having been used as knives and projectiles. The percentages of mesial and proximal transverse fractures (indicative of use as knives) and unambiguous distal impact fractures (indicative of use as projectiles) remained constant throughout different environmental settings . . . despite collection biases, suggesting that Perkiomen points were not specialized tools associated with riverine environments. This finding contrasts sharply with several previous interpretations (Kinsey 1972:346–47; Cook 1976; Custer 1978:11–13, 1984a:79, 1984b:40; Snethkamp 1981:73). Perkiomen points exhibited fractures indicative of use as projectiles. This eliminates the need to suggest that other narrow-bladed Late Archaic point types served as projectiles among groups which used Perkiomen points (see Custer 1984a:79). The fact that these points are associated with a variety of functional activities and occur in association with a diverse tool kit suggests that Perkiomen points were produced by a socially autonomous group (see Cavallo 1987:VIII) and were not merely specialized tools adopted into an existing Perkiomen tradition tool kit (cf. Custer 1984a:79).

Truncer was careful to note that generalizations about other broadspears cannot be made based on his study of Perkiomen points. Each point type must be studied individually.

Problems for the Current Study

The preceding observations and comments on Transitional components recognized either by diagnostic artifacts or actual datings by David Rue and Christopher Bergman, Joseph Blondino, William Gardner, W. Fred Kinsey, Herbert Kraft, William Ritchie, James Truncer, and Jack Cresson from different regions and sites discussed above show that the entire trait list did not travel as a package. Typologically similar bifaces can be found in different econiches where people manufactured a variety of implements from different lithics (e.g., rhyolite, argillite, jasper, and chert) and constructed a variety of facilities for resource procurement and processing. One might justify the differences by saying that co-occurrence does not equal association. Multiple occupations at the same site might be commingled and mistaken archaeologically for a single component. One type might not equal one band. Lithic preferences might well have been determined by local availability. Rather than attempting to trivialize the contexts by assuming admixture, I stepped back for a longer, temporal perspective.

Since the huge Perkiomen and Orient hearths I had seen in the Upper Delaware Valley were found on the floodplain, they could have been used for large-scale fish processing, but fish bones were lacking in the hearths, as were large amounts of charcoal. Despite the lack of definitive evidence, however, the assumption was that these were specialized occupations. Were the hearths and broadspears used for one activity set, with the other implements used for other activities? Did each hearth represent a single camp or a composite from repeated occupations? Large hearths did not always have broadspears, Orient fishtail points, or both, but the same points were also found at sites lacking large hearths. The bifaces were used in both hearth- and non-hearth-related activities. If broadspears were associated with hearths on the floodplain, the hearths were more likely to be large than small.

The problem had now expanded into new realms: Transitional components, hearths, non-Transitional hearths, stone boiler accumulations, or fire-cracked rock dumps and their associated artifacts and ecofacts. In an effort to better understand the roles of hearths and broadspears during the Transitional period, I recalled my years of experience in the Upper Delaware Valley excavating sites and analyzing collections from them. Late Archaic components had small rock-lined hearths (if any at all), ground-stone implements, and argillite, quartzite, or chert bifaces (Kinsey 1972:332–43). Transitional components had very large hearths with intensely fire-cracked rock; they sometimes had steatite bowls or Vinette I pottery; their bifaces, scrapers, knives, and drills were made from jasper and chert (Kinsey 1972:343–61). Middle Woodland components might contain small pieces of fire-cracked rock in shallow pits or scattered across a living floor, net-impressed pottery, and bifaces made of jasper and chert (Kinsey 1972:363–74). With the exception of a few middens, for example, those at the Zimmerman Site (Werner 1972:58), Late Woodland components were almost always recognized from pit features containing small amounts of fire-cracked rock, pottery, bifaces, debitage, and ecofacts, such as carbonized seeds, mussel shells, and mammal bones (Moeller 2011:Table 9). Although each of the periods is defined by distinctive diagnostic implements, the frequently associated features and contexts varied. If all who came to the floodplain did so for the same purpose, then they approached that purpose in different ways. If they were not there for the same purpose, at the same time of year, with the same number of people or the same technology, then the differences were more understandable. The archaeological problem becomes one of determining how to weight each of these factors in creating a model of prehistoric behavior.

Analysis

The use of projectile point typologies to define temporal periods is common in archaeological analysis. The best use of typology is to create an easy-to-remember mnemonic for a group of traits believed to uniquely refer to a particular class of objects. Rather than repeatedly saying "a long, slender, relatively thin biface made of a cryptocrystalline lithic having a base resembling that of a fish's tail and found associated with contexts likely dating between 3300 and 2700 BP," it is easier to say, "Orient or possibly Dry Brook fishtail." The problem comes in believing that a merely heuristic device can reliably assign function, exclusivity, and cultural affiliation. This is how Orient fishtails and broadspears became associated with large hearths on the floodplains of major rivers and their tributaries. What began as a co-occurrence in some locales became part of a cultural package. It did not matter that the type site on Long Island did not have large hearths, but did have a wide variety of sea fauna and land mammals not found at inland and upland sites. The repeated co-occurrences reinforced the stereotype, yet the sites having these bifaces and lacking hearths did not degrade the stereotype. The mere possibility that the large hearths and the broadspears were a necessary package for a specialized adaptation became a "fact."

I have always combined the broadspears (e.g., Perkiomen, Susquehanna, Lehigh, Koens-Crispin, Snook Kill) with the fishtails (Orient and Dry Brook) when thinking about Transitional settlement patterns and subsistence. Considering them as individual types, I realized the great variability within and between archaeological components or levels at stratified sites. Certainly, broadspears are different from all other Late Archaic points or knives (e.g., Lackawaxen, Bare Island, Brewerton, Lamoka). Lithic preferences are also evident, with jasper, rhyolite, argillite, or quartzite being more likely to occur among broadspears than among other Late Archaic point types in some places. Confusion arises when supposed Late Archaic points found in Transitional contexts or bifaces diagnostic of one component are made from the "wrong" lithics. We recorded the contexts as precisely as possible and decided to figure out what it meant in the lab.

We found that, if we split the broadspears into discrete types rather than clustering them, including only the associated bifaces, lithic types, and ground-stone tools found in each component, the pattern changes. Not all sites in the greater Middle Atlantic region have broadspears associated with large hearths. Not all sites with approximately the same radiocarbon dates have broadspears. Why not consider temporally proximate clusters with different artifacts and features as functionally discrete elements in a larger settlement system?

Although there is a clustering of radiocarbon dates for Orient and Perkiomen bifaces, other types intervene in the earlier portion of the Transitional period in the Upper Delaware Valley (Table 7.1). Did these types represent discrete groups moving through the region and encountering the locals? This question goes well beyond who "invented" the Perkiomen type or why the Susquehanna broadspear was replaced by the Orient fishtail. Regardless of what a collection of attributes really meant to the people making the bifaces, something happened to make Orient points the only ones in this bracket in the Upper Delaware Valley. Does this mean a period of cooperation, where disparate bands are spending enough time together to decide the appropriate attributes for a biface—or a period of exclusion, where only a single resident band camps, procures, and processes? Other authors have different approaches to the question.

A Normanskill occupation dates between the Perkiomen and Orient phases of the Transitional period at the Brodhead-Heller Site. If broadspears represent a separate tradition, temporal marker, or specialized adaptation in a particular econiche, then how can they be contemporaneous with Lackawaxen and Normanskill points? Jay Custer (1996:173) uses the apparent mixture of broadspears and stemmed types

TABLE 7.1 Transitional sites and dates in Upper Delaware Valley

Type Name	Radiocarbon Date	Calibrated Dates	Site	State	Reference
Orient	2760 ± 100 BP	3159–2729 BP or 1210–780 BC	Faucett	Pennsylvania	Kinsey (1972:433)
Orient	2920 ± 30 BP	3160–2969 BP or 1211–1020 BC	Driftstone	Pennsylvania	Blondino (2008:169)
Orient	3070 ± 80 BP	3452–3057 BP or 1503–1108 BC	Driftstone	Pennsylvania	Blondino (2008:169)
Orient/Dry Brook	3120 ± 120 BP	3594–2993 BP or 1645–1044 BC	Brodhead-Heller	Pennsylvania	Kinsey (1972:433)
Orient	3170 ± 120 BP	3646–3065 BP or 1697–1116 BC	Miller Field	New Jersey	Kinsey (1972:433)
Dry Brook	3230 ± 120 BP	3726–3158 BP or 1777–1209 BC	Zimmerman	Pennsylvania	Kinsey (1972:432)
Perkiomen?	3270 ± 30 BP	3571–3445 BP or 1622–1496 BC	Driftstone	Pennsylvania	Blondino (2008:169)
Normanskill	3390 ± 100 BP	3886–3441 BP or 1937–1492 BC	Brodhead-Heller	Pennsylvania	Kinsey (1972:416)
Perkiomen	3450 ± 120 BP	3992–3445 BP or 2043–1496 BC	Faucett	Pennsylvania	Kinsey (1972:427)
Perkiomen	3590 ± 100 BP	4156–3632 BP or 2207–1683 BC	Miller Field	New Jersey	Kinsey (1972:33)
Perkiomen	3570 ± 100 BP	4101–3612 BP or 2152–1663 BC	Brodhead-Heller	Pennsylvania	Kinsey (1972:427)
Susquehanna	3600 ± 80 BP	4098–3693 BP or 2149–1744 BC	Zimmerman	Pennsylvania	Kinsey (1972:430)
Lackawaxen	3660 ± 120 BP	4299–3689 BP or 2350–1740 BC	Brodhead-Heller	Pennsylvania	Kinsey (1972:414)
Lehigh	3670 ± 100 BP	4293–3704 BP or 2344–1755 BC	Peters-Albrecht	Pennsylvania	Kinsey (1972:426)
Perkiomen	3670 ± 120 BP	4300–3695 BP or 2351–1746 BC	Miller Field	New Jersey	Kinsey (1972:427)
Lehigh/Snook Kill	3740 ± 70 BP	4159–3982 BP or 2348–1943 BC	Driftstone	Pennsylvania	Blondino (2008:169)

Note: Dates calibrated using Calib 7.0.

to develop his hypothesis that broadspears represent a specialized tool type in various regional Late Archaic assemblages by noting that there are similar mixtures of broadspears and Late Archaic points at a number of sites in the Middle Atlantic region. Although Cresson (1990:125) and Truncer (1990: 33–34) separately concluded that broadspears with breakage were most likely used as projectiles, this does not mean that broadspears and Late Archaic points could not both be used as projectiles at the same site during the same occupation. Specialization does not necessarily imply exclusivity. The appearance or continuance of the Late Archaic points might indicate that they were serving a specialized function in the established Broadspear occupation.

The supposition of specialization is based on the association of distinctive points with large hearths. The Late Archaic period, which lasted for thousands of years, forms the baseline culture for the region. The basic hammerstone, general stemmed point, and rough flakes are common occurrences in surface collections. Nearly every site has evidence of a Late Archaic presence. All of a sudden, the broadspears appear, with their flashy, exotic lithics, distinctive blades and bases, and fine knapping, associated with large hearths. The broadspears are thought of as "specialized" because of the time it obviously took to find the exotic lithics and the skills employed in knapping. Why go to all that effort unless it was for something special? What we really mean, however, is that the association of hearths and points is special, not the culture itself.

No one cares if multiple Late Archaic biface types are found close to one another. Broadspears are not special just because they are sometimes found with large hearths, whereas Late Archaic points are usually not. Large hearths are what make the Transitional culture different. The reason they are not always found is that not all sites needed them. The real questions are why did large hearths appear at this time and not earlier in the Late Archaic? And why did they all but disappear in the Early Woodland? The exception is the Ohio River drainage basin in western Pennsylvania (Paul Raber, personal communication, April 2013).

The time range and association of each point type can be highly misleading because traits moved individually and not in clusters. And because not all camps served the same purpose, the same tool kit was not necessary at each. But the larger the number of purposes served, the greater the variety in the tool kit. The longer the stay, the greater the number and diversity of implements manufactured, employed, and discarded. The primary point of commonality among all the components is the distinctive biface. Each band occupied numerous camps as part of the seasonal round. Throughout the Northeast and Middle Atlantic regions, riverside, lakeside, inland, upland, mortuary, fishing, hunting, and gathering camps are known. Confusion is caused by creating a composite of all associated artifacts and features rather than taking each component individually. By selecting individual, resource-specific components, however, an entire settlement system can be modeled.

This collection of traits at sites having broadspears is different from that for a generic "Late Archaic" adaptation. Although there are precedents for recognizing specialized adaptations during the Archaic (e.g., Maritime, Desert, Piedmont), the co-occurrence of broadspears and hearths does not necessarily imply specialization. I do not think that the broadspears are more a part of a specialized adaptation than any other biface found on the floodplain. Broadspears just happen to be the style of bifaces people were using for a variety of functions. We credit Transitional foragers with specialization because large hearths and broadspears did not appear before nor did they recur afterward except in a few notable locales (e.g., Abbott Farm). These bifaces would not appear as special if they were found with the same associations as other Late Archaic biface types in the absence of large hearths.

Looking at components obviously later than the Transitional period, Middle Woodland sites are more likely than Late Archaic or Transitional ones to have preserved post molds, suggesting house patterns. The pottery is better fired and likely to be net impressed. Corner notching is used for some bifaces. Many things changed between the Late Archaic and Middle Woodland periods, but the changes did not happen all at once. The Early Woodland sites vary widely depending on whether they are in western, central, eastern, northern, or southern Pennsylvania. Some sites are considered Early Woodland only because of a few bits of pottery and material dated too late to be Transitional. The degree of change is more apparent when seen at Middle Woodland sites.

The large hearths are the key to understanding the Transitional settlement system. Why are they not found in the Late Archaic period? Why are they nearly absent in the post-Orient Early Woodland period? Of all the Middle Woodland sites I have researched, I recall only Abbott Farm (Trenton, New Jersey) having major amounts of fire-cracked rock. John Cavallo (1984:114) reported hearths 4.2 meters in length. In attempting to create a model for the various dates and associations of Transitional hearths, I realized I did not know what a hearth is and how it was formed.

What Is a Hearth?

The generic term "hearth" might refer to a platform hearth, pit hearth, rock-lined feature, stone-boiling dump, or any combination of these. One might ask whether platform hearths are truly different from stone-boiling dumps or merely at opposite ends on a continuum of use history. John Cavallo and Shari Kondrup (1985) conducted hot-rock boiling experiments and concluded that, from their distribution and appearance, the piles of fire-cracked rocks seen at the Abbott Farm Area B Site (28ME1-B) should be considered stone-boiling dumps rather than hearths. R. Michael Stewart (2005, 2008) and Kathie Gonick (2003) discuss the factors determining the nature of heated stones. And Joseph Blondino (2008:172–73) discusses various logical indicators for determining the actual function of a specific hearth, including soil reddening, stone sooting, stone cracking, available containers for stone boiling, and the presence of charcoal or of charred or burned bones or seeds. Large hearths might have appeared because of accumulations from recurring seasonal, intensive short-term, or continuous long-term use. For all the discussion of this matter, however, there still needs to be a scientific typology to compare an experimental analysis of hearths to actual archaeological features. Although the analysis to develop this typology is beyond the scope of this chapter, the point of such an analysis should be a processual one: what were the processes behind the construction and utilization of these features?

What Was the Function of Large Hearths?

Arguably related cultures transformed their cooking vessels from hide bags to steatite bowls and crude pottery in less than 400 years. The change was so fast (in archaeological time) that not all components at all sites reflect this process. At some sites, there is an obvious ending of one lifestyle, tool kit, and level of technology and the equally obvious beginning of the next. Using fire to transform clay into watertight ceramic vessels is a vast technological leap forward, but it was not perfected quickly. Some groups sharing a common biface were technologically lagging. Good-quality pottery is rarely found in valid association with large or numerous hearths within a single component, but steatite fragments are. Does this mean that pottery vessels were better for cooking, rendering, reducing, or processing than steatite ones? Did the heat-cracked rock come from stone boiling in hide bags or hide-lined pits? Since people cooking with steatite bowls and good-quality ceramic pots could place them directly over a fire, they would not need to stone boil. Is it possible that pottery vessels were a replacement for steatite ones because they were much larger and easier to transport? Another issue to be addressed in this analysis would be whether hearths grew large because of repeated, intensive, short-term (i.e., one-season) use by many people or because of repeated, continuous, intensive, long-term use by fewer people?

Regardless of how many people or days are represented by a single huge hearth, the size of the resident group is a factor.

Population Size

Most population curves I have seen for the Northeast and Middle Atlantic regions show population peaking in the Late Archaic period, descending into a deep trough during the Early Woodland period, gradually increasing in the Middle Woodland, and growing more rapidly in the Late Woodland. See, for example, the population curve constructed by Kurt Carr from the entire PASS file (see Figures 3.6 and 3.7). The periods, defined by diagnostic artifacts, are not broken into phases.

Population curves based on site counts using projectile point and pottery typologies are flawed. The fallacy in using projectile point types is that modern humans are creating a typology for artifacts made by prehistoric humans thousands of years ago. The most widespread points (e.g., Lamoka, small-stemmed, side-notched points) have too wide a geographic distribution, are too generic to reflect their being made by knappers following a specific mental template, have temporal spans of thousands of years, or have clones appearing in other time periods. Counting sites where these more generic types are found will always result in higher numbers of these sites than of sites having more specific types used for shorter periods of time in other time periods. Although specific types could be used and a statistical correction factor applied for the different time spans of the periods (Carr, Chapter 3), at least five other factors need to be addressed in assigning sites to specific periods.

The second factor inflating the counts of Late Archaic sites is that Late Archaic culture is the baseline culture. The basic procurement and processing implements (e.g., projectile points, knives, grinding stones, hammerstones) do not change rapidly between periods. The shape of projectile points or knives might change, but not their functions. Hammerstones and grinding stones are not affected by the same forces for improving efficiency or adapting to new lithics. Any site might appear to have a Late Archaic component until pottery or well-defined, temporally specific, diagnostic points are found.

The third factor inflating the counts of Late Archaic sites is the misconception that post–Late Archaic sites in one area need to look like those in other areas. One expects Early Woodland sites to be more than Late Archaic sites with pottery, but what if that is exactly what they are? While doing background research for an article on the Early Woodland period in the main-stem valley of the Susquehanna River, I was quite surprised to find scant mention of exotic trade items, exotic raw materials, or diagnostic artifacts indicative of the Adena culture. The surveys by Paul Raber (2008) and Gary Coppock (2008) on the west side of the Susquehanna River and in the Juniata River drainage basin have revealed sites that would have been characterized as Late Archaic had they not had Early Woodland AMS radiocarbon dates. Early Woodland sites in the Susquehanna River Valley south of the West and North Branches are not likely to have much pottery or even diagnostic Adena bifaces. The unlikelihood of finding tiny bits of poorly fired pottery in surveys of this area would merely add to the count of Late Archaic sites. Not all sites needed pottery. Since the Early Woodland pottery in this region is very poorly fired and friable, its survival rate during long-distance transport must have been low.

The fourth factor is that Middle Woodland components follow the pattern of Early Woodland components. In the absence of actual datings (not just artifactual comparisons), Middle Woodland sites are easily overlooked or misassigned. Hopewell artifacts are not common in the interior of Pennsylvania. The fifth factor is that Late Archaic foragers are going to be visiting more procurement stations on their seasonal rounds than the increasingly sedentary, budding (pun intended) horticultural Early Woodland foragers are. And the sixth factor is climate. According to the research of Frank Vento (Chapter 1), the climate of the Transitional period was warm and dry. Interior streams would not have been reliable. People would have depended on the larger streams for water. With an increasing focus on foraging closer to the floodplains, the previous foraging range would have diminished. Fewer interior sites would have been occupied. The increasing frequency of streamside or floodplain visitation would have increased archaeological visibility.

Unless one can prove the intervening presence of one or more of the Four Horsemen of the Apocalypse (pestilence, war, famine, death), then I will side with Thomas Malthus: food production increases arithmetically and population increases geometrically. Population increases faster than food production through time. The post–Late Archaic/pre–Middle Woodland period had a larger population than the pre-Transitional/Late Archaic period did.

If the population was actually increasing, then it seems reasonable that foragers might have sought an abundant, storable resource. Since they did not have any domesticated crops and were not practicing vegeculture at the advent of the Transitional period, they needed to intensify their hunting and gathering. There are few economies of scale with plant food collecting. Fish can be harvested much more intensively using dams, weirs, and larger nets with macroband cooperation. The popularity of huge hearths for relatively short periods of time in a few locations suggests that great quantities of fish could be processed quickly by large numbers of people. But we might not recognize facilities for procuring and processing larger amounts of game, nuts, berries, shoots, and roots because their archaeological visibility is too low.

William Schindler's (2006) dissertation and many speakers at the Middle Atlantic Archaeological Conference have presented extraordinary detail regarding ethnographic, archaeological, experimental, and biological/ecological data related to the availability and processing of fish resources in the Delaware Valley. The conundrum facing archaeologists is to explain how such intensive, short-term, but possibly repeated use of hearths left so little trace evidence beyond the fire-cracked rock. The excavation and flotation of many hearths on the floodplain of the Delaware River need to be done.

The problem with the idea of intensified fish use is that great quantities of firewood would be necessary to dry and smoke the fish during the spring or late fall fish runs. The summer's heat would have been enough to rapidly desiccate fish without nearly as much firewood, but the fish would not be nearly as abundant then. People must have soon realized the downside: once the fish were dried, they would have to be kept dry until they were prepared for eating. Since there is no evidence for long-term or winter housing on the floodplain, large amounts of dried fish would have to be transported to a structure where they could be stored and kept dry, requiring that people live with a store of dried fish that attracted skunks, raccoons, and bears.

Why Did Large Hearths Disappear Before the Middle Woodland Period?

My hypothesis is that large hearths declined in popularity because of the drawbacks to large-scale fish procurement and storage and because of the advent of vegeculture or nearly true horticulture in Orient times. People were already familiar with basic gathering techniques; plant stewardship and early domesticates would have increased the yield. If Vento's climatic model is correct, the warm and dry conditions of the Transitional period that had forced people closer to the reliable water supply of major streams opened interior locations for more intensive settlement. Base camps might have been located on the rivers, but the procurement catchment areas would be extended inland.

Patricia Miller and colleagues (2010) found extensive evidence of early plant food processing at Calver Island in the Middle Susquehanna River, including an AMS radiocarbon date of 3980 ± 40 BP (4530–4348 BP or 2581–2399 BC calibrated) on *Chenopodium* seeds bearing characteristics of domestication. There is evidence for diverse plant foods being processed in steatite bowls found on-site:

> Residue analysis of steatite bowl fragments support the use of native seeds by the Calver Island occupants (Cummings and Varney 2006). Steatite residues included starches of the *Hordeum/Elymus* type, indicating that seeds from grasses such as little barley or wild rye were processed in the vessels. . . . Residue analysis of Calver Island ceramics and steatite also revealed evidence of the roots of the lily family (Liliaceae) in the Transitional and Early Woodland periods. The use of geophyte resources (tubers, rhizomes, roots, bulbs, and corms) as a food resource by Native Americans has been well-documented in the ethnohistorical record. (Miller et al. 2010:99, 99–10)

Timothy Messner (2008, 2011) summarizes and discusses these data and their implications in great detail for the Eastern Woodlands.

Plant foods can be obtained in a wider variety of locales than fish without labor-intensive facility construction and macroband cooperative procurement. Plants are easier to transport, less attractive to scavengers, and more easily stored, but large, transportable, sturdy, waterproof, fire-resistant containers are needed for processing, preparing, and storing plant foods. Steatite bowls served well for a relatively short time before pottery was introduced, but they were very heavy. Pottery was more efficient and more portable, but it took time to perfect its manufacture.

Summary

One of the basic tenets of the intelligence and law enforcement fields is that you know you have a problem when your suspect is described as a "tall, short, balding man with long, red hair dressed as a woman." If there are too many contradictions in the description, then you must reexamine your evidence. The same is true for descriptions of the Transitional period. Attempts to offer a one-size-fits-all model for the diverse manifestations in the Middle Atlantic, New England, Northeast, and Midwest regions have masked what I believe is the truly important factor during this period. Population increase was forcing people to practice the intensive fishing evidenced by the large hearths, but this was only one part of their seasonal round. This adaptation lasted for less than a thousand years until ceramic technology made vegeculture and early horticulture a more viable alternative.

REFERENCES

Blondino, Joseph R.

2008 How Can You Mend a Broken Hearth? Preliminary Results of Excavations at the Driftstone Site. *Journal Middle Atlantic Archaeology* 24:167–75.

Botwick, Bradford, and Robert D. Wall

1994 Prehistoric Settlement in the Uplands of the Upper Delaware Valley: Recent Surveys and Testing in the Delaware Water Gap National Recreation Area. *Journal of Middle Atlantic Archaeology* 10:63–73.

Cavallo, John A.

1984 Fish, Fires, and Foresight: Middle Woodland Economic Adaptations in the Abbott Farm National Landmark. *North American Archaeologist* 5 (2): 111–38.

1987 *Area B (28Me1-B), Data Recovery*. Trenton Complex Archaeology: Report 8. Prepared for Federal Highway Administration and New Jersey Department of Transportation, Bureau of Environmental Analysis, Trenton. Cultural Resource Group, Louis Berger & Associates, Inc., East Orange, New Jersey.

Cavallo, John A., and Shari L. Kondrup

1985 A Replicative Analysis of Fire-Cracked Rock Features. Paper presented at Middle Atlantic Archaeological Conference, Rehoboth Beach, Delaware.

Cook, Thomas Genn

1976 Broadpoint: Culture, Phase, Horizon, Tradition, or Knife? *Journal of Anthropological Research* 32 (1): 337–57.

Coppock, Gary F.

2008 Shriver Chert Acquisition: A Case Study from Snyder County, Pennsylvania. *Journal of Middle Atlantic Archaeology* 24:113–40.

Cresson, Jack

1990 Broadspear Lithic Technology: Some Aspects of Biface Manufacture, Form, and Use History with Insights Towards Understanding Assemblage Diversity. In *Experiments and Observations on the Terminal Archaic of the Middle Atlantic Region*, edited by Roger W. Moeller, 105–30. Archaeological Services, Bethlehem, Connecticut.

Cummings, Linda Scott, and R. A. Varney

2006 *Pollen, Starch, and Phytolith Analysis for the Calver Island Site (36DA89), Pennsylvania: Stratigraphic Columns and Ceramic and Steatite Sherds.* Technical Report 06-09, prepared for KCI Technologies, Mechanicsburg, Pennsylvania. Paleo Research Institute, Golden, Colorado.

Custer, Jay F.

1978 Broadspears and Netsinkers: Late Archaic Adaptation Indicated by Depositional Sequences from Four Middle Atlantic Archaeological Sites. Paper presented at Middle Atlantic Archaeological Conference, Rehoboth Beach, Delaware.

1984a *Delaware Prehistoric Archaeology*. University of Delaware Press, Newark.

1984b Paleoecology of the Late Archaic: Exchange and Adaptation. *Pennsylvania Archaeologist* 54 (3–4): 32–47.

1996 *Prehistoric Cultures of Eastern Pennsylvania*. Anthropological Series 7. Pennsylvania Historical and Museum Commission, Harrisburg.

Gardner, William M.

1976 *Excavations at 18PR141, 18PR142, 18PR143, near Piscataway, Maryland.* Report submitted to Washington Suburban Sanitary Commission. Thunderbird Research, Front Royal, Virginia.

1987 Comparison of Ridge and Valley, Blue Ridge, Piedmont, and Coastal Plain Archaic Period Site Distribution: An Idealized Transect (Preliminary Model). *Journal of Middle Atlantic Archaeology* 3:49–80.

Gonick, Kathie

2003 Fire Altered Rock as Artifacts: Two Experiments—Fire and Water; Their Effects on Quartz and Quartzite. *Journal of Middle Atlantic Archaeology* 19:151–62.

Kinsey, W. Fred, III (editor)

1972 *Archeology in the Upper Delaware Valley*. Anthropological Series 2. Pennsylvania Historical and Museum Commission, Harrisburg.

Kraft, Herbert C.

1972 The Miller Field Site. In *Archeology in the Upper Delaware Valley*, edited by W. Fred Kinsey III, 1–54. Anthropological Series 2. Pennsylvania Historical and Museum Commission, Harrisburg.

1975 *The Archaeology of the Tocks Island Area*. Archaeological Research Center, Seton Hall University Museum, South Orange, New Jersey.

1990 The Terminal Archaic in the Upper Delaware Valley: A Broad and Narrow Perspective. In *Experiments and Observations on the Terminal Archaic of the Middle Atlantic Region*, edited by Roger W. Moeller, 63–84. Archaeological Services, Bethlehem, Connecticut.

2001 *The Lenape-Delaware Indian Heritage: 10,000 BC to AD 2,000*. Lenape Books, Stanhope, New Jersey.

Messner, Timothy C.

2008 *Woodland Period People and Plant Interactions: New Insights from Starch Grain Analysis*. Ph.D. dissertation, Department of Anthropology, Temple University, Philadelphia. University Microfilms, Ann Arbor, Michigan.

2011 *Acorns and Bitter Roots: Starch Grain Research in the Prehistoric Eastern Woodlands*. University of Alabama Press, Tuscaloosa.

Miller, Patricia E., James T. Marine, Justine Woodard McKnight, and Frank J. Vento

2010 Archaeological Investigations on Calver Island (36DA89), a Stratified Site in the Lower Susquehanna River Valley. *Journal Middle Atlantic Archaeology* 26:81–103.

Miller, Patricia E., James T. Marine, and Frank J. Vento

2004 *Phase III Archaeological Data Recovery, Route 11/15 Improvements (SR 0011, Section 008), Juniata and Perry Counties, Pennsylvania*, Volume 4: *36Pe61*. Report prepared for Pennsylvania Department of Transportation, Engineering District 8-0, Harrisburg. KCI Technologies, Inc., Mechanicsburg, Pennsylvania.

2007 *Phase III Archaeological Data Recovery, Route 11/15 Improvements (SR 0011, Section 008), Juniata and Perry Counties, Pennsylvania*, Volume 2: *36Pe16*. Report prepared for Pennsylvania Department of Transportation, Engineering District 8-0, Harrisburg. KCI Technologies, Inc., Mechanicsburg, Pennsylvania.

Miller, Patricia E., Frank J. Vento, James T. Marine, and Eloisa A. Pollack

2003 *Phase III Archaeological Data Recovery, Route 11/15 Improvements (SR 0011, Section 008), Juniata and Perry Counties, Pennsylvania*, Volume 3: *36Pe60*. Report prepared for Pennsylvania Department of Transportation, Engineering District 8-0, Harrisburg. KCI Technologies, Inc., Mechanicsburg, Pennsylvania.

Moeller, Roger W.

2009 Rethinking the Terminal Archaic in Pennsylvania: Hearths, Fish, and Pottery. Paper presented at Annual Middle Atlantic Archaeological Conference, Ocean City, Maryland.

2011 *Analyzing and Interpreting Late Woodland Features*. Occasional Publications in Northeastern Anthropology 12. Archaeological Services, Bethlehem, Connecticut.

Raber, Paul A.

2008 The Early and Middle Woodland in the Upper Juniata River Drainage: Archaeological Visibility and Regional Population. *Pennsylvania Archaeologist* 78 (1): 16–40.

Ritchie, William A.

1965 *The Archaeology of New York State*. Natural History Press, Garden City, New York.

Rue, David J., and Christopher A. Bergman

1991 Contemporaneity of Late Archaic Piedmont Projectile Point Forms: The Woodward Site (36-CH-374), Chester County, Pennsylvania. *Journal of Middle Atlantic Archaeology* 7:127–53.

Schindler, William

2006 *Middle Woodland Exploitation of Migratory Fish in the Delaware Valley*. Ph.D. dissertation, Department of Anthropology, Temple University, Philadelphia. University Microfilms, Ann Arbor, Michigan.

Snethkamp, Pandora E.

1981 *Late Archaic Hunter-Gatherers in the Pennsylvania Piedmont*. Ph.D. dissertation, Department of Anthropology, State University of New York at Binghamton. University Microfilms, Ann Arbor, Michigan.

Staats, F. Dayton

1986 Function of the Perkiomen Broad Point: Another Point of View. *Pennsylvania Archaeologist* 56 (1–2): 7–41.

Stewart, R. Michael

2005 Thoughts on Fire-Altered Rock. *Bulletin of the Archaeological Society of New Jersey* 60:37–42.

2008 Formation of Hearth Basin Features: Implications for the Interpretation of Paleoindian and Later Archaeological Sites in the Middle Atlantic Region, Eastern United States. Paper presented at 73rd Annual Meeting of Society for American Archaeology, Vancouver, British Columbia.

Truncer, James J.

1990 Perkiomen Points: A Study in Variability. In *Experiments and Observations on the Terminal Archaic of the Middle Atlantic Region*, edited by Roger W. Moeller, 1–62. Archaeological Services, Bethlehem, Connecticut.

Turnbaugh, William A.

1975 Toward an Explanation of the Broadpoint Dispersal in Eastern North American Prehistory. *Journal of Anthropological Research* 31 (1): 51–68.

Wall, Robert D.

2000 *Phase III Archaeological Investigations, 36Un82, Allenwood Federal Correctional Complex, Sanitary Water Treatment Facility, Union County, Pennsylvania*. Report prepared for U.S. Department of Justice, Federal Bureau of Prisons, Washington, D.C. Cultural Resource Group, Louis Berger & Associates, Inc., East Orange, New Jersey.

Werner, David J.

1972 The Zimmerman Site 36-Pi-14. In *Archeology in the Upper Delaware Valley*, edited by W. Fred Kinsey III, 55–130. Anthropological Series 2. Pennsylvania Historical and Museum Commission, Harrisburg.

Wholey, Heather A.

2009 A Population Approach to the Middle Atlantic Archaic. *North American Archaeologist* 30 (1): 1–21.

LIST OF CONTRIBUTORS

Joseph R. Blondino is a Project Archaeologist with Dovetail Cultural Resource Group in Fredericksburg, Virginia. He has more than fifteen years of experience doing both academic and cultural resource management archaeology in the Middle Atlantic region. Blondino embraces a multidisciplinary approach to archaeology, particularly with regard to the earth and environmental sciences. Believing that an understanding of landscapes and their formation processes is critical to interpreting past human behavior, he has sought extensive training in geology, geomorphology, and soil science. His interest in Transitional Archaic site location and its relationship to subsistence was the focus of his graduate research at Temple University. His other research interests include culture contact, the Colonial period, and military sites archaeology.

Kurt W. Carr has been with the Pennsylvania Historical and Museum Commission since 1980, serving as the Chief of the Division of Archaeology and Protection between 1988 and 2005. As Senior Curator of Archaeology at the State Museum of Pennsylvania since 2007 with a staff of eight archaeologists, Carr supervises curation of the museum's archaeological collections (with more than 8 million artifacts), plans exhibits, develops a variety of public outreach programs, and conducts field research on significant issues in Pennsylvania archaeology. His research interests include Early Holocene Native American cultural adaptations, the role of population density in cultural change, lithic technology and quarries, settlement pattern analysis, geomorphology, and environmental reconstructions.

Patricia E. Miller received her Ph.D. in Anthropology from the Pennsylvania State University in 1993. She worked in cultural resource management for Archaeological and Historical Consultants, KCI Technologies, and URS Corporation before retiring in 2013. During her twenty-five-year career, Miller was privileged to direct data recovery investigations at a number of stratified sites in the Susquehanna and Ohio River valleys for clients such as the Pennsylvania Department of Transportation, the Pennsylvania Turnpike Commission, and the U.S. Army Corps of Engineers.

Roger Moeller received his Anthropology degrees from Franklin and Marshall College (B.A.) and the State University of New York at Buffalo (M.A. and Ph.D.). He has conducted research on prehistoric sites in Iowa, New York, Connecticut, New Jersey, Massachusetts, Delaware, and Pennsylvania, with components ranging in age from the Paleoindian through the Contact period. Most of his research in Connecticut was done while Moeller was Director of Research at the American Indian Archaeological Institute (now known as the "Institute for American Indian Studies"). He has been or is currently the editor of *Journal of Middle Atlantic Archaeology*, *North American Archaeologist*, *Bulletin of the Archaeological Society of Connecticut*, *Abstracts in Anthropology*, *Bulletin of the Eastern States Archaeological Federation*, *Occasional Publications in Northeastern Anthropology*, and *A Current Bibliography on African Affairs*. Most recently, Moeller is the webmaster for http://esaf-archeology.org/, http://www.pennarchcouncil.org/, http://siftings.com/, http://www.quad50.com/, http://www.pennsylvaniaarchaeology.com/, http://quad50.com/Beauchamp/, and http://www.maacmidatlanticarchaeology.org/.

Paul A. Raber is the series editor of Recent Research in Pennsylvania Archaeology and co-editor of two previous volumes in the series. He serves as Senior Archaeologist and Director of Archaeological Services with Heberling Associates, Inc., Alexandria, Pennsylvania. His research interests include the evolution of technology and the archaeology of hunter-gatherers and early horticulturalists in eastern North America. He holds an M.A. and Ph.D. in Anthropology from the Pennsylvania State University and has published in *North American Archaeologist*, *Archaeology of Eastern North America*, *Pennsylvania Archaeologist*, and the *Journal of Field Archaeology*.

R. Michael Stewart has a long record of research and publication dealing with the archaeology of American Indians, from the Paleoindian period (13,000 years ago) through the Contact period and the interaction of Native Americans with Europeans in the Middle Atlantic and Northeast regions. His research interests include human ecology, trade, pottery technology, paleoenvironmental reconstruction, and the integration of archaeology and environmental sciences. With degrees in Anthropology from the University of Delaware (B.A.) and the Catholic University of America (M.A., Ph.D.), Stewart is Associate Professor Emeritus of Anthropology at Temple University. An archaeologist at the New Jersey Historic Preservation Office, he maintains ongoing field projects throughout the Delaware Valley of Pennsylvania and New Jersey.

Frank J. Vento, a licensed professional geologist and registered professional archaeologist, is Research Professor of Geology and Director of Graduate Studies in Geoarchaeology at Mercyhurst University and Professor Emeritus of Anthropology, Geography, and Earth Science at Clarion University of Pennsylvania. He taught for thirty-one years in the State University of Pennsylvania system. Vento has had grants and contracts with the National Park Service, U.S. Forest Service, Pennsylvania Bureau for Historic Preservation, U.S. Army Corps of Engineers, Baltimore and Pittsburgh Districts, Pennsylvania Department of Transportation, and Maryland Highway Administration, as well as other local, state, and federal agencies and numerous private consulting firms. He has served for more than seven years as a Statewide Geomorphologist for the Pennsylvania Department of Transportation. His research focuses primarily on fluvial geomorphology (genetic stratigraphy) and the effects of climate on fluvial systems (soil development, terrace formation) as they relate to the formation and occurrence of archaeological sites. He has worked extensively in the northeastern, southeastern, and western United States, the Caribbean, the Upper Orinoco River valley in Venezuela, in Malta, and in the Sieve, Ombrone, Garigliano, and Simeto River valleys of Italy.

Robert D. Wall holds a B.A. degree in Anthropology from the University of Maryland and an M.A. and Ph.D. in Anthropology from the Catholic University of America; he teaches Anthropology full time at Towson University. With more than thirty-five years of experience in Northeast, Great Lakes, and Middle Atlantic archaeology and several decades in cultural resource management, Wall has developed specializations in lithic and prehistoric ceramics analysis. He has worked extensively on archaeological survey and excavation projects throughout the Upper Potomac Valley since 1980 and on the Barton Site Archaeological Field School excavations since 1993. In 2001, he received the William B. Marye Award for contributions to Maryland archaeology, and he currently serves on the Maryland Advisory Committee on Archeology and the Executive Board of the Council for Maryland Archaeology.

Heather A. Wholey received her Anthropology degrees from the State University of New York at Albany (B.A.) and the Catholic University of America (M.A. and Ph.D.). She has conducted research on prehistoric sites throughout the Eastern Woodlands, with components from the Paleoindian through Contact periods in academic and cultural resource management contexts. Her research is primarily focused on the Archaic and Transitional Archaic periods from a multidisciplinary perspective. Wholey's research interests include human population ecology, the application of earth sciences to archaeology, and settlement patterns and human landscapes. She is currently Professor of Anthropology at West Chester University.

INDEX